WEALTH BEYOND MEASURE

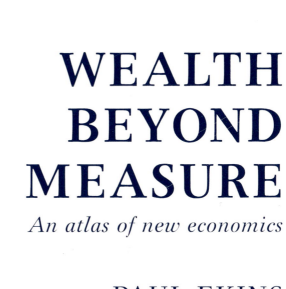

WEALTH
BEYOND
MEASURE

An atlas of new economics

PAUL EKINS
Mayer Hillman and Robert Hutchison

Gaia Books Limited

A GAIA ORIGINAL

Conceived by
Joss Pearson

Series editor
Norman Myers

Project editor
Jonathan Hilton

Production editor
Katherine Pate

Design
Andrew Barker

Direction
Joss Pearson
Patrick Nugent

DEDICATION

To our four children
John Paul, Josh, Sarah and Saul
in the hope that the ideas in this book will be
implemented

Paul Ekins   Mayer Hillman   Robert Hutchison

First published in the United Kingdom in 1992 by
Gaia Books Limited
66 Charlotte Street
London W1P 1LR

Printed by Mateu Cromo, Madrid, Spain

A catalogue record for this book is available from
The British Library

ISBN 1 85675 050 7

10 9 8 7 6 5 4 3 2 1

Paul Ekins is a Research Fellow of
Birkbeck College, London, Co-founder of
The Other Economic Summit (TOES),
founder of the Living Economy Network
and of New Consumer, and Research
Director for the Right Livelihood Award
(the "Alternative Nobel Prize").

Mayer Hillman is head of the
Environment and Quality of Life
Programme at the Policy Studies Institute
(PSI), London. He specializes in
transport, energy, and health policies.

Robert Hutchison is a Senior Research
Fellow at the PSI, specializing in
information technology, media, and
politics.

Foreword

Economic progress, in the form we now know it, is doomed. It already threatens the ecosystems on which it depends. And its vision for the future is that everyone, in a human population twice as large as now, should aspire to the high-consumption, high-pollution way of life of the rich minority today.

This conventional economic vision is hopelessly false, and not only for ecological reasons. Today more people than ever before live in absolute poverty – well over one billion – and the number continues to rise. This is no accident. Conventional economic progress systematically transfers wealth from the poor to the rich. Its way of creating wealth creates poverty too.

We have to change to a new path of economic progress, directed to the wellbeing of people and the Earth, to quality of life rather than quantity of consumption and accumulation. The new economics must enable people to develop their own sustainable ways of living, in the context of their own cultures. It must value and cherish the resources and blessings bestowed by nature. It must recognize that the wealth-of-nations era is passing, and that today's one-world human community now has a one-world economy to manage and understand. It must bring back ethical and spiritual values into economic life and thought, from which they have been excluded by conventional pseudo-scientific economics.

Paul Ekins, as the first director of The Other Economic Summit (TOES) and in other ways, has played an important part in the worldwide new economics movement that has gathered strength in the last few years. I congratulate him, together with his co-authors and Gaia Books, on this further fine contribution. *Wealth Beyond Measure* will encourage many readers to take up the challenge of the new economics. And that is one of the most urgent – and most exciting – ethical, political and intellectual challenges of our time.

James Robertson

James Robertson is an independent writer, speaker and consultant on alternative futures and economic and social change. His books include *The Sane Alternative* (J Robertson, 1978, 1983), *Future Work (M T Smith 1985)* and *Future Wealth* (Cassell 1990). He was one of the founders of The Other Economic Summit (TOES) in 1984.

Contents

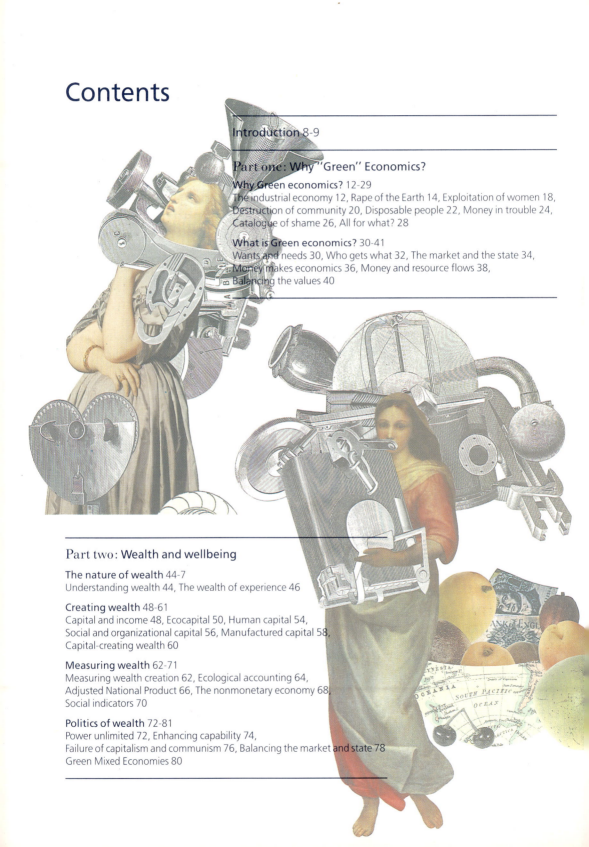

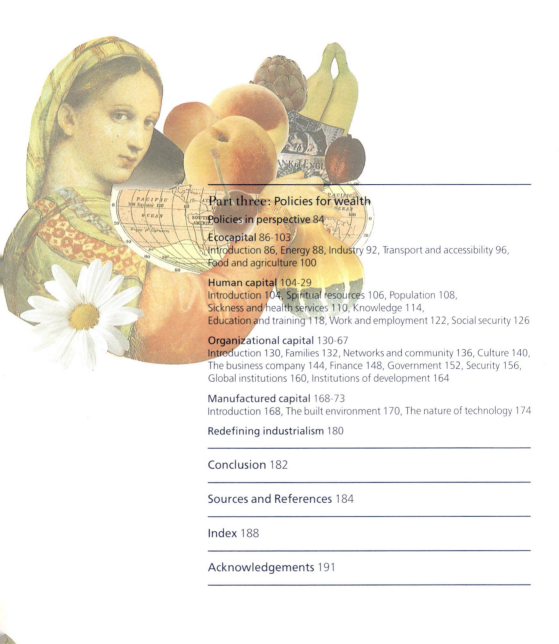

Introduction

Humanity is now living through a period of enormous change, turmoil, and challenge in which one of the few safe predictions is that the future will not be like either the present or the past. The accelerating changes are simultaneously environmental, demographic, technological, economic, social, and cultural. The Earth's atmosphere is warming at an unprecedented rate and the extinction rate is larger than at the time of the death of the dinosaurs some 65 million years ago, while human population is still exploding. Technological revolutions with increasingly profound implications are now occurring every few decades, precipitating ever more disruptive economic and social restructuring. The slow evolution of many diverse human cultures has been shattered by global cultural homogenization in the Western mould as peoples are torn from millennia of traditional living and thrust into the world market economy and consumer society.

The forces behind the changes have been acting with increasing power at least since Columbus sailed to the Americas 500 years ago. It is apparent that the trends they have engendered are patently unsustainable. We can confidently expect the future course of human lives to be increasingly disrupted by environmental calamity and social upheaval unless and until the human species attains a new equilibrium with its environment. Decisions taken over the next decade or two will do much to determine the population level and the human quality of life at that equilibrium.

In attempting to understand the present human predicament, the conventional Western scientific approach will only be of limited use. The American philosopher of science Willis Harman has most cogently argued that the powerful reductionism of this approach is only perfectly suited to the inorganic sciences. He has postulated other forms of scientific enquiry, involving an increasingly holistic and participatory approach, appropriate to the life sciences, the social sciences, including economics, and the spiritual sciences. This book seeks to follow such an approach, integrating the ethical, social, ecological, and economic dimensions of human experience in an effort to expose how much current economic practice actually destroys more wealth than it creates; and seeks to chart a new methodology of wealth creation that is able to address the roots of the global economic crisis.

From the rhetoric of Western leaders one would be forgiven for not noticing that there was such a crisis. The purpose of Part One is, thus, firstly to expose the nature of the crisis, especially since it has been caused by economic activity and the economic theory that underlies it. Here the argument is made for a new economics. The second chapter of this part then describes the principal features of this new economics compared with those of the conventional theory it is seeking to replace.

Part Two explores the concept of wealth, its nature, how it is created and how it can be measured. The fact that some of the most important aspects of wealth are beyond measure limits the scope of technical decision making and emphasizes the role of politics in wealth creation, in deciding how much wealth of what type is created, and for whom.

Part Three progresses to policies for wealth, in many different sectors. With few exceptions, each sector is discussed in two two-page parts – the first analyzing the problems and dominant trends in that sector, and the second outlining appropriate policy responses with the objectives of economic justice, democracy, and sustainability.

Throughout the book, an economy with these characteristics is called a Green economy, while Green economics is the body of theory and policy through which it can be promoted. Many examples are also given of Green economic practice, which should decisively expel the notion that the discussion is only of abstract relevance. This book is primarily intended for the general reader and citizen, on whose efforts and commitment the construction of a Green economy depends. In small and large ways the Green economy already exists in the lives of perhaps the majority of the world's people. As importantly, Green economics often emerges as a restatement in different form of some of the most basic traditional wisdom of humankind. The objective of this book is to help relocate Green economic experience from the margins to the centre of contemporary life.

This work has drawn on the ideas of many others, some of whom are mentioned in the acknowledgements; the work of others is listed under Sources and References. These are organized according to the pages to which they relate. Where there are many references for a particular page, some ambiguity may exist, which we regret, but this was considered preferable to the distraction of numbered footnotes.

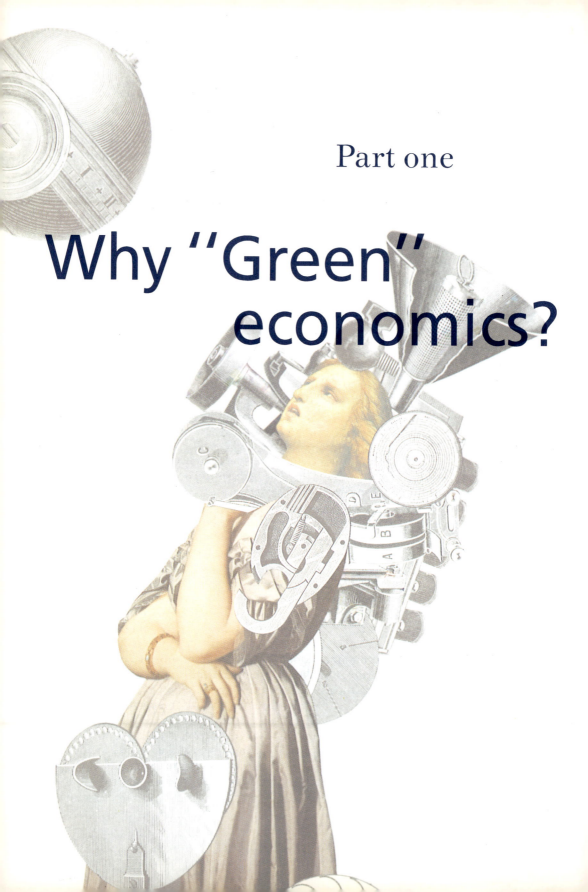

Part one

Why "Green" economics?

Manfred Max-Neef is the Founder and Executive Director of the Development Alternatives Centre (CEPAUR), in Santiago, Chile. As well as being the author of some seven books and more than a hundred essays and papers on alternative economic policies, many of which have been translated and published throughout the world, he was the creator of the principles of "Barefoot Economics", for which he received the Right Livelihood Award, the "alternative" Nobel Prize, in 1983. In 1986 he published his theory of Human Scale Development (see pp. 46-7). His professional posts are many and varied: Professor of Ecological Economics, Schumacher College, England; Member of the Scientific Committee of the Leopold Kohr Academy, Austria; and Lecturer at the University of California during the early 1960s, and Visiting Professor at several US and Latin American universities. As well, Manfred is a Member of the Club of Rome and former General Economist for the FAO, Head of Mission of the ILO, and Consultant for both UNICEF and UNDP.

Life is probably the result of a Universe that needs to discover itself in order to have significance. Without a Universe there would be no life, and without life the cosmic unfolding would be meaningless. Today, scientific evidence increasingly indicates that such a mirror-image relationship is not the product of chance.

There are about 20 fundamental physical constants, such as the speed of light, the gravitational constant, Planck's constant, and Boltzmann's constant. These constants are not independent, and it has been estimated that the probability for their unique inter-relationship to occur is something like $1/10^{200}$ (one in ten to the power of 200). Furthermore, the most infinitesimal change in the value of those constants, or in the relation that holds between them, would make the Universe unstable and bring it to an end.

In relation to life, it is known that a living cell is composed of some 2000 specific enzymes. Biologists have calculated that the probability for the unique combination of all of these elements to occur in order to produce a living cell over a period of a million years of evolution, is something like $1/10^{1000}$. Such incredible magnitudes of chance lead to only one far-reaching conclusion: that our being is the product of an infinite improbability of being.

We are, therefore, a part of life that is today the only scientifically provable miracle – and the greatest possible miracle for that matter. Not only have we not grasped that idea – which is deeply worrying – but we actually take life, and everything that goes with it, for granted, as if all that we destroy or deplete were mechanically reversible. Our economic activity, and its theoretical justification, is in many respects a perfect example of this absurd behaviour. It is becoming increasingly clear that through the applied dominant economic rationality – our notions of value, progress, profit, and the rest – our capacity to destroy the infinitely improbable is becoming a certainty.

That we need a radically new economic rationality is, at this stage of history, overwhelmingly self-evident. A Green economics – or ecological economics, as I prefer to call it – transforms our destructive economic logic because it subordinates economics to the processes of life, rather than, as has been the rule so far, placing life at the service of economics.

Manfred Max-Neef,
Founder and Executive Director, CEPAUR

The industrial economy

The foundations of modern economics are rooted in the Industrial Revolution. Its father was the Scottish moral philosopher and economist Adam Smith, whose book, *An Inquiry into the Nature and Causes of the Wealth of Nations*, was published in 1776. As now, this period was a time of social turmoil. The traditional sources of power and authority – the Church and aristocracy – were under increasing pressure: Voltaire was preaching a new humanism; Francis Bacon had foreseen the total subjugation of the natural world; the scientific worldview of Newton and Descartes was being articulated; the French Revolution was in prospect; and a great new force was being established in Britain – the power of productive capital that turned the fledgling wheels of the new industry.

The new industrialists took comfort from Smith's words. They wanted the freedom to make profits, and Smith not only said that they should have this freedom, he identified them as the new saviours of society, the wealth creators. He endorsed their pursuit of self-interest, with qualifications, as being conducive to the greatest general good. The modern industrial economy was being built.

Two hundred and more years on we can take stock. For most of those years, Europe and, later, North America, have had practically all the resources of the planet at their command. Mountains of production have arisen that the world has never seen before. One-quarter of the world's population has a lifestyle beyond all previous imagination. The global market that supplies them now reaches into every aspect of human life in practically every society on Earth.

Industrial consumerism on such a scale has exacted a terrible price. As the subsequent pages show, it has become an infernal machine that eats away at the foundations of human society and life on Earth, bringing the economic system it has constructed to the brink of collapse.

Few people have anything to gain from such a collapse, so interdependent has the world economy become. It would be far better to use the experience and skills we have acquired to build a materially more modest, culturally more diverse way of life – community based, convivial, sustainable and on a human scale – in which all people can participate and find fulfilment. That in essence is what this book is about.

The infernal machine

Out of the industrial economy issues the dazzling variety of consumer goods that make for the affluent society. To produce them, it sucks up, like an enormous vacuum cleaner, life on Earth and, indeed, the Earth itself. It lays nature waste, exploits women, undermines family and community, and impoverishes hundreds of millions of people. It is socially, culturally, environmentally, and economically unsustainable.

Adam Smith

Adam Smith lived from 1723 to 1790, his life spanning the first great inventions of the Industrial Revolution. He is now mainly remembered for his recommendation that individual economic self-interest be allowed to work through the market, when, as by an "invisible hand", it would also be led to serve the common good. Too often forgotten are Smith's other observations on human nature published in *The Theory of Moral Sentiments* in 1759, when Smith was Professor of Moral Philosophy at the University of Glasgow. He identified the individual conscience and "fellow feeling" – a sympathy with others – as balancing human characteristics to self-love. These needed to be embodied in a system of justice to restrain the excesses of self-interest if a congenial society was to be achieved. Nationally, all such systems of justice still leave much to be desired. Internationally, the complete absence of such a system has permitted the great international exploitation and injustices in the world today.

Rape of the Earth

It is hard to imagine the 18th-century world of Adam Smith (see pp. 12-13) as he sat musing on the marvels of self-interest: a human population of 1 billion; birds, beasts, and fish in profusion; a vastly productive land mass rich in diverse plant life; and large expanses swathed in an ample forest green.

In two hundred years industrial society, powered by that same self-interest, has penetrated the farthest, darkest corners of the land and sea and deep into space. It is irreversibly changing the great natural systems that support life on Earth – old forests topple, new deserts spread, plant and animal species are extinguished, industrial poisons penetrate even through the polar ice, billions of tonnes of topsoil are washed away. And all this in a mere one-twenty-thousandth of the time that human life has existed on Earth.

"Today the very conditions of life on our planet are threatened by the severe attacks to which the earth's atmosphere is subjected." *Hague Declaration,* March 1989, which was signed by senior representatives of 24 countries, including 17 heads of state

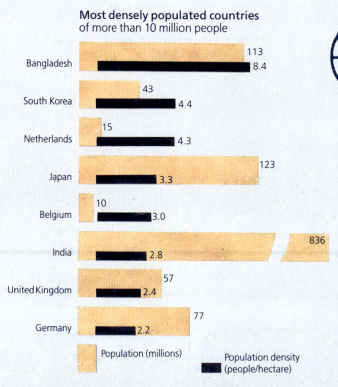

Most densely populated countries
of more than 10 million people

Country	Population (millions)	Population density (people/hectare)
Bangladesh	113	8.4
South Korea	43	4.4
Netherlands	15	4.3
Japan	123	3.3
Belgium	10	3.0
India	836	2.8
United Kingdom	57	2.4
Germany	77	2.2

Population (millions)

Population density (people/hectare)

Ozone depletion
The ozone layer shields us from the full effects of the sun's ultraviolet radiation. Greater levels of UV could severely affect human health, plant growth, and basic forms of aquatic life vital to the food chain and the balance of carbon dioxide in the atmosphere. The ozone layer is being depleted by a range of chemicals, principally chlorofluorocarbons (CFCs), used in aerosols, refrigerators, air conditioners, and foam blowing. Over the Antarctic, 97.5% of the ozone is missing, and there is the start of a similar "hole" over the Arctic. Elsewhere, depletion varies from 2 to 6%. The US Environmental Protection Agency (EPA) has called for an immediate 100% worldwide cut in CFCs. The Montreal Protocol of 1990 permits CFC use until 2000, and allows for their substitution by other, less-powerful ozone depleters, which are also greenhouse gases.

Greenhouse gas	Source	Greenhouse effect (GE) compared with CO_2	Rate of annual increase (%)	Approx contribution to GE (%)	IPCC recommended reduction (%)
Carbon dioxide (CO_2)	fossil fuel burning (77%) deforestation (23%)	1	0.5	52	>60
Chlorofluorocarbons (CFCs) Related gases (HFCs, HCFCs)	various industrial uses e.g. refrigerators	approx 10,000	4.0	22	75 / 40-50
Methane (CH_4)	rice paddies livestock digestion gas leakage	30	0.9	13	15-20
Nitrous oxide (N_2O)	biomass burning fertilizer use fossil fuel burning	150	0.8	5	70-80
Ozone (ground level)	fossil fuel burning	2000		8	

The greenhouse effect

The warming of the atmosphere known as the greenhouse effect is caused by the accumulation of gases that retain heat from the sun as it is reradiated by the Earth. Carbon dioxide, methane, and nitrous oxide are all rising above naturally occurring levels, and CFCs are an artificial factor. The Intergovernmental Panel on Climate Change (IPCC) agreed in 1990 that global warming of up to 3°C by the year 2100 was likely. The speed of this warming – 1°C every 30 years – is unprecedented in human history and is likely to lead to massive changes in climate patterns: floods, droughts, storms, and crop failures.

Acid rain

Sulphur dioxide (SO_2), from burning coal and oil, and nitrogen oxides, from coal, oil, and vehicle exhausts, form acid rain. The main effects are acidification of lakes, die-back of forests, stunting of crops, and erosion of buildings. In southern Norway, 80% of the lakes and streams are either dead or critical; Canada has 14,000 strongly acidified lakes; 52% of Germany's forests show signs of die-back; 35% of Europe's forests in 15 countries is affected; and acid erosion is destroying some European monuments. Acid rain is also acute in parts of India and China. Timber losses in Germany cost $5 billion a year; crop damage in the US, $5.4 billion; erosion costs in OECD countries, $20 billion a year. Acid rain is transnational: 96% of

SO$_2$ exports (1000 tonnes/year)
* = member of 30% club

USSR*	7922
UK	3750
E Germany*	2888
Poland	2576
W Germany*	2338
Czechoslovakia*	2100
France*	2042
Italy*	1804
Hungary*	1178
Belgium*	638

Norway's sulphur deposition is imported, while the UK exports 71% of its output. In Europe exports range from 61 to 75%. In the 1980s the 30% club of countries pledged to reduce SO_2 output by 1993 to 70% of 1980 levels. It had 19 signatories by 1985. A 1988 EC directive imposed larger cuts over a longer period, but nowhere near the 90% reductions in sulphur and nitrogen emissions now thought necessary.

Cause and effect

The cause of all this is too many people, some of whom are consuming too much. Pollution and water depletion spring directly from industrialization; they are the result of the consumer appetites of the quarter of the world's population in industrial societies and the industrial elites that exist in all predominantly nonindustrial societies.

The causes of deforestation and desertification are more complex, but the demands of the wealthy are a major component. Tropical timber from nearly 5 million hectares is shipped annually from poor to rich countries. In the ten years from 1974 to 1984 the amount of land in developing countries devoted to the major export crops rose by 11 per cent. In Brazil the percentage of land used for growing food for domestic consumption fell from 63 per cent to 55 per cent between 1967 and 1979 as the cultivation of export crops increased.

The appropriation by the rich of the resources of developing countries leaves less and less for the indigenous poor, who are forced into the forests or on to marginal or fragile soils that simply cannot sustainably support them. Thus the environment analysts Paul and Anne Ehrlich write: "Industrialization of agriculture in southern Brazil has created an army of landless people whom the government funnels towards the frontier of the Amazon." And the environmental authority Norman Myers estimates that there may be 250 million of these shifted cultivators who are destroying tomorrow's Earth in order that they can stay alive today.

Population growth has complex causes, too, chief among them being that industrialization seems to cause death rates to decline well before birth rates fall off. In industrializing Europe it took more than a hundred years for populations to stabilize, and it was growth there that was largely responsible for the doubling of world population to 2 billion people in the 130 years from 1800. Indeed, European countries still account for half the eight highest population densities in countries with more than 10 million people. The "demographic transition" to population stability in poor countries is likely, today as then, to depend on them achieving economic security for their inhabitants (see pp. 108-9).

Deforestation
Forests once covered 75% of the planet's land area. The figure is now less than 30%. Tropical forests alone once covered 14% of the land, today less than 7%. The still rising rate of tropical deforestation has increased by 90% over the last decade. At current rates of 14.2 million hectares destroyed annually, and 15 million hectares degraded, tropical forests will have all but disappeared in 25 years.

Species extinction
Estimates vary, but probably 50-100 animal and one plant species are being extinguished every day, with the rate rising rapidly. Tropical forests contain 70-95% of all Earth's perhaps 30 million species. If, by 2020, these forests are all but gone, millions of species will have been lost forever. This greatest-ever mass extinction, with incalculable consequences for humanity and future evolution, will have been brought about by the species that considers itself to be the most intelligent in nature.

"The earth is slowly dying, and the inconceivable, the end of life itself, is actually becoming conceivable. We human beings have become a threat to our planet." Queen Beatrix of the Netherlands in her Christmas message to the people of Holland, 1988

Toxic chemicals

Some 70,000 chemicals are in common use with 500-1000 new ones added annually. From 1945 to 1985 the production of synthetic organic chemicals in the US rose 15 times to 102 million tonnes, and the US National Research Council estimates that no information on toxicity is available for 79% of the 48,500 plus chemicals listed by the EPA. Pesticides and herbicides kill 10-40,000 people annually in the Third World, the traditional dumping ground for chemicals banned in the West. The breast milk of Nicaraguan women has been shown to contain DDT at 45 times the WHO tolerance limit. Pesticides on food in the US could be causing 20,000 additional cancers per year. And their persistent use leads to resistant strains of pest: crop losses from some types are back at the 30% level pertaining before the chemical age. Moves to nontoxic, biological control and integrated pest-management techniques have had some striking results. Other hazardous materials are also produced as a byproduct of many industrial processes. The dumping of these wastes poses a particular threat to groundwater in many industrial nations. West Germany is thought to have 35,000 problem sites and Denmark 2000. And cleaning up "priority sites" in the US could cost $100 billion. The export of wastes also threatens Third World countries. However, the amount of dangerous waste can be diminished. In Japan in 1983 only 18% of industrial wastes required disposal. The remainder was reused or recycled.

Desertification

Each year desertification claims 6 million hectares worldwide and another 20 million become degraded. The UN Environment Programme judges 4.5 billion hectares – 35% of Earth's land surface – to be at risk from desertification, including 66% of Australia's agricultural land. Worldwide, 24 billion tonnes of topsoil are washed away annually. The principal causes of degradation are overgrazing, overcultivation, waterlogging and salinization, and deforestation. In 1950, 278 million Africans kept 272 million livestock animals. By 1987 604 million Africans had 543 million animals. The real roots of the problem are excessive population densities and the displacement of poor people on to fragile lands. However, all but the worst examples of soil degradation can be reversed. In China's Loess Plateau 10 million hectares were stabilized in seven years from 1979. Trees and pastures were planted, and a 17% greater crop was yielded from half the cropland. UNEP estimates that $4.5 billion a year (less than two days' worth of world military spending) for 20 years is needed to control the problem.

Water depletion

Farming accounts for 70% of global water use, which, through irrigation, underpins the large food output necessary to feed more than 5 billion people. This function, however, is now experiencing severe constraints:

○ Project costs – the costs of canal schemes in India have doubled in real terms between 1950 and 1980.
○ Salinization – 24% of the world's irrigated land has been damaged by the build-up of salt.
○ Social and environmental costs – increasing local and international opposition to large schemes such as China's Three Gorges dam project, which will displace 750,000 people.
○ Scarcity – worsening water shortages in North and East Africa, China, India, the Middle East, and, due to falling water tables, the US.

The result is declining output per head; for world grain, this fell by 7% from 1984 to 1989, a trend presaging mass famines. Water for direct human consumption has been no less affected by abuse and overuse. A 1987 UNEP report estimated that pollution and population increase could cut per capita availability of water in the Third World by up to 50%, while 2 billion people already suffer chronic water shortages. In the US, drinking water has been found to contain 129 dangerous chemicals. In terms of overuse, by the end of the 1980s each American was flushing 34,000 litres of drinking water per year away, to remove 500 litres of body wastes.

Exploitation of women

Women do most of the world's work for little material return. An increasing proportion of women in almost all societies now earn money and, in industrial countries, comprise around 40 per cent of all those in paid work. However, women mainly earn less than men doing comparable work, or they are concentrated in the low-paying sectors, especially in the service industries, or they work part-time. And most such women will also experience the "double burden" of having paid employment as well as doing the major part of housework and caring for children or elderly relatives.

The exploitation of women's productive capacity is repeated with their sexuality. All too often, women have little or no choice over the timing or number of their pregnancies. Large numbers of women are sold to their partners; others are forced into prostitution; others still are mutilated by female circumcision. In the US the FBI estimates that wife battery occurs at three times the rate of rape (not including rape within marriage), and a rape is reported every six minutes. And many rapes are never reported at all.

Many crucial home-based tasks, which are overwhelmingly performed by women, are not only unpaid, they are nearly always ignored in economic analysis. Those who perform these tasks full time are categorized as "economically inactive". The fetching of water and the collection of firewood, growing food for the family, housework, caring for the children and other dependants, are all systematically excluded from the national accounts. The flawed economic perceptions formed by such omissions are deeply discriminatory. One result is the waste of much so-called development aid. In Malawi, for example, men were invited to attend agricultural demonstrations organized as part of an aid programme. They dutifully did so but agricultural productivity remained unchanged. Closer examination revealed that the farmers in these communities growing food for their households were in fact women. Even in industrial countries, unpaid household production has a value of 25-40 per cent of gross national product.

Women at work and play

Sociologists at the University of California, studying whether women's work performance could explain their lower wages, found that women gave more time and attention to their jobs than men, despite spending twice as much time on housework. A time-budget study of 12 countries in Europe and North America found that employed women had an average 14.5 leisure hours per week, only 43 per cent of employed men's leisure time.

"Women comprise about half the world's population . . .

. . . perform about two-thirds of its work . . .

. . . receive only one-tenth of its income . . .

. . . and own less than one-hundredth of world assets."

State of World Women 1979

"In Vanuatu there is a sort of joke about girls: they are called 'Toyotas' because the market-price for a young bride equals a new car for her family."
If Women Counted, Marilyn Waring

Prostitution

In 1982 more than 1 million Japanese tourists visited Thailand, the Philippines, South Korea, Taiwan, and Hong Kong on "trips for men only", which explicitly included visits to brothels. An estimated 60% of 2 million tourists visiting Thailand each year are allegedly drawn by bargain-price sex. In Bangkok alone in 1981, 300,000 women and children worked in establishments offering sexual services. While in Bangkok researching her book, *If Women Counted*, Marilyn Waring "watched ten, twelve and sixteen year old girls dancing in numbered swimming costumes, or in nothing at all, along cat-walks. They are sold to these places by their parents. They live, eat and sleep here and are enslaved not only in theory. In 1984 when one of these bars burned down, the skeletons of six girls aged between ten and sixteen were found among the ruins, chained to the beds."

Relationships of poverty, US style

In the US in 1980, 50% of marriages ended in divorce, a figure expected to rise to 66%. About 45% of American employed women are household heads; and 35% of American single mothers live below the poverty line. Only between 5 and 10% of divorced women receive alimony and 70% of divorced women with custody of children receive no child support. The author Sylvia Ann Hewlett has concluded that, having lost the protection and guarantees of traditional marriage and still locked into low-paying jobs, in the US today: "most women are in worse economic shape than their mothers were."

Destruction of community

The exploitation of women is not only an injustice in itself (see pp. 18-19), it has knock-on effects on the community, and on the family, an institution of which women are traditionally the backbone. With women now the sole breadwinners in 25-30 per cent of families worldwide and increasingly shouldering a triple workload – housework, paid employment, and reproduction – as well as working on average about 25 per cent longer than men, it is not surprising that families are cracking under the strain.

The model family runs counter to the ideology of free-market self-interest in many ways. Those within it share their money on the basis of need. They feed, clothe, shelter, and care for each other free of charge, giving particular care to those with special needs – the young, the old, the disabled. They make real sacrifices when such are called for. It is these qualities that have made the family an appropriate institution for the nurturing of children. When the exploitation of women undermines the family, when family motivations are eroded by the individualistic spirit of the time, then families diminish to their nucleus, and then that breaks up, too. Children suffer most – neglected, bought off, exploited, or abused.

As with the family, so with the community, the webs of relationships that connect people to people and people to places. Industrial projects can uproot people and divide or destroy communities when they come and go. The need to move to where the jobs are fractures communities farther. In many communities in cities of both industrial countries and the Third World there are no jobs nor any possibility to move. Then able-bodied, able-minded men and women waste away their lives or eke out a subsistence from garbage heaps and street corners. Community is not necessarily destroyed by these conditions. Indeed, it is only through community action that they are likely to be ameliorated. But community action through settled communities cannot become a sustaining root of culture while the economic terms continue to be dictated by destructive development and redevelopment, industrial restructuring, and international competitiveness.

The end of the family?

In Western society it was the close-knit extended family that attenuated and has now all but disappeared. Now it seems as if the same process could be happening to the family itself. In the US in 1988, more than one in five children lived only with their mothers, double the proportion in 1970. For the black community the figure was over half. In the UK, with one of the highest family-breakdown rates in Europe, the divorce rate has increased sixfold since 1961 and, on present trends, more than one in three marriages will end in divorce. Lone parents in 1988 already headed 16% of all families with dependent children, up from 6% in 1961. Childbearing outside of marriage doubled between 1980 and 1988 to 25%.

Migration

Due to poverty, war, repression, or ecological degradation, there are some 80 million migrants in the world. Only 25% migrate legally; the rest represent a pool of exploitable labour. While remittances home of migrant workers abroad can be more than half what countries such as Pakistan earn in exports, migration is profoundly disruptive of family and community. Rural-to-urban migration within countries is little better: because of desertification, 10 million African farmers are thought to have moved to urban centres in the 1980s. The only ways to halt these movements are through greater economic opportunity in poor countries, civil stability, respect for human rights, and ecological regeneration.

Measuring "community"

So little importance has been attached to community that there are no generally accepted indicators of community wellbeing. A rare attempt to throw light on this area was UK sociologist Peter Townsend's 1985 survey, which included questions about "lack of integration into community" on topics such as loneliness, neighbourhood safety, racial harassment, neighbourly help proffered or expected, and frequency of change of residence. A further set of questions explored participation in social institutions. Lack of funds prevented the analysis of the data generated. Until attention to community ranks equally with profit margins, we can expect it to continue being sacrificed for individual enrichment.

The adolescent time bomb

"The mobility of American families, the need for second incomes . . . and increases in poverty have robbed too many young people of stable families and communities . . ." As a result, in the US 10% of boys and 18% of girls attempt suicide; homicide is the leading cause of death among 15-19-year-old blacks; 30% of all youth have experimented with drugs; the number of 14-17 year olds arrested each year has increased nearly 30 fold since 1950; by 1989 23% of children under six were living in poverty. For the first time in US history, "young people are *less* healthy and *less* prepared to take their place in society than were their parents". National Association of State Boards of Education 1990

Crime and drugs

Crime figures from the UK and the US indicate an erosion of community. Notifiable offences recorded in the UK increased fivefold from 1956 to 1989, those of violence against the person went up nearly 400% from 1971 to 1989. In the US homicides went from 4.7 to 8.7 per 100,000 people from 1960 to 1987. The rape rate more than doubled from 1970 to 1988, as did cases of child neglect or abuse from 1980 to 1987. The link between US drugs and crime is strong. In 1988 in Chicago over 75% of people arrested for serious nondrug offences gave positive drug tests, and other cities show similar results. Estimates indicate that in the US there are 10 million regular marijuana and 8-20 million cocaine users, and 500,000 heroin addicts, involved in a drugs business worth $100 billion a year.

Disposable people

The free market industrial economy perceives people as either usable or disposable. The economic language, developed in the 19th century, is remarkably explicit, talking of labour as a factor of production, of labour inputs, of labour-intensive technology. This is a language in which people are raw material for the process of production. Many of those used as such have often had to, and still have to, endure conditions of harshness and brutality, their skills overexploited or denied in mindless mass production, their health undermined, while they receive only a fraction of the value of their product. Where such conditions have been bettered, it has largely been through labour organizations in the teeth of sometimes violent intimidation by employers. Employment itself does not generate an escape from poverty. In Britain in 1989, two out of five full-time workers were living on low pay as were 78 per cent of the part-time workforce. In the US average wages fell 9 per cent between 1980 and 1989, and in 1987, 31.5 per cent of the workforce was receiving poverty-level pay.

To be raw material for the industrial economy can be bad; to be rejected material is probably worse. Rejection can take two forms. One comes from the restless profit-seeking drive for innovations: new products, new technologies, new skills. Those who cannot learn those skills, or who live in areas companies do not favour, are shoved aside by the market to live the rest of their lives in disadvantaged circumstances. These are the unemployed, 6.7 per cent of the workforce in OECD countries in 1988, and many more than that in the Third World.

The second form of rejection is probably worst of all, afflicting those for whom industrialism has never had any use at all. These are the real "development refugees", the indigenous peoples and subsistence farmers around the world who do not fit in with industry's harsh regimen. But although industrialism has no use for these people's labour, it has plenty of uses for the resources that sustain them: the fields, forests, or fishes on which they subsist, or the even greater subsoil wealth beneath their land. So in the name of "development", these resources are taken and turned into market goods, which the dispossessed can never hope to buy.

A tale of three cities

Homeless families with children in London increased fourfold through the 1980s, to 400,000 people. Another 120,000 single people are also homeless. At the same time government leaders were boasting of an "economic miracle".

In the US Reaganomics has had similar results, as described by S Berkoff in his article "A Hell of a Town": "When you stroll here (New York) you have to pretend not to notice some ex-human propped up every few yards against a wall as he rots away . . ." Up to 3 million people in the US are now homeless. In the ten years to 1988 the number of Americans living below the poverty line increased by 7.5 million to 32 million (13.1%).

In Bombay there are 100,000 street dwellers. In Darryl D'Monte's article "The Pavement Dwellers of Bombay" the scene is described: "Women pick lice from each other's hair. The boys beg . . . Typically they have been pushed off their plots because of environmental degradation." In Calcutta there are 600,000 such people.

Oustees and the World Bank

In 1990 some 70 ongoing projects of the World Bank were forcibly displacing 1.5 million people. In almost every case the "oustees" will end up impoverished by the "resettlement and rehabilitation" process. In Indonesia the Bank-backed Kedung Ombo dam displaced 20,000; the 12,500 oustees of the Ruzizi II dam on the Zaire/Rwanda border were inadequately compensated; the 6000 displaced by Kenya's Kiambere hydroelectric project got nothing. Bruce Rich of Washington's Environmental Defense Fund visited the Singrauli industrial area in India and saw the devastation of a Bank-funded mine: "At one edge of the mine we saw a large pile of overburden . . . which the giant dumpers were continually adding to. The pile engulfed remaining forest areas and a small valley which was the home of a small village called Hardlawa . . . The grazing land and tracks of villagers' livestock were being engulfed . . . . The village itself would start to be engulfed in a few days. These people had no place to go and would receive no compensation . . ."

Genocide of native peoples

Since the beginning of European and then Western expansion and economic "development", tribal peoples have been dispossessed, enslaved, and exterminated: North American Indians displaced; Australian Aborigines hunted down by the British; the Brazilian Indian population decimated. The Dayaks of Sarawak and the Yanomami of Brazil epitomize the struggle for survival of two indigenous peoples.

Sarawak, the world's largest exporter of hardwood logs, is felling its rainforests at a rate of 1100 hectares a day. Unless halted, they could be gone in seven years, and with them the home of 220,000 Dayaks. In an appeal to the West for help in 1990, Unga Paran, a tribal elder, said: "You must help us before it's too late. Our forest is your life support system."

The 20,000 Yanomami of the Amazon are among the few indigenous peoples to survive with their culture and way of life essentially intact. But in the last three years government orders have fragmented their land and what remains has been illegally invaded by up to 40,000 gold miners. In these same three years, 15% of the Yanomami have died from diseases introduced by the miners. Without official recognition of their lands they cannot survive.

Money in trouble

Money makes the modern economic world go round. In societies where markets are the law of life, money is the circulating blood of the organism. We consume and money changes hands and calls forth more production. The money we save in the bank is lent to others to produce, who buy machines to make their businesses more productive. More goods are made; profits result; and new technologies come into use. Flows of money support all this.

In recent years, however, a number of signs of sickness have developed in the body economic. Making money out of money independently of productive activity or real wealth creation has become a debilitating virus in the economic system. An example of this is the explosion of debt of all types – personal, corporate, and government – that has taken place over the last decade. In the Third World billions of dollars of loans have been stolen or squandered by governments under the eyes of the lending institutions. Now the lives of millions of people and whole economies are laid waste so that these debts can be repaid.

Another example is speculative currency trading. Currencies change one for another at a certain rate – the exchange rate. Currency exchange via these rates is the key mechanism in international trade. However, trade-related currency exchange is now dwarfed by that undertaken for currency speculation, a process that undermines confidence in the real use and purpose of money as a value base for useful economic activity. It also creates exchange-rate instability, which disrupts the plans of governments without any regard to their real performance. And currency speculation also makes life more uncertain for those in the business of real trade, for which the system was designed.

A last example is the recent plethora of mergers and takeovers. These have chillingly confirmed Marx's century-old perception that capitalism's principal tendency is the concentration and centralization of wealth and power. Such activities confer little economic benefit. They are mainly to do with power, about decreasing competition, and capturing whole markets – objectives that strike at the root and *raison d'etre* of the market system.

World debt

Third World debt, consumer debt, US-government debt – all have reached unprecedented levels. In the US, public (governmental) debt hit $2 trillion in 1986; private consumer debt (excluding mortgages) in 1988 was $640 billion; corporate debt was $2.6 trillion. In the UK, consumer debt (excluding mortgages) quadrupled in the 1980s to nearly $3800 per household. The number of house repossessions rose 900% from 1979 to 1987, and the National Consumer Council described debt as "the single most important social problem of the decade". Other European countries showed a similar substantial rise in consumer debt.

Increasing levels of debt are the product of easy loans. Banks lend many times more money than they have on deposit, in a sense creating money in order to charge interest on it. It is becoming clear that this great power should be more explicitly harnessed to the public interest rather than the profit motive.

Foreign exchange speculation

In 1989 nearly $600 billion was going through the main foreign exchange markets every day, more than double the amount of only three years before. At least half this exchange is not to buy goods; it is to buy money in order to make more money. Dollars buy yen today, the yen moves up in price tomorrow, the yen is sold the next day, and somebody is richer without having contributed a cent's-worth of useful goods or services to humanity. Unproductive, speculative errands such as this make a mockery of the purpose of money.

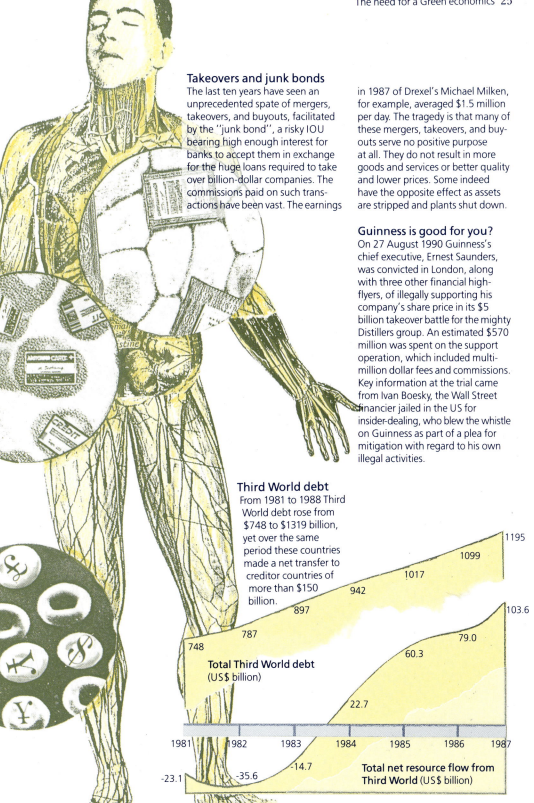

Takeovers and junk bonds

The last ten years have seen an unprecedented spate of mergers, takeovers, and buyouts, facilitated by the "junk bond", a risky IOU bearing high enough interest for banks to accept them in exchange for the huge loans required to take over billion-dollar companies. The commissions paid on such trans-actions have been vast. The earnings in 1987 of Drexel's Michael Milken, for example, averaged $1.5 million per day. The tragedy is that many of these mergers, takeovers, and buy-outs serve no positive purpose at all. They do not result in more goods and services or better quality and lower prices. Some indeed have the opposite effect as assets are stripped and plants shut down.

Guinness is good for you?

On 27 August 1990 Guinness's chief executive, Ernest Saunders, was convicted in London, along with three other financial high-flyers, of illegally supporting his company's share price in its $5 billion takeover battle for the mighty Distillers group. An estimated $570 million was spent on the support operation, which included multi-million dollar fees and commissions. Key information at the trial came from Ivan Boesky, the Wall Street financier jailed in the US for insider-dealing, who blew the whistle on Guinness as part of a plea for mitigation with regard to his own illegal activities.

Third World debt

From 1981 to 1988 Third World debt rose from $748 to $1319 billion, yet over the same period these countries made a net transfer to creditor countries of more than $150 billion.

Total Third World debt
(US$ billion)

748
787
897
942
1017
1099
1195

Total net resource flow from Third World (US$ billion)

-23.1
-35.6
-14.7
22.7
60.3
79.0
103.6

1981 1982 1983 1984 1985 1986 1987

Catalogue of shame

Most of the ravaging by the industrial economy of the planet, its people and communities is an unexceptional part of the system's operation. It has been occurring since industrialism was invented, from the smoke-filled, life-decaying slums of the early European and US industrial centres to the barrios, favelas, and shanty towns of the exploding Third World megacities today, and the continuing removal of indigenous peoples from their lands in Brazil and many other countries. However, punctuating this ongoing violence against people and nature there have been exceptional incidents of appalling damage, of increasing size and frequency.

The incidents here represent only a tiny portion of the suffering the industrial economy has caused in its blinkered pursuit of profit, production, and "development", but serve as grim reminders of the infernal aspects of the Faustian bargain industrialism has struck with humankind: pleasure for some people certainly, here on Earth; but hell for many, too, and, for many of the other species unfortunate enough to share the planet with us, torment and probable extinction.

Oil spills

The first large oil spill in Europe was in 1967 from the *Torrey Canyon,* wrecked off the Isles of Scilly. The dispersant sprayed on the slick was more toxic than the oil and did untold damage to marine life. Hundreds of kilometres of coastline were affected for several years.

In 1978 the *Amoco Cadiz* was wrecked off the coast of Brittany, releasing 200,000 tonnes of crude into the sea. More recently, in 1989 the *Exxon Valdez* ran aground in Prince William Sound, Alaska, spilling 11 million gallons of crude. Bird life suffered 300,000 casualties and there was massive ecological damage, the costs of which will run to tens of millions of dollars. And worst of all, the 1991 spill during the Gulf War, released 7 million tonnes of crude.

Hi-tech militarism

Industrialism has made a special contribution to warfare. It has made conventional arms more deadly and added to them the nuclear, chemical, and biological weapons of mass destruction. In 1988 global military expenditure reached $1 trillion, and military payrolls employed some 50 million people. In 1987, the world's arms trade was worth $47 billion. Militarism has become part of the industrial way of life.

Agent Orange

During the Vietnam War, from 1961 to 1970, the US army sprayed the vegetation of South Vietnam with massive amounts of defoliants in order to reveal the hiding places of the Vietcong. The most destructive substance of both people and environment was Agent Orange, containing dioxin. It left a bitter legacy for the survivors in the form of malignant growths and grossly deformed children and various forms of cancer.

"Threatened with the ruin of the biosphere, pollution of the air, water and soil, we realize that freedom should also be the possibility to live in non-devastated surroundings."
Polish environmental group

Development debacles

Two names bring into sharp focus the patent unsustainability of much current "development". The Narmada River in central India is the subject of the largest water development scheme ever proposed, comprising 30 major dams and hundreds of smaller ones. The largest two dams, one partially funded by the World Bank, will displace 200,000 people. The project is being resisted by those affected, which is leading to widespread human rights violations by the state governments involved. Critics claim that inadequate attention has been paid to the dams' waterlogging, siltation, and salinization problems, so that they will not even yield their projected drinking water, irrigation, and hydropower benefits.

In 1982 the World Bank funded the Carajas Iron Ore Project in Brazil involving, in addition to mining and processing plants, the building of a 900km railway to deep-port facilities at Ponta da Madeira. The completed infrastructure of the development has brought about an explosion of industrial activity, threatening to devastate 5.8 million hectares of rainforest, and its 10,000-strong Indian population. The nine pig-iron smelters and two cement factories already approved will use 1.1 million tonnes of charcoal a year, and will be economically viable only if virgin forests are used to provide the wood rather than plantations.

Nuclear power

The world's first serious nuclear accident occurred in the UK in 1957 at Windscale, now renamed Sellafield. A reactor fire raged for more than 24 hours releasing large amounts of radiation. Since then, Sellafield has remained a major radiation polluter and has been linked to significantly higher rates of leukaemia in the area.

The next major reactor accident was in 1979 at Three Mile Island, Pennsylvania. A total reactor melt-down was only just avoided and again large amounts of radiation were released. From 1979 to 1982 Pennsylvania had a death rate for elderly people 3.6 times the national rate, and as many as 130,000 may have prematurely died.

The worst reactor accident was seven years later at Chernobyl, with a massive release of radiation. Approximately 200,000 people have been permanently evacuated, most from the 30km exclusion zone that is to be indefinitely enforced. The senior scientist at Chernobyl has said that 7-10,000 miners and soldiers died from radiation exposure during the cleaning-up operation; and that the 3.5 million citizens of Kiev received radiation doses hundreds of times the normal safety levels. The winds ensured that most European countries were contaminated, with agricultural costs of $250 million in West Germany alone. The Soviets have officially put the cost of the disaster at $14 billion. Estimates of eventual cancer deaths range from a few thousand from nuclear industry sources to more than a million from Professor John Gofman at the University of California.

Chemical poisonings

The first instance of mass chemical poisoning was in Japan in the early 1950s, when the Chisso Corporation released methyl mercury directly into Minamata Bay. Since 1953, 1000 people have died and between 6000 and 9000 have been crippled by convulsions, blindness, and brain damage.

In Seveso, Italy in 1976 an explosion at a Hoffman La Roche factory released a cloud of deadly dioxin into the atmosphere. About 900 people were evacuated and increased birth defects were reported locally the following year. Ten years later the soil was still contaminated.

In the years leading up to 1953 the Hooker Chemicals and Plastic Corporation had used the area of Love Canal, USA, as a dump for over 40,000 tonnes of waste, much of it carcinogenic. The area was later developed for housing until, in 1978, leakage from the old dump became evident. Love Canal was declared a Federal Disaster Area with estimated clean-up costs of $250 million. Three other dumps nearby are also leaking into or near the Niagara River, the source of drinking water for 6 million people.

These incidents are nothing compared with the release, in 1984, of methyl isocyanate from the Union Carbide factory in Bhopal, India. Official figures in 1990 put the number killed at 3677. Unofficial estimates go beyond 10,000, and there are 80,000 people seriously affected, with one related death still each day. The victims claimed damages from Union Carbide of $3.3 billion. The company paid nothing until February 1989 when the Indian government decided to accept $470 million in full and final settlement, a decision overturned in 1990 when the new government decided to continue to press Union Carbide for more.

Less than two years after Bhopal, a fire at a Sandoz factory in Switzerland caused 30 tonnes of pesticides and other chemicals to be washed into the Rhine. As a result the river was rendered lifeless for 100-200 km. About 500,000 fish were killed and the drinking water for all those in the Rhine Basin may be at risk for years to come. The investigation following the Sandoz fire brought to light 12 other major Rhine pollution incidents, involving Ciba-Geigy, Hoechst, BASF, and Lonza, among others.

Water abuse

The Aral Sea is situated in the USSR, and was the world's fourth largest lake. Due to massive diversion of its feeder rivers for irrigation, its area has shrunk by 40% and its volume by 65%; its salinity has tripled and all native fish species are dead, as is the fishing industry that once thrived on its shores. Between 40 and 70 million tonnes of salt from the Aral's now exposed lake bed are distributed by winds annually and dropped over 20 million hectares of neighbouring land—the very land the waters were diverted to nourish. Further damage is caused by the local climate changes due to the Aral's contraction: in 1989, 500,000 hectares of cotton plants were killed, 70% of all grain fields lost, and many other crops and livestock damaged by freak snow in May.

Lake Balaton is the only large body of water available to land-locked Hungary. "In one year from 1987 following the introduction of chemically intensive farming", according to Janos Szentagothai, President Emeritus of the Hungarian Academy of Sciences, "the lake was dead and the surrounding woods were silent and lifeless". Drinking water has been so badly affected that, as reported by the Blue List environmental group, 400 villages had to be supplied with bottled water because babies were dying from high nitrate levels.

All for what?

The industrial economy was built at a heavy cost, much of which is still to be paid. Countless lives have fed its processes of production, and it has laid waste countless more. Hardly a person in the world today is beyond its reach. Much of the planet's accumulated wealth, its fossil fuels, has now been spent. And the systems on which life itself depends are undergoing fundamental change. Has it been worth it? What new dimensions of human culture has it helped to bring about?

To answer these questions we must go to that paradigm society of the Individual, to the most "developed" culture of the postwar years, which has been emulated worldwide – in short, to the United States of America and, in particular, to its middle classes.

The principal leisure activities of middle-class Americans, in terms of time spent, are watching television and shopping. Television occupies the undivided attention of the average American for 15 hours per week, rising to 20 hours or 50 per cent of average free time, when watching TV while eating, reading, or socializing is included. Shopping, on average, occupies six hours per week and has been described by a former director of the Metropolitan Museum of Modern Art as America's chief cultural activity. The link between shopping and television is direct – television accounts for a major part of the $130 billion, which works out as $500 per person, that the US spends on media advertizing.

Shopping takes place chiefly in large malls that have been built all over North America in the last 30 years. There are 35,000 such malls in the US and they account for 55 per cent of non-automobile sales and 14 per cent of GNP. Americans spend more time in them than anywhere else except at home, in school, or at their job. The largest, when it opens in 1992, will be the Mall of America in Minnesota. Its 75-acre site will contain eight department stores, 800 specialty stores, an entertainment park, miniature golf course, 14 movie screens, nightclubs, and restaurants. The mall has been called "the cathedral of postwar culture", and "the culmination of all the American dreams".

The vast range of goods Americans are buying does not include happiness. Surveys by the National Opinion Research Center at the University of Chicago show that the number of Americans describing themselves as "very happy" has fluctuated around 30 per cent since 1957, and levels of general satisfaction have actually fallen. In 1978 a major US study of happiness led to the conclusion: "Above the poverty level, the relationship between income and happiness is remarkably small." Oxford psychologist Michael Argyle has shown that the main determinants of happiness have nothing to do with income and consumption at all. They are satisfaction with family life, followed by satisfaction with work, leisure, and friendship.

Argyle's study also shows that the source of money's satisfaction in a competitive society is not simply being rich; it is also being richer than other people. If so, one individual's gain makes others worse off; and the consumer society's entire frenzied spiral of accumulation, sucking in lives, community, and Earth, has resulted in no overall benefit at all.

The mall becoming the cathedral of the consumer society is a perfect example of means becoming ends. Many enlightened capitalists, and socialists who connived with them for the sake of economic growth, thought that solving the problems of production would lead people, having enough, to turn toward the higher things in life: beauty, spirit, art, love. They were wrong. Making the market the principal instrument of human betterment has transformed it, as shopping, into the consumer society's principal cultural expression.

Changing this situation will be no easy task. It will be no good changing the goals of the economy, from growth to basic needs or sustainability, for example, if the means, the economics, remain the same. It is the means that determine where we end up. The challenge for Green economics is not only to decide on another destination. Its task is also to design an economics, and a development process to go with it, that is as sustainable, equitable, participatory, and satisfying as the end that is in view. Such an economics, and such a process, are the subjects of the rest of this book.

Wants and needs

The purpose of economics is to help society decide how to create, distribute, and consume wealth. Its usefulness is based on two assumptions. First, scarcity of resources: there are simply not enough for us to be able to do everything we might want to do. Second, competition between uses: resources used in one way will not be available for use in another. As a "science" economics seeks to pose the choices between these uses in a neutral, value-free way.

The choices we actually make, however, depend crucially on what we think the economy is for, what economic activity is intended to achieve, how it will help us attain "the good life". The answers of economics to these sorts of questions are based on the goal of increasing human welfare.

Now, human welfare is a slippery concept, including as it does such factors as health, environment, family life, and so on, as well as the more readily identifiable economic aspects such as income and savings. To cope with this, economics calls *all* the components of welfare "wants". Moreover, it assumes that if something is good, that is, it satisfies a want, then more of it is better. In economics you cannot have too much of a good thing. Further, this definition assumes that there is no end to our potential wants.

Such a view of economics is certainly good for economists. If infinite wants forever seek to put scarce resources to competing uses, economists are always going to be important and necessary people.

The wheel of welfare
Human welfare has many different components that are affected by the economy: health, environment, leisure, employment, income, and so on (see below). By placing almost all the emphasis on consumption (and therefore production), conventional economics gives a distorted picture of welfare. Green Economics aims to get the balance right.

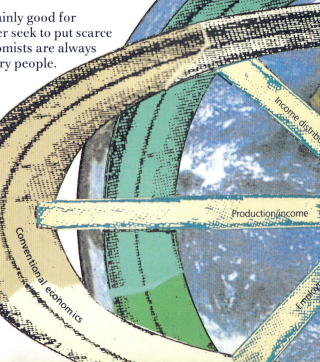

Income distribut

Production/income

Conventional economics

Employm

"Values are always with us. Disinterested research there has never been and never can be. Prior to answers there must be questions. There can be no view except from a view-point. In the questions raised the view-point has been chosen and the valuations implied."
Nobel-prize-winning economist Gunnar Myrdal

The Green approach Green economics accepts the scarcity of and competition for resources, but insists that economics cannot be value free. The selection, presentation, and interpretation of economic "facts" depend on the objectives and attitudes of those involved. The role of the economist is as much to expose the values and assumptions underlying economic choices as it is to give guidance about the choices themselves. Green economics also draws a distinction between wants and needs – an unsatisfied need, material or nonmaterial, leads to damage of the individual. This distinction produces a much richer analysis of welfare creation than simply the increasing satisfaction of an expanding number of wants.

Welfare comes, firstly, from the satisfaction of needs. The more simply and cheaply needs can be satisfied, the greater the proportion of need-satisfaction that will result. Regarding wants, welfare can come not only from their satisfaction but also from their diminution. One way to satisfy the wanting of something is to stop wanting it. And there is the moral dimension, codes that rule out of court certain options, however pleasurable they might be as satisfiers of needs or wants.

Finally, in Green economics both needs and wants can be satisfied. There is no place here for the treadmill of infinitely expanding, insatiable wants. Green economics is the economics of enough.

Leisure

Working conditions

Environment

Safety of the future

Health

Green economics

Turning wants to needs
A triumph of marketing in a capitalist economy is to make people "need" products. At Christmas, 1983, thousands of American parents and children became hysterical when stores sold out of the "cabbage patch" dolls that advertizing had hyped. More broadly, the "Breadline Britain" survey of 1983 found that more than 66% of Britons regarded a washing machine as a necessity, and 43% felt the same way about a telephone: by 1990 the figures were 92% and 57% respectively. As time goes on, it seems that people in consumer societies need more and more things.

Who gets what

The principal focus of economics is production and consumption: what we decide to produce, how, and how much (allocation); and the division of the product among those who helped make it (distribution). Conventionally there are three ingredients of this economic cake, known collectively as the "factors of production": *land*, including energy, minerals, and all other natural resources; *capital*, including machines and the technology infrastructure; and *labour*, the human effort that goes into production.

Since the Industrial Revolution the trend has been to substitute capital and land for labour, a process that has vastly increased the amount one person can produce, and so raised average incomes. It has also resulted in continual restructuring of industry and thus insecurity for workers and communities alike.

Once the cake is baked and sold, the proceeds are divided up among the various types of producers: the workers (wages); landowners (rents); bankers (interest); entrepreneurs (profits). But the proportions in which the cake is divided depend on many factors, which conventional economics seeks to relate to the "marginal productivity" of each – the amount that a single extra unit of land, labour, or capital can produce.

The size of the economic cake
"(This century) the global economy has grown twentyfold, and fossil fuel use tenfold. It took all of human history for the world economy to reach $600 billion in 1900, but it now grows by more than this sum every two years." (*Promoting Environmentally Sound Economic Progress*, Robert Repetto) "On average, the additional economic output in each of the last four decades has matched that added from the beginning of civilisation until 1950." (*State of the World 1990*, Lester Brown) Humanity now appropriates some 40% of all land-based plant growth. Further increase will eventually eliminate ecological diversity and lead to ecosystem collapse: the economic cake will sink the ecological boat.

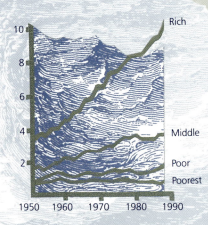

The income gap
In 1950 people in rich nations could, on average, buy about ten times as much as those in poor nations; by 1988 it was nearly 30 times as much. The figures of income per person in this graph (right) are adjusted to reflect purchasing power for four economic classes of countries. The income gap can be about as great within countries as it is between them. In Brazil, for example, the richest 20% earn 28 times as much as the poorest 20%; in Turkey the figure is 16 times; in the US 12 times; in Japan 4 times; in China 3 times. Great disparities in wealth do not contribute to economic success.

(1980 $000s)

Rich
Middle
Poor
Poorest

1950 1960 1970 1980 1990

The Green approach   Green economics has two central objectives in its thinking about allocation and distribution: the elimination of poverty and the maintenance of the economy at its optimal ecological size. Poverty destroys motivation and potential and fosters anger and alienation. Poverty also tends to perpetuate itself. The elimination of poverty can be justified on grounds of both economic efficiency and social justice. And because poverty is a relative as well as an absolute condition, this does not just mean enabling the poorest to satisfy their needs: it also means reducing the gap between and within societies.

The optimal size of the economy depends on its relation to the relevant ecosystem, which, for the human economy, is the entire biosphere. Broadly, its size will be inversely related to the economy's environmental impact, which will, in turn, depend on the number of people and the damage they inflict. It will also depend on the dominant ethical perception of the people/nature relationship: do living things have a right to exist independently of their usefulness to humanity, or can humanity reorder nature solely according to its contribution to human convenience?

The carbon Plimsoll line
The bar chart on the left shows the average carbon emissions from primary fossil fuels per head of population for a range of countries. The minimum 60% reductions in carbon emissions recommended by the IPPC will lead to a carbon "Plimsoll line" of 0.45 tonnes per person. To achieve this, a country such as the US will have to reduce its emissions by more than 90%.

The economic Plimsoll line
The optimal loading of a cargo ship depends not only on the balanced distribution of the load to give the craft stability, but also on not exceeding the cargo's maximum safe weight. Boats have a Plimsoll line on their hulls to indicate how low in the water they can safely be weighed down. Green economics recognizes the importance of having a well-defined economic "Plimsoll line" to stop the economy overburdening its sustaining environment.

tonnes

5.13 4.08 3.75 2.78 1.81 1.13 0.97 0.57 0.38 0.19 0.09 0.03

0.45

USA Australia USSR UK Italy World Mexico China Brazil India Nigeria Zaire

The market and the state

Conventional economics assumes that baking the economic cake is best done by either the market *or* the state. The market is favoured by those who believe that individual consumers should decide; the state by the diminishing number who believe that governments can effectively organize production themselves. There are many conditions for the market to work well, chief among them being that prices must reflect the full costs of product in question. But prices will also be determined by the interaction of supply and demand.

In market theory the role of the state is both to define the context of the market, by allocating property rights and enforcing contracts, and to correct its deficiencies. It should ensure that consumers are truthfully informed and that the market remains competitive. It must also ensure that prices really do reflect full costs. However, bad social and environmental "externalities" – pollution and all sorts of disruption – are often left out of prices, making them too low. Vested interests, the supporters of the "free market", profit from this situation. Calls for state intervention to rectify it can make the market and state appear to be in conflict concerning basic questions of purpose and direction.

What price the car?

The more than 400 million cars in the world impose greater externalities than any other product – at least $300 billion a year in the US alone. Some specific examples include the following.

○ *Air pollution:* in OECD countries road vehicles contribute 75% of carbon monoxide, 48% of nitrogen oxides, and 40% of hydrocarbons. Worldwide they contribute 17% of CO_2 emissions.

○ *Health:* in the US medical costs of pollution from vehicle and industrial fuel combustion are estimated at $40 billion annually.

○ *Resource depletion:* in 1986 cars used 200 billion gallons of fuel.

○ *Congestion:* jams in and around London in 1988 cost $20 billion.

○ *Death and injury:* an estimated 250,000 people die in road accidents each year, and over ten times that number are badly injured.

○ *Blight:* excessive road networks disfigure cities and landscapes, destroy communities, and are the principal areas of danger for children.

Market

State

The "free market"

Although markets are not free, being based on enforceable property rights and contracts, the free market is one of capitalism's most hallowed concepts, implying freedom for all. In fact, it bestows freedom only on property owners at the expense of non-property owners and third parties on the receiving end of the externalities property owners often impose. Whether the free market is socially desirable, therefore, depends on whether the distribution of property is fair, and whether externalities have been internalized into the market. Where this is not so, the state has cause to intervene in the name of social justice and economic efficiency on behalf of those against whom the market is discriminating.

The Green approach Here, the market and the state are seen as complementary. Without the state's context-setting role there can be no market. Without its correction of market failures, the market will not deliver to society value for money or meaningful choices. The state also has an acknowledged redistributive role. Current distributions of wealth and income are not seen as fair, and the state has an obligation to make possible improvements.

The state in Green economics is seen as having three key levels: *local*, corresponding to the idea of a local economy, amenable to a detailed analysis of local needs and resources and able to draw on the attachments of people to each other and their locality; *national*, corresponding to the nation-state, the current focus of most politico-economic analysis; and *international*, reflecting the growing interdependencies in the world, the global nature of many problems, such as security or the environment, and an emerging planetary awareness. Concentration on the local level highlights another important area of Green economic concern – the nonmonetary economy, to which due recognition must start to be given if present trends of decline of family and community are to be reversed.

The nonmonetary economy

The nonmonetary social economy of households and voluntary organizations is the foundation of wealth creation. Office and factory work is made possible only by those, largely women, who maintain home and community. For this, they receive low status and no remuneration. Little wonder that escape from the social economy is a priority for most parents and homemakers, resulting in the institutionalization of care and the breakdown of family and community.

Nonmonetary economy

Local

National

International

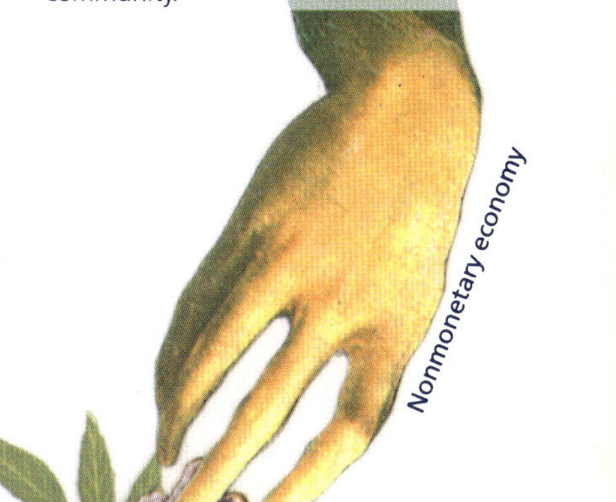

The principle of subsidiarity

Decision making in society should be located at the lowest appropriate level. This core tenet of decentralization was first articulated by Pope Pius XI in *Quadragesimo Anno* in 1931: "It is an injustice and at the same time a grave evil and disturbance of right order to assign to a greater and higher association what lesser and subordinate organizations can do." "Subsidiarity" refers to the perception that the higher organizations are subsidiary to the smaller ones and should be at their service, rather than the reverse.

Money makes economics

Money is the measuring rod of economics. Oscar Wilde's identification of a cynic as a person who knows the price of everything and the value of nothing could easily apply to the conventional economist, for whom price *is* value.

In economics money has three uses. The first is as a unit of value. Second, as a means of exchange – the ability to be able to swap goods for money rather than having to barter goods for goods. Third, as a store of value – it allows the saving in a convenient form of resources that do not need to be consumed immediately. Conventional economics expresses all of these in money terms. Those that are not or cannot be thus expressed tend to be left out of the analysis on the grounds that they are not "economic" values at all.

Economics has two crucial price-based techniques of analysis used to guide decision making. The first, applied to individual projects, is cost-benefit analysis, which involves adding up all a project's costs and benefits and describing it as "economic" if the benefit/cost ratio exceeds a certain figure. The second, applied to the whole material economy, is Gross Domestic Product (GDP) and its derivatives, Gross National Product (GNP) and Net National Product (NNP). GDP is the sum total of all money-based goods and services produced by the domestic economy in a year.

Gross National Product

GNP is calculated, with a few adjustments, from the market prices for which goods and services are sold. But it fails to measure the total output of the economy for several reasons. For example, nonmarketed goods and services, produced in the home, have no price and are thus excluded from GDP. So are activities such as "moonlighting", "informal" trading, or trafficking in drugs in which cash transactions are undeclared. A different type of error is that GNP is widely used as a measure of economic welfare. This is a double mistake, firstly because welfare depends on factors other than production and, secondly, there are many costs – pollution, traffic accidents, commuting – associated with production of GNP goods and services that are either excluded from or even added to GNP (see pp. 66-7). Thus GNP systematically overstates the benefits of market-based production.

Grameen Bank
The Grameen Bank of Bangladesh was founded in 1976 by economics professor Muhammed Yunus specifically to prove the bankability of the poor. By October 1990 Grameen had lent $278 million, and was lending nearly $8 million a month, to its 830,000 members, 90% of whom are women and all of whom are classified as very poor, with a repayment rate of 98%. The benefits that the bank's tiny loans, often only around $50, bring its members in terms of proportional additions to their income and savings are immense. Grameen Bank has doubled in size in the last two years and is still growing fast. It has proved that "development banking" can work on a large scale and is sponsoring many similar initiatives in other countries (see pp. 148-9).

The Green approach Green economics does not deny the usefulness of money in its conventional functions, but believes there are aspects of the financial system in urgent need of reform. First, Green money must reflect wealth created by real goods and services rather than being generated by speculative arbitrage or unproductive paper transactions. Second, those who can make productive use of money must have access to it through an appropriate banking system, whether they are rich or poor or want to borrow much or little. Third, Green money must be tough on inflation, implying strict financial discipline in government and equally strict controls on consumer credit.

Thus the Green approach emphasizes that money is a tool, an enabler of economic activity and a useful store for some types of wealth. It is not, emphatically, wealth itself. There are many values that cannot be meaningfully expressed as prices. It has already been noted that many economic effects – the externalities – fail to get into prices at all. Some of these effects should be estimated so that allowance can be made for them in cost-benefit analysis (see below). But the uncertainties involved mean that financial calculations should only ever be used as an approximate guide to decision making. The actual decision making should be explicitly recognized as the political act that making decisions about society always really is.

Cost-benefit analysis
CBA has traditionally taken an extremely limited view of which costs and benefits of a project to include and has often ignored environmental matters altogether. Thus in tropical forestry the focus has tended to be entirely on the value of harvested timber. This is simply bad CBA. The examples of the analysis used in the Korup (Cameroon) and Oban (Nigeria) National Parks Projects show how good CBA can express some of the values of conservation. The benefit-producing environmental functions of these forests were first grouped under four headings. Under the first, *Regulatory*, are such things as climate regulation; waterflow regulation; and erosion prevention. *Carrier* functions include habitat for indigenous peoples; cultivation areas; nature conservation areas. The *Production* functions yielded timber; other wood products; and genetic resources. And under *Information* account was taken of the forests' spiritual, cultural, educational, and scientific importance. In the event, money values could be given only to a minority of these wider forest benefits, but even so the CBAs showed the conservation values of the parks were $20 million (Korup) and $55 million (Oban), or 20 and 2 times the respective forests' timber values. Thus, in taking a broad view of costs and benefits, good CBA not only puts figures on some of them, it also helps to clarify what has been left out so that this, too, can be considered in the final decision making.

Money and resource flows

The basic way of depicting the economy in conventional economics is as a circular flow of money. The simplest picture is of households receiving income (Y) from companies and either buying goods from those companies (C) or saving. Those savings are invested (I) by financial markets, which buy capital goods also from companies. The income/expenditure equation is then: $Y = C + I$. When the government is added (see below), the picture becomes more complex. The government is funded by taxes on households (T) and government borrowing (Br). Out of this it buys goods and services from private companies (G1) and from the public sector (G2). The income/expenditure equation then becomes: $Y = C + I + G$ (where $G = G1 + G2$).

From this it can be seen that part of the total savings of households (I + Br) has been diverted to government borrowing. Government spending (G) can also be seen to be the difference between the sum of taxes and borrowing and transfers to households, such as social security benefits and pensions (Tr): $G = T + Br - Tr$. Although it is not shown here, the picture can be additionally complicated by the inclusion of transactions with other countries, introducing imports and exports, balance of payments, and foreign currency flows mediated by exchange rates. The importance of the international dimension has increased enormously in recent decades to the point where national management of the economy can be greatly constrained by international money markets.

"In the art of acquiring riches its end has no limits, for its object is money and possessions; but economy has a boundary, for acquiring riches is not its real end . . . For the mere getting of money differs from natural wealth and the latter is the true object of economy."   Aristotle

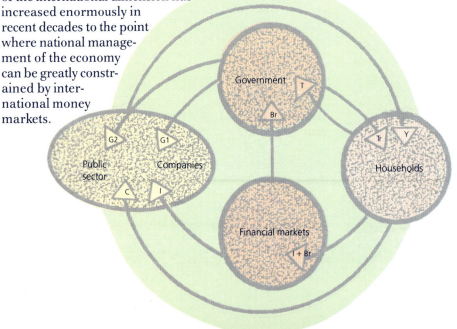

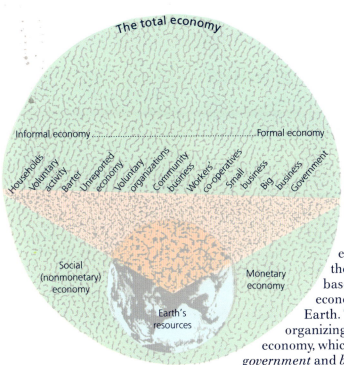

The total economy

Informal economy .... Formal economy

Households · Voluntary activity · Barter · Unreported economy · Voluntary organizations · Community business · Workers' co-operatives · Small business · Big business · Government

Social (nonmonetary) economy

Monetary economy

Earth's resources

The Green approach

Here, too, the flow of money between companies, households, and government is considered an important topic for economic analysis, but it is not nearly the whole story. It leaves out the social economy completely, fails to distinguish between types of economic activity, and divorces the economy from its resource base. First and foremost, the total economy (see left) is supported by Earth. Then come the main organizing principles: the *social* economy, which does not use money, and the *government* and *business* economies, which do.

Households, producing the equivalent of about a third of GNP, and voluntary activity outside of them, are based on nonmonetary, mutual self-help. Barter, or skill exchanges, allow goods and services to be exchanged without financial mediation. Barter in world trade is now estimated at 10 per cent of total trade. The unreported economy is huge and includes drug dealing and other illegal activity, tax evasion, and all the street-based activity in the Third World.

Further along the scale are voluntary organizations and community businesses with predominantly social objectives, and then come employee-owned businesses, which are geared to profit making but which often have social objectives, too. Still further along are the small and big companies, normally purely monetized. They pay for their inputs, sell their output, and have formal employee-employer wage relations. Finally come government and the public sector, which pay for all their inputs and are structured with managers and employees. But a significant part of government output can be the provision of such services as health care and education, which in many countries are distributed more or less freely because of the desirability of universal access.

Lima's unreported economy

In Lima bureaucratic procedures are such that it can take 289 days and more than $1200 (32 times the survival wage) to set up a small business. The economist Hernando de Soto has described how an informal economy has mushroomed out from under this morass of red tape. About 48% of the city's economically active population, contributing 61% of the working hours, is employed in the informal economy, proportions thought to represent Latin America as a whole. More than 40% of the houses were built illegally by invading wasteland; 91% of public transport vehicles are owned and operated informally; 90,000 street sellers have an estimated turnover of more than $300 million a year. Overall, Lima's informal economy is thought to produce the equivalent of nearly 40% of Peru's official GDP.

Balancing the values

In modern industrial societies, and increasingly in the rest of the world, the economy is regarded as the single most important aspect of public policy. The economy has also been separated conceptually from the ethical, social, and ecological aspects of life. It is regarded as a large machine that generates "the good life" of increasing consumption more or less independently of the society of which it is a part. With the economic dimension supreme, it is no surprise that a prime characteristic of the modern world is the destruction of social and ecological values, and the wealth to which they give rise. Industrial humanity is behaving like King Midas, who turned his daughter to gold before he realized the limitations of this conception of wealth.

Nothing better illustrates the economization of human existence than the concept of "development". Not only was development defined as economic development, it also provided a single scale, with industrial countries at the top, against which the diversity of human culture could henceforth be evaluated. Whole societies, many with rich and varied histories, were classified as "underdeveloped", and then "developing", so that in the course of time they could become "developed", as epitomized by the US. For the first time in history, human life was classified as a league table along economic lines.

Four-dimensional human space

Consider a pyramid with four key words at its corners. Any point of the space inside the pyramid can be assigned four co-ordinates: the closer to any one corner the higher that co-ordinate relative to the others. At each corner the co-ordinates are zero except for that relating to that corner. Along the lines joining two corners, the co-ordinates of the other two dimensions are zero. These co-ordinates make comparison without oversimplification possible for many different conditions of human life.

Economy

Human Development Index (HDI)

Dissatisfaction with GNP as a welfare indicator has prompted several alternatives. HDI, developed by the UN Development Programme, combines three standard indicators into a single index. The indicators are real GDP per person, adjusted for purchasing power, the adult literacy rate, and life expectancy. Sri Lanka, China, and Vietnam perform best on HDI relative to GDP per head; Oman, the United Arab Emirates, and Gabon the worst.

Industrial Midas

The industrial economy is turning into commodities, the equivalent of Midas's gold, the wealth of the planet. Meanwhile community withers in the atmosphere of the marketplace; complex ethical codes are reduced to simply the rights of property owners; and a stream of effluent is produced that is undermining the conditions for a healthy human existence.

Society

The Green approach   The economy here is viewed as only one of the four essential dimensions of the human condition – the other three being society, ecology, and ethics. The economy shapes and is shaped by the society and ecology of which it is a part. And all human activity is guided by ethical considerations, although ethical norms will change in response to economic, social, and ecological influences.

Most human situations have these four dimensions. Analysis taking all of them into account still permits comparisons of different situations, but because the dimensions are maintained distinct with no single unit of measurement, no league table can be constructed. Whether one situation is better than another will depend on the subjective judgements of those concerned, based on their goals and priorities. "Development" in this context is defined as progress of the society toward the goals it itself has set. Wealth is what makes this "development" possible.

Ecology

Green wealth
The following pages unfold this view of wealth. It will reject neither money nor goods. But it will embed them in a broad context, acknowledging the rich diversity of human experience and the fact that money can contribute only to part of it. It will put the Midas touch at the service of a humanity that also knows how to value the human spirit, the bonds of community, and the other forms of life on Earth.

Ethics

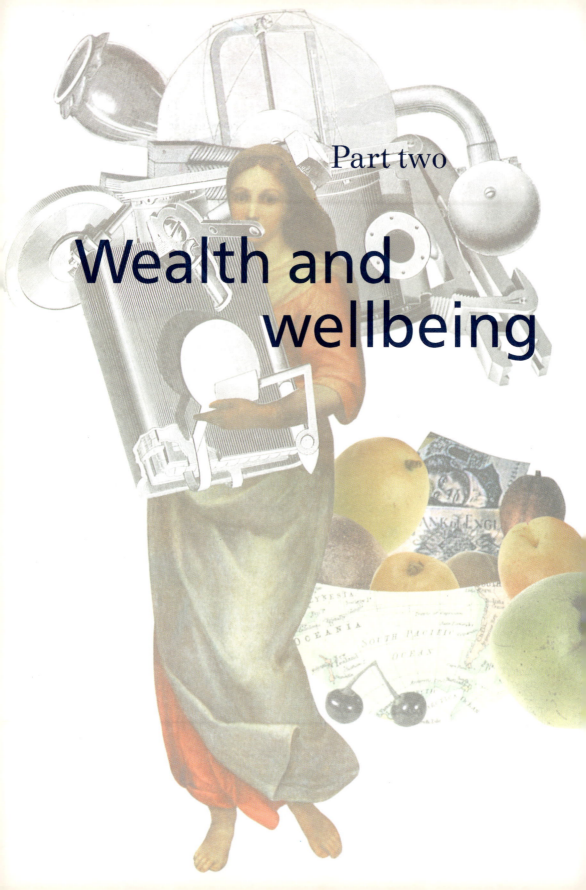

Part two

Wealth and wellbeing

Signs of the planet's deteriorating health are all around us. Some, like global warming and the thinning ozone shield, seem remote and can be understood only with the help of scientists. Others, such as receding forests, contaminated water, and worsening air pollution are painfully real – especially to the rural women who must now walk a kilometre farther to gather enough fuelwood for the evening meal or to the urbanite who lives and breathes in a choking pall of smog.

"Progress", as defined by modern economies, is destroying the very natural systems upon which we depend for health and prosperity. In the same way as an autoimmune disease, in which the body's own defence system attacks and destroys vital tissue, the human economy is assaulting the very life-support systems that keep it functioning. That we persist in calling this progress is the grossest fiction – and the greatest danger – of our time.

Nothing less than a fundamental overhaul of the way we define, pursue, and measure wellbeing will enable us to halt the self-destruction. Use of the Gross National Product, the total output of goods and services in an economy, as the prime indicator of whether people are becoming better off is increasingly deceptive. Among other things, the accounting methods used to produce GNP ignore the destruction of forests, soil, water supplies, and other natural assets. A country can be on the brink of ecological bankruptcy and still register GNP growth, and thus appear to be making progress.

We all know that human wellbeing depends on much more than producing and consuming things valued in the marketplace. Good health, satisfying work, a sense of community, freedom of expression, equal opportunity, and a healthy environment shape overall welfare as much as income does, often more so. Helping us to see and understand wealth in its many dimensions – and how we might begin to measure it better – is what Part Two of this book is about.

Nothing lasting can be gained by economic growth that diminishes the health of the planet or its people. Part Two offers insights into building wealth in all its richest forms – and making real progress.

Sandra Postel
Worldwatch Institute

Sandra Postel is Vice-President for Research at the Worldwatch Institute, an environmental research organization in Washington DC. Her research and writing focus primarily on water and forestry issues, and the economics of environmental sustainability. As well as contributing to all eight of the Institute's annual *State of the World* reports, she has for the last three years served as associate project director for the book, which is now translated into 20 languages. She has also had articles and features published in more than 30 news-papers in the US, and has lectured at several leading US universities, including Stanford, Harvard, and Yale. Ms Postel studied geology and political science at Wittenberg University and resource economics and policy at Duke University.

Understanding wealth

Wealth for the Green economist is broadly conceived as anything that makes us individually and collectively better off. While money is wealth, it is clear that wealth has many other sources.

Three types of wealth, two economic and one noneconomic, can be imagined. Economic wealth can be monetary or nonmonetary. Monetary wealth is anything that can be bought and sold, anything in which there is a market. The market reflects a commodity's price but not necessarily its worth, as the example of water shows (see right). Nonmonetary economic wealth refers to things for which there is a demand and that depend on scarce resources. But since they are not provided in the market, they do not have a price. Much government expenditure seeks to provide nonmonetary economic wealth. Defence spending is supposed to increase security; spending on schools to increase education, and on hospitals, health. But there is no agreement on what any of these is "worth", nor sometimes, as with nuclear weapons (see right), on whether the expenditure on them has even yielded a useful output.

Economists always try to find ways to "price" nonmonetary wealth by reference to markets. Thus the value of beautiful scenery (positive) or of living under an airport's flight path (negative) can be estimated by analysing house prices in these areas compared with others. Attempts have also been made to measure the "option value" of preserving resources for the future, or the "existence value" of an endangered species. As with cost-benefit analysis (see pp. 36-7), these are useful techniques to give weight to environmental values, but dangerous if they imply that all environmental values can be measured in this way. As with the ozone layer, many cannot.

Other nonmonetary wealth-creating values are those pertaining to community, family, and other social structures that potentially engender wellbeing. This concept shades into the noneconomic type of wealth, sources of wellbeing that it makes no sense to relate to ideas of "resource scarcity". The values of love, friendship, religion, and the spirit are obvious examples. Only the most fanatical economists seek to explain such values in terms of scarce resources and competing uses, indicating again the extent to which the economic dimension has attempted to dominate the other, non-economic aspects of life.

Love and marriage?
Gary Becker has been Professor of Economics at the University of Chicago since 1970. The following is from his 1976 book *The Economic Approach to Human Behaviour*.

"Since many men and women compete as they seek mates, a *market* in marriages can be presumed to exist. Each person tries to find the best mate, subject to the restrictions imposed by market conditions. . . .

"Household-produced commodities are numerous and include the quality of meals, the quality and quantity of children, prestige, recreation, companionship, love and health status. . . .

"At an abstract level, love and other emotional attachments, such as sexual activity or frequent close contact with a particular person, can be considered particular, non-marketable commodities. . . . That is, if an important set of commodities produced by households result from 'love', the sorting of mates that maximises total commodity output over all marriages is partly determined by the sorting that maximises the output of these economies. . . .

"Most people, no doubt, find applying the concept of a market allocation of commodities to beloved mates strange and unrealistic." To the Green economist, that is because it is!

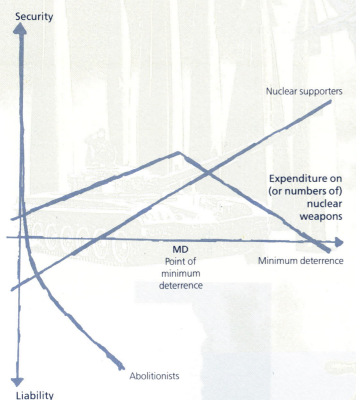

Security

Nuclear supporters

Expenditure on
(or numbers of)
nuclear
weapons

MD
Point of
minimum
deterrence

Minimum deterrence

Abolitionists

Liability

Nuclear security
The wealth in terms of security
generated by expenditure on nuclear
weapons depends totally on your
point of view. This graph (left)
identifies three positions: Nuclear
supporters – the more nuclear
weapons a country has, the greater
the security; Minimum deterrence –
beyond the MD point, nuclear
weapons diminish security; Nuclear
abolitionists – any nuclear weapons
are a liability for security.

"Wealth is what Nature gives us
and what a reasonable man can
make out of the gifts of Nature
for his reasonable use."
William Morris

The value of water
In temperate industrial countries
water is widely available without
charge, making its price zero.
However, as a sustainer of all life
water's value can be thought of as
being close to infinite. Its price will
be low only if there is an abundant
supply at low cost to fulfil this
life-support function. If supply were
to fall to a level of deprivation then
an enormous increase in price
would be expected. In this situation
the market would cease to function
and either the government would
ration water or brute force would
prevail. Price, therefore, indicates
exchange value under certain
conditions at a certain time. But it is
not at all a good indicator of value
in terms of usefulness or necessity
(see right).

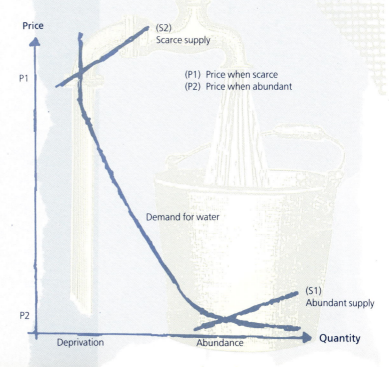

Price

(S2)
Scarce supply

P1

(P1) Price when scarce
(P2) Price when abundant

Demand for water

(S1)
Abundant supply

P2

Deprivation

Abundance

Quantity

The wealth of experience

Wealth is a means to an end, a means by which people can develop their innate potential and lead fulfilling and satisfying lives. Economists call this end "welfare"; its components obviously include income, health, the quality and quantity of work and leisure, environmental quality, personal and social security, and an individual's emotional and spiritual life. It is likely that the components of welfare are directly related to wellbeing, or happiness, but there is no automatic relationship between them. Wellbeing is a subjective condition. Some people experience wellbeing in conditions that others find profoundly uncomfortable. The ideas of objective welfare and subjective wellbeing can be related through the concept of human needs.

In the system of fundamental human needs developed by Manfred Max-Neef, the needs are objective: unchanging, universal, and classifiable. These needs comprise subsistence, protection, affection, understanding, participation, creation, recreation, identity, and freedom. It is the means by which these needs are satisfied, their *satisfiers*, that vary over time, between cultures, and between individuals. Moreover, each need has satisfiers relating to the four modes of human experience: being, doing, having, and interacting. The needs and their modes of satisfaction can be represented by a 36-square matrix.

The matrix shown opposite is an illustrative example only, which could vary greatly depending on the group to which it is applied. The derivation of such matrices has proved a valuable technique in Latin America and elsewhere to help people, ranging from academics and government officials to grassroots groups, to identify those conditions that are either inhibiting or contributing to the satisfaction of people's needs, or might do so.

Envisaging needs and their satisfaction in this way has become a sophisticated and powerful but accessible means for people of all types to understand some of the most profound aspects of their lives and how they can be improved. Such understanding is a fundamental precondition for the creation of real wealth.

Matrix of needs and satisfiers

This matrix relates Max-Neef's nine fundamental human needs to the four ways in which they can be satisfied. Each square contains the satisfiers that relate a particular need to a mode of satisfaction. The Being column, for example, registers personal or collective *attributes*, Having registers *institutions, norms, mechanisms*. The Doing column registers *actions* and Interacting registers *relationships* in space or time. Relatively few of the satisfiers can be appropriately provided by money or ownership of things, except insofar as these lead to higher levels of personal or social development. Emphasizing money and things is actually likely to inhibit need satisfaction in most of the boxes of the matrix.

"Most psychological data show that the main determinants of happiness in life are not related to consumption at all: prominent among them are satisfaction with family life, especially marriage, followed by satisfaction with work, leisure and friendships."
Alan Durning, Worldwatch Institute

Modes of experience / Fundamental human needs	Being	Having	Doing	Interacting
Subsistence	1 Physical health, mental health, equilibrium, sense of humour, adaptability	2 Food, shelter, work	3 Feed, procreate, rest, work	4 Living environment, social setting
Protection	5 Care, adaptability, autonomy, equilibrium, solidarity	6 Insurance systems, savings, social security, health systems, rights, family, work	7 Co-operate, prevent, plan, take care of, cure, help	8 Living space, social environment, dwelling
Affection	9 Self-esteem, determination, generosity, receptiveness, passion, sensuality, sense of humour, tolerance, solidarity, respect	10 Friendships, family partnerships, relationships with nature	11 Make love, caress, express emotions, share, take care of, cultivate, appreciate	12 Privacy, intimacy, home, spaces of togetherness
Understanding	13 Critical conscience, receptiveness, curiosity, astonishment, discipline, intuition, rationality	14 Literature, teachers, method, educational policies, communication policies	15 Investigate, study, experiment, educate, analyse, meditate	16 Settings of formative interaction, schools, universities, academies, groups, communities, family
Participation	17 Adaptability, receptiveness, solidarity, willingness, determination, dedication, respect, passion, sense of humour	18 Rights, responsibilities, duties, privileges, work	19 Become affiliated, co-operate, propose, share, dissent, obey, interact, agree on, express opinions	20 Settings of participative interaction, parties, associations, churches, communities, neighbourhoods, family
Creation	21 Passion, determination, intuition, imagination, boldness, rationality, inventiveness, autonomy, curiosity	22 Abilities, skills, method, work	23 Work, invent, build, design, compose, interpret	24 Productive and feedback settings, workshops, cultural groups, audiences, spaces for expression, temporal freedom
Recreation	25 Curiosity, sense of humour, receptiveness, imagination, recklessness, tranquillity, sensuality	26 Games, spectacles, clubs, parties, peace of mind	27 Daydream, brood, dream, recall old times, give way to fantasies, remember, relax, have fun, play	28 Privacy, intimacy, spaces of closeness, free time, surroundings, landscapes
Identity	29 Sense of belonging, consistency, differentiation, self-esteem, assertiveness	30 Symbols, language, religion, habits, customs, reference groups, sexuality, values, norms, historical memory, work	31 Commit oneself, integrate oneself, confront, decide on, get to know oneself, recognize oneself, actualize oneself, grow	32 Social rhythms, everyday settings, setting to which one belongs, maturation stages
Freedom	33 Autonomy, self-esteem, determination, passion, assertiveness, open mindedness, boldness, rebelliousness, tolerance	34 Equal rights	35 Dissent, choose, be different from, run risks, develop awareness, commit oneself, disobey	36 Temporal/spatial plasticity

Capital and income

A fundamental distinction in all economics is that between capital and income. In broad terms capital is the stock of resources of all sorts that makes possible and generates a flow of production. It is the farmer's seedcorn, tractor, hoes, and other equipment; the industrialist's factories and machines; the homemaker's house, cooker, and refrigerator. Income is defined as that part of people's production that can be consumed without making them worse off.

In the process of production some of the stock of capital is consumed. Seedcorn is sown, machines deteriorate: the capital depreciates. To sustain production this capital must be replaced through investment of some of the production that it has generated. The part of the production flow that remains after making good for depreciation is the income. So income is by definition *sustainable*. A positive income assumes that the capital base that generated it has been left intact. Consuming more than the income calculated in this way is equivalent to consuming capital, which cannot then be reinvested to make up for depreciation and therefore guarantees a lower production in the future.

The four-capital model of wealth creation, which will be elaborated in detail on pages 52-61, builds on, but also substantially differs from, the three-capital model of conventional economics (see opposite). Land is replaced by ecological capital. Labour becomes human capital. Manufactured capital is retained, but a fourth form of capital is added: social and organizational capital.

The interaction between these capitals is also perceived to be more complex than in the conventional model, with pervasive feedback effects and welfare deriving from several different sources. Among other effects, this means that an increase in production can actually lower welfare. In his book *The Costs of Economic Growth*, London School of Economics economist Ezra Mishan gave a forceful and detailed analysis of how an increasing GNP can actually hide the fact that society is becoming worse off. Clearly, under these circumstances, the use of the conventional model can be positively counterproductive and more conducive to wealth destruction than the reverse.

A three-capital model

Conventional economics identifies three types of capital, referred to earlier as "the factors of production" (see pp. 32-3): land, labour, and capital. These three are combined in different proportions in economic processes, which give rise to a stream of goods and services. Part of this stream is invested to replace the machines and sustain the workers. Part of it is consumed to give people pleasure: that is, to increase their economic welfare or utility. Where more is invested than was strictly necessary to allow for depreciation, the capital stock rises so that future production will also rise. When the sole determinant of welfare is taken to be production, as in the model right, an increase in production, reflected by a rising GNP, will inevitably increase welfare. This is an assumption often made in conventional economic analysis with, as will be seen, very misleading results.

John Hicks

John Hicks was born in 1904 and received a British knighthood in 1964 and the Nobel Prize for Economics in 1972. The main reason for the Nobel was his book *Value and Capital*, which first appeared in 1939 and is, in the words of *Palgrave*: "a work so rich in ideas that a short account of it cannot hope to do it justice". One of these seminal ideas was what has now come to be the standard definition of income. "A person's income is what he can consume during the week and still expect to be as well off at the end of the week as he was at the beginning." Income is, therefore, defined as being sustainable: only that part of production that can be consumed after having made up for capital depreciation. It is a very great pity that countries' Net National Products, often called their National

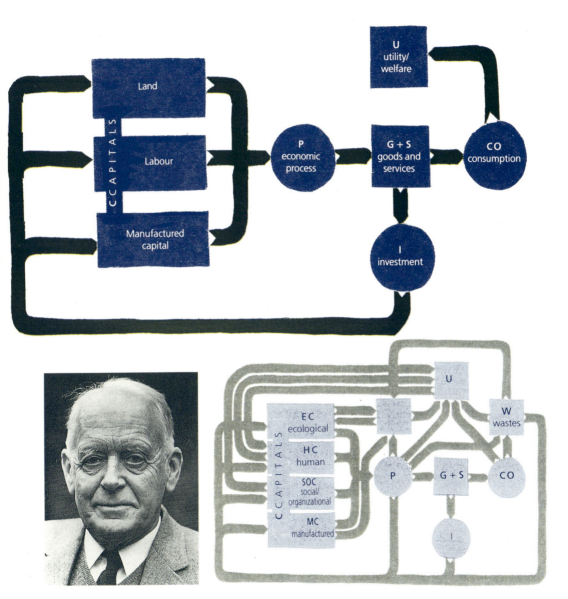

A four-capital model

Income, have not been constructed with this definition rigorously in mind. Their routine treatment of natural capital as income by failing to account for the costs of destruction and depletion of the environment augurs badly for wealth creation in the future.

In this model, only the definition of manufactured capital is substantially unchanged from the three-capital case. Ecological capital embodies a more realistic perception than "land" as to how the biosphere sustains the economy. Human capital emphasizes the roles in wealth creation of health, knowledge, skill, and motivation. And the new category of social and organizational capital reflects the importance of many kinds of groups in helping people working together to be more productive than they could be as isolated individuals.

Ecocapital

To refer to the Earth, including its wealth of living systems, as "ecological capital" is already to devalue it and reduce it to the status of some instrument for human use, a factor of production like any other. Such an implication needs constantly to be corrected, for it is an obvious fact that this "capital" is the precondition not only of production but of life itself.

There are also fundamental ethical questions concerning the intrinsic value of the natural world, its right to exist irrespective of its use to people. Is it really true, as Oxford University economist Wilfred Beckerman has written, that: ". . . effluence entering into some remote stream might harm the fish in it, but if the fish were never to be the object of human satisfaction, this would be of no practical consequence"? Such an attitude places humanity as firmly at the centre of life on Earth as the Earth was once placed at the centre of the universe. It is a prime expression of the modern view that the Earth, and its creatures, only matter insofar as they are useful to people, a view so different from the ancient concept of the Earth as humanity's nurturing mother.

It seems likely that a solution to the ecological crisis will require a general shift to a biocentric worldview, one in which humanity is seen as a dependent part of a larger whole, and other species and their habitats have value in their own right. The great natural ecosystems and life processes are so complex, and human understanding of them still so rudimentary, that any hubristic attempt to "maximize" or "optimize" their use for humanity will, for the foreseeable future, run the gravest risks of catastrophic instabilities. These instabilities could result in the perhaps irreversible destruction of crucial life-support mechanisms of which even the best scientists were unaware. Never were caution and humility in the face of the imponderable more justified. The "great experiment" with the planetary system and thus its own survival, on which the former UK Prime Minister Margaret Thatcher perceives humanity to be currently engaged (see far right), resembles more a once-and-for-all spending spree than a thoughtful quest for scientific knowledge.

Before humanity seeks to "manage the planet" it would do better to learn to manage itself, and discover how to align itself with the forces of life on Earth, following the examples in the natural world, rather than always seeking to improve on or second guess them.

The ecocapital cycle

ECOPRODUCTION

plant
fish, hydroelectricity
crop
income

Nature's no-waste economy

It is paradoxical that humanity's attempts at production should be undermining its natural foundations because, in fact, nature itself provides the archetype of a high-productivity, sustainable economic system (see diagram right). The key to its success is that it is a totally renewable, no-waste economy powered by the sun, whose duration is the only limit on sustainability. Inorganic substances – trace elements – are used in such small quantities as effectively to be renewable, and each "waste" from one process becomes the raw material for another.

Humanity in its wisdom has chosen instead a linear economic

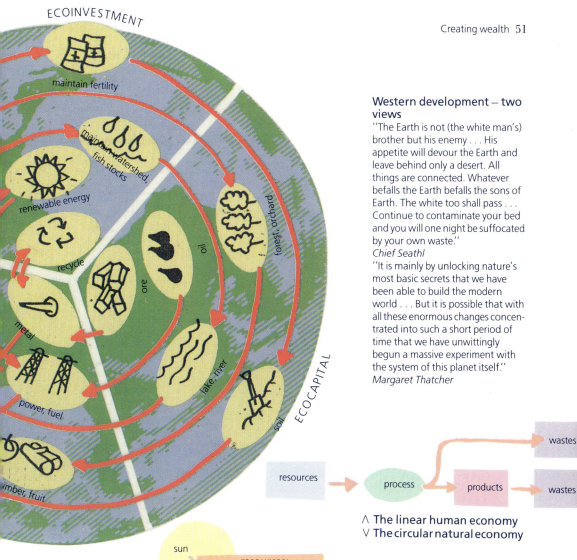

ECOINVESTMENT

maintain fertility

maintain watershed, fish stocks

renewable energy

recycle

ore

oil

forest, orchard

metal

power, fuel

lake, river

soil

ECOCAPITAL

timber, fruit

Western development – two views

"The Earth is not (the white man's) brother but his enemy . . . His appetite will devour the Earth and leave behind only a desert. All things are connected. Whatever befalls the Earth befalls the sons of Earth. The white too shall pass . . . Continue to contaminate your bed and you will one night be suffocated by your own waste."
Chief Seathl

"It is mainly by unlocking nature's most basic secrets that we have been able to build the modern world . . . But it is possible that with all these enormous changes concentrated into such a short period of time that we have unwittingly begun a massive experiment with the system of this planet itself."
Margaret Thatcher

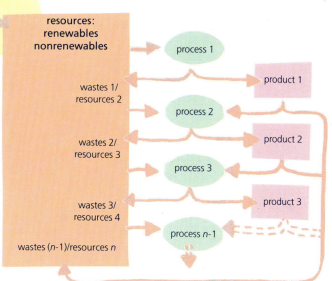

resources → process → products → wastes / wastes

∧ **The linear human economy**
∨ **The circular natural economy**

sun

resources: renewables nonrenewables

process 1

wastes 1/ resources 2

product 1

process 2

wastes 2/ resources 3

product 2

process 3

wastes 3/ resources 4

product 3

process n-1

wastes (n-1)/resources n

model in which resources and wastes are disconnected. The inevitable result, as soon as throughput is sufficiently increased, is resource shortages on the one hand and pollution problems on the other.

This situation can be remedied only by learning, or relearning, nature's way: rely on renewable resources; ensure that they are indeed renewed; and refrain from producing wastes that cannot become resources. Unfortunately, from the high-consumption, high-effluent economic situation in which we find ourselves and to which we have become habituated, such a lesson is more easily recited than acted on.

Accounting for the environment

In economic terms the planet makes three basic contributions to human welfare, as shown in the diagram opposite. First, it provides resources for production (ECp). Some of these, such as timber, grain, fish, and water, can, if not overexploited, be renewed year after year. Others, such as oil and minerals, cannot. Minerals at least can be recycled. Energy, once spent, is dissipated forever. Second, the environment absorbs, neutralizes, or recycles the wastes of the economy (Wec), which derive from production (Pw) and consumption (COw). The third economic contribution the planet makes is in providing various "services" independently of human activity (ECe). Some of these, such as climatic regulation or the protection afforded by the ozone layer, are literally survival services. Others, such as wilderness, scenery, or amenity, are of an aesthetic or a recreational nature. These can be important sources of utility through their satisfaction of the needs of "being" (Eu) (see pp. 36-7). This function can be seriously impaired by effects from the economic process (Pe), such as noise or the visual intrusion of factories.

These economic functions of the environment interact at every level, and it is their interactions that are at the root of all the great environmental challenges described on pages 14-17. Thus the survival services, such as climate, have a crucial effect on renewable resources (Eec) through desertification, for example, as of course do wastes (Wec), through such effects as acid rain and toxic pollution. The wastes also affect the survival services (We), by causing global warming and ozone depletion. The failure to renew potentially renewable resources by, for example, tropical deforestation, affects both the survival services through global warming and the ability to produce such resources in the future because of soil erosion. Wastes can also have a direct impact on welfare (Wu), usually negatively as with litter.

The size of all these effects depends on three basic variables: the population level, per capita consumption, and the environmental impact of the technology through which the consumption is delivered. Different technologies exhibit enormous differences in resource efficiency, pollution intensity, and in whether they reinforce or disrupt natural processes.

The eco-eco connection
The diagram (right) clearly reveals the pervasive interaction of the global ecosystem with the human economy. In this diagram, and in those on pages 54-9, the relationships and factors emphasized and annotated are only those explained in the accompanying text. The full version of the four-capital model is given on pages 60-1. In the notation of flows, upper case letters indicate sources, and lower case letters destinations.

The capital consumers
Seven countries – the US, Japan, USSR, the UK, France, West Germany (as was), and Italy – are among the top ten consumers of all the resources shown on the right. These countries had just 16.8% of the 1990 world population. The diagram shows the proportion of 1988 world consumption of the metals listed, and 1987 world consumption of energy, for which the seven countries were responsible. It also gives the years before exhaustion of the resources at current production rates. For energy this is calculated from proven reserves. For the other resources two figures are given: in I the calculation has been made on the basis of the known reserves that could be viably extracted at current prices with current technology; in II the reserve figures used are totals that are known to exist, but their extraction may be more costly and problematic.

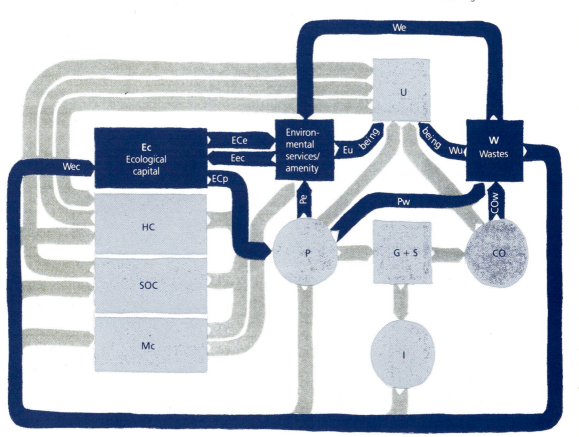

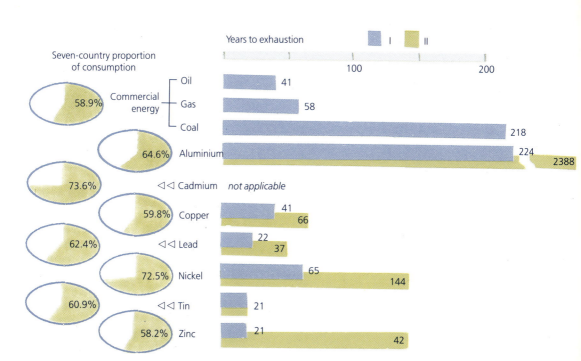

Seven-country proportion of consumption

Years to exhaustion   I   II

100   200

Commercial energy
┌ Oil   41
├ Gas   58
└ Coal   218

58.9%

64.6%   Aluminium   224   2388

73.6%   ◁◁ Cadmium   *not applicable*

59.8%   Copper   41   66

62.4%   ◁◁ Lead   22   37

72.5%   Nickel   65   144

60.9%   ◁◁ Tin   21

58.2%   Zinc   21   42

Human capital

Referring to people as "human capital" runs the same risk of devaluation as calling the Earth "ecological capital" (see pp. 50-3). People are clearly more than instruments of production. But just as an analysis of the global environment's contribution to the human economy helps to elucidate its crucial importance, so explaining the role of people in production as "human capital", rather than just "labour", provides a richer and more useful perspective, which emphasizes the growing importance of people to production.

In the early years of industrialism, labour was widely expected to remain close to a subsistence standard of living. Labour often actually lived *below* subsistence level: the workers' health was generally poor and they and many of their children died young or achieved well below their potential, a situation being perpetuated by the crisis in the Third World today. In the 1980s, standards of nutrition, health, and education in most of Latin America and sub-Saharan Africa fell for the first time in four decades. UNICEF Deputy Director Richard Jolly commented: "For the young child there is no second chance. The underemphasised tragedy of the disinvestment in human capital in the 1980s is that the results will be carried forward in stunted bodies and deficient educations well into the 21st century." This was, and is, industrialization red in tooth and claw, with people as disposable inputs of production.

Apart from being morally indefensible, this treatment of people is also economically inefficient when they are regarded as human capital whose capacities could be developed and engaged in the production process. People then become a valuable resource. Jolly says bluntly: "Human capital is a more important factor for achieving economic growth than physical capital."

Finally, there must be some mention of human capital and work, the activity through which it is deployed. In economics, work is usually regarded as an unpleasant requirement to gain an income. In Green economics, however, work is not only a means to a livelihood. Fulfilment through work and relationships at work make it one of the most important potential "satisfiers" of a wide range of needs related to "doing" and "interacting". In Max-Neef's matrix (see pp. 46-7), work appears five times – more than any other word. Its potential contribution to human welfare is immense.

Renewing human capital

According to Allan Gilmour, Executive Vice-President Ford Motor Co: "The key resource that most companies have is the brains, energy and ambition . . . of their people." To be fully productive, people must be healthy, motivated, and appropriately skilled, qualities that need constantly to be renewed. An essential part of good management today is the provision of schemes to ensure that this renewal is an integral part of working life. Companies are starting to introduce staff counselling and health and fitness centres, career guidance, integrated production units, decentralization of authority, opportunities for worker initiatives and involvement, and profit sharing and other incentive schemes. And, of course, high levels of training and retraining have become standard practice in many companies. As Professor Charles Handy of the London Business School has pointed out: "Companies are uncomfortably aware that people are assets which could walk out the door. Now *there* is a reason for showing proper concern for our employees."

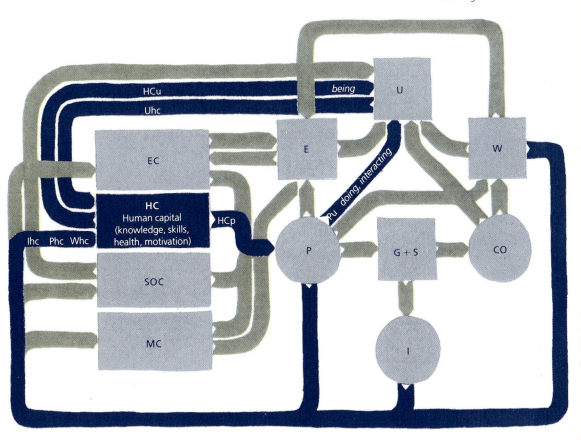

The three components

Human capital has three components: health, knowledge and skills, and motivation (see above). All three are required for productive work (HCp). The potential contribution of work to human welfare through job satisfaction and working relationships is shown by Pu. Human capital and welfare also have an important direct interaction. A healthy, skilled, and motivated person is likely to be happier than one without these attributes (HCu); and a happy person is more likely to remain healthy, skilled, and motivated than an unsatisfied one (Uhc). Enhancing human capital thus becomes an objective of, as well as a means to, a productive economy, through investment in education and training (Ihc) and stimulating work experience (Phc). By damaging health by, for example, pollution, wastes can have a negative effect on human capital (Whc).

New School Programme

The New School Programme was designed in Colombia in 1978 by a team of rural educators led by Vicky Colbert. The Programme is based on "active instruction" – small groups with self-instruction workbooks and a practical, problem-solving approach. The schools are integrated into the community and adapted to people's lifestyles: for example, time is allowed for pupils to help with the harvest. By 1987, when it was chosen by the World Bank as an outstanding primary education initiative, the Programme was being implemented by 35,000 co-ordinators and 26,000 teachers in 15,000 rural schools reaching 750,000 children a year. Further expansion is planned to take it to the remaining 10,000 rural schools and into marginal urban areas.

Human capital formation

Though education is more than learning to be productive, the formation of human capital is one of its functions. Given the resources devoted to them, most education systems' achievement in terms of human capital formation seems low. A recent World Bank report cited evidence that "in many countries the average dollar invested in primary education returns twice as much as one invested in higher education. Yet governments . . . heavily subsidise higher education at the expense of primary education" (see pp. 118-21). Perhaps an emphasis on health education and on teaching skills appropriate to students' lives and experiences would act to correct the imbalance and realize education's economic benefits. It could also provide a powerful impulse toward education's wider goal of personal development.

Social and organizational capital

Very few working situations involve the human capital of isolated individuals (see pp. 54-5). In most cases people work together, and the quality of the relationships between them, and the way in which they are structured, make an enormous difference to both the quality and quantity of the work produced. Whatever the human capital involved, the organizational framework within which it operates is crucial to its productivity.

Organizations are not just sums of individuals. They have their own habits, norms, procedures, traditions, memories, and cultures. They are communities. These characteristics largely determine the effectiveness of those within the organizations. Where they foster efficiency, motivation, dynamism, and creativity they become very real contributors to the process of wealth creation. Increasingly, they are causing organizations themselves to be seen as a form of capital.

The most obvious form of organizational capital is that exhibited in businesses or such related economic structures as trade associations, co-operatives, and trade unions. But the productive potential inherent in people's relationships and their organizational structures is by no means confined to the business world. By keeping the focus firmly on the total economy it is possible to see capital, too, in household and family relationships, and in community and voluntary organizations of all types. Such capital is also present in a country's legal and political structures and, internationally, in treaties that provide for wealth conservation or creation, such as the Montreal Ozone Protocol or the Law of the Sea.

Community organization

The phenomenon of the "nongovernmental organization" (NGO) is a clear example of how people organized together can bring about improvements in their lives that would have been unattainable individually. Even Senior Vice-President of the World Bank, Moeen Quereshi, has acknowledged: "NGOs are telling us that more involvement by grassroots NGOs in our operations will improve the Bank's impact on both poverty and environmental aspects of development. And their advice squares with our own experience."

Villa el Salvador

The wealth-creating power of community is well illustrated in Lima's largest squatter settlement, Villa el Salvador. A large area of state-owned desert land has, over a period of 15 years, been transformed into a thriving, self-governing community of 300,000 people. At the heart of the development has been CUAVES (the Self-Management Urban Community of Villa el Salvador), Villa's own community organization. The organization's democratic structure gives representation to each block and a vast network of women's groups, through which citizens have planted 500,000 trees and built 26 schools, 150 daycare centres, and 300 community kitchens. Training and education has reduced illiteracy to 3% and infant mortality to 40% below the national average. This is despite the fact that one-third of residents live on lower-than-subsistence incomes, compared with only 10% in Lima as a whole.

Law of the Sea

After ten years of negotiations, the Convention of the Law of the Sea was signed in April 1982 by 119 nations, 35 of which had ratified it by 1988. Although the UK, US, and USSR have refused to sign, the Convention has already had an important conservation effect on "the common heritage of mankind" – the world's oceans. Its 320-kilometre (200-mile) exclusive economic zones around coastal nations have led to, at least the possibility of, responsible management of these now national resources. In the northwest Atlantic, for example, the cod catch by long-range fleets has been cut by at least 90%. The Convention also calls for new laws to enforce a reduction in the dumping of toxic substances at sea, and could well become an effective framework for the enactment and enforcement of these laws when they come into effect.

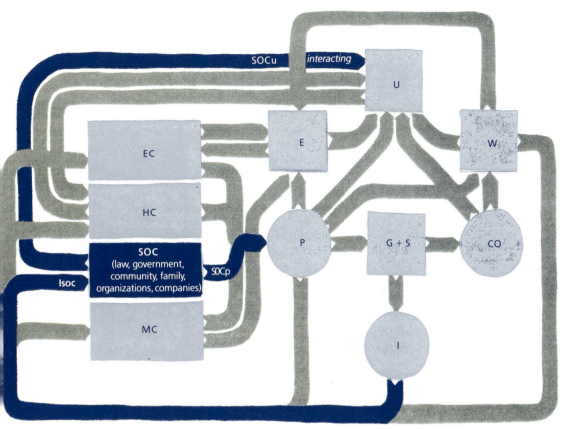

SOCu interacting

U

E

W

EC

HC

SOC
(law, government,
community, family,
organizations, companies)

P

G + S

CO

SOCp

Isoc

MC

I

The role of social and organizational capital (SOC)

Social and organizational capital (above) is a crucial ingredient in the economic process (SOCp) through the structures of the economy and the working relationships they generate. An example of investment of this type of capital (Isoc) is the employment by companies of management consultants to improve their organizational structure and efficiency. The relationships embodied in social and organizational capital, whether at work or in the home or community, also have an important direct effect on utility (SOCu). Through the greater political bargaining or productive power that community organization confers, it seems certain to increase in importance as a means whereby people can defend their rights and work for improvement in their quality of life. It is the generation of such power that entitles people's organizations to be called social capital.

Companies, trade unions, bureaucracies

Not all organizations are productive. Logging or extractive companies in rainforests are clear examples of organizations destroying more wealth than they create. But within businesses, intelligent, humane, and efficient organization remains the principal way of enhancing the quality of work and minimizing the environmental impact of economic activity. Trade unions have similar positive and negative features. Through them people have managed to win great improvements in both their remuneration and conditions of work. Where this has improved the workers' health and productivity, their human capital, unions can be seen as wealth creators. But unions committed to industrial conflict can also destroy wealth both for their members and society at large. Labour-capital partnerships, as in Germany and Japan, rather than institutionalized confrontation, would appear to be the way to maximize the organizational capital of businesses. Similarly with government bureaucracy: it can be enabling and supportive of business and community endeavour; or it can stifle it. UK industrialist George Goyder has expressed the desirable situation thus: "We need in industry a framework of law which is able to command the confidence of employees, financial backers, customers and the community at large. The creation of a sense of partnership in industry and commerce is the most urgent task facing us in domestic politics."

Manufactured capital

The fourth type of capital is the one economists usually refer to simply as "capital": all the tools, machines, buildings, technologies, and infrastructure that enhance productivity. It is to the increasing stock of this capital that production growth is usually attributed.

As manufactured capital is accumulated and people become more productive, average wages rise. Two conclusions follow: first, each workplace needs a greater capital investment to become established; second, more savings are required to maintain the capital base. Both these conclusions have some worrying implications.

With regard to the greater cost of workplaces, countries with high unemployment or underemployment are likely to find it almost impossible to find the capital to achieve full employment using modern, capital-intensive technologies. Countries will increasingly tend to have a "dual economy" – a high-tech sector of capital-intensive production and relatively high wages, and a low-tech sector of low-paid services and traditional or outdated production methods. This phenomenon is becoming more evident in all economies, and the two sectors coexist uneasily. The modern sector is continually destroying the viability of the other and failing to employ all those made unemployed. At the same time, workers' expectations rise according to the new technologies, so that the older methods become unattractive. The result is widespread dislocation as migrants are drawn to cities in search of elusive jobs, and growing discontent as the economy fails to deliver to ever-larger numbers of people what television and other advertising have taught them to expect of it.

Regarding savings, it is hard to avoid the impression that the "born-to-shop" ethic of the consumer society is seriously affecting the attitude of thrifty investment on which all capital-intensive societies are founded. The proportion of income saved (savings ratio) as opposed to consumed has declined markedly in industrial countries in the last two decades, with high levels of consumer credit, amounting to the present consumption of future income, exacerbating the trend. Developing countries' savings have also fallen since the mid 1970s, largely reflecting their debt burden and deteriorating terms of trade (see pp. 164-7). If savings continue to decline the outlook for both per capita output and the environmental restructuring of production must be bleak.

The role of manufactured capital

In its contribution to the productive process (MCp), wear and tear causes manufactured capital to depreciate (Pmc) and, to remain constant or increasing, it always needs to be replenished through investment (Imc) of this amount or more. Through buildings and the built environment generally, manufactured capital can also be an important contributor to environmental beauty and amenity, or the reverse, (MCe), although this function often tends to be ignored in favour of more economistic criteria when sites are redeveloped.

Household capital

With manufactured capital, as with so much else, economic analysis and procedures discriminate against the household in favour of the monetary sector. All the productive capital in the industrial-country household – for example, refrigerator, vacuum cleaner, iron, cooker, and countless other tools – are treated as consumer rather than investment goods. As such they do not qualify for tax relief, just as those who work with these tools (predominantly women) tend to be classed as "economically inactive".

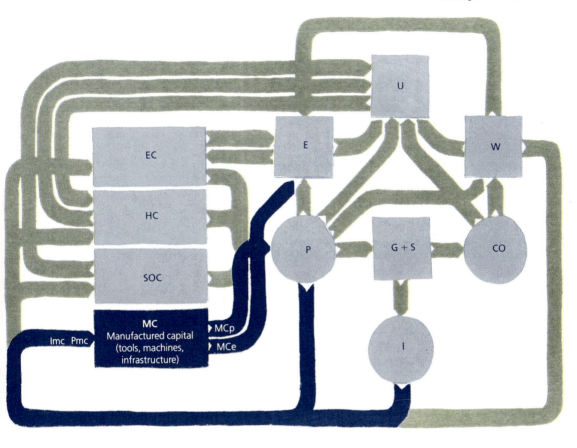

Declining savings

Both savings and investment as a percentage of GNP have been on a downward trend in both industrial and Third World countries since the mid 1970s (see right). While economists still argue about the implications of this for long-term production growth, it is a worrying trend in view of the immense *environmental* investment that is required to reverse current ecological decline. Such investment needs to improve the environmental performance of production technologies by a factor of 4 over the next 50 years, even without production growth in industrial countries (see pp. 180-1). It is hard to see how such investment will come about without a considerable increase in both public and private savings stimulated by determined public policy.

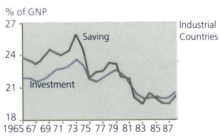

% of GNP

Industrial Countries

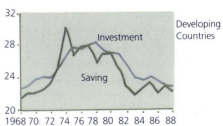

Developing Countries

Capital-creating wealth

Putting together the four capitals already looked at in detail – ecological, human, social/organizational, and manufactured (see pp. 50-9) – leads us to a model of wealth creation (see right) far richer than the land-labour-capital model favoured by conventional economics.

This richness is not an optional extra. It is absolutely necessary if the model is to reflect the realities of the modern global economy and help us to understand and act within it. The model readily encompasses many of the issues that have been encountered earlier.

○ The multiple sources of human welfare, or utility, deriving from different parts of the economic cycle and from all the modes of experience: being, doing, having, interacting, as well as having (COu).

○ The more precise definition of each type of capital, in particular identifying the detailed contribution of the environment and including social and organizational factors to balance the individualism inherent in much economic treatment of "labour" and "human capital".

○ The pervasive feedback effects from practically everything to practically everything else – the hallmark of a system as opposed to a linear process. Above all, this permits an explanation of how consumption can go up while human welfare goes down. It also shows the different effects on capital stock from the economic process (Pc), the wastes (Wc), and, more conventionally, investment (Ic).

The description of the four capitals is also important because it permits another challenge to orthodox economics, concerning the "substitutability" of one capital for another. The model reveals the unique qualities of each form of capital and, therefore, the limited scope for substitution that actually exists. In particular, the environment, with its multiplicity of functions, is shown to be irreplaceable in many vital respects. With all our technology, we are still nowhere near creating a possible substitute for the ozone layer or the Earth's great climatic processes. We do not even understand the basic operation of many ecosystems, nor can we recreate their elements, individual species, once they have been extinguished. All of these insights from the model point to the necessity of preserving intact all key environmental features if human welfare is to be secured into the future.

A balanced life

Thinking of welfare generation as depicted in the diagram, right, is as relevant to individuals as to whole societies. Everybody has to choose how to apportion their time and energy between their families, friends, and colleagues *(interaction)*, solitude and interaction with nature *(being)*, work satisfaction *(doing)*, and income and what it can buy *(having)*. In a consumer society, there is relentless pressure to trade off being, interacting, and doing for more having, with a consequent proliferation of pseudo-satisfiers that cannot really take the place of relationships and fulfilling work. Green economics suggests that the "good life" is much more likely to be had by seeking to strike an appropriate balance between the four modes of experience than by maximizing one of them at the expense of the others. Between individuals the chosen balance is likely to vary markedly according to taste and preference. However, for societies the balance is likely to be within a narrow band of possibilities if stability and sustainability are to be achieved.

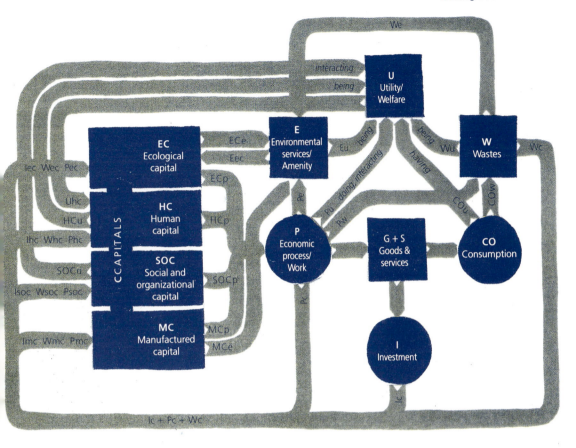

More growth, worse off

The model above provides an explanation for what may be one of the most significant processes in today's economy: an increase in Gross National Product (GNP) but a decline in human welfare. In the conventional, three-capital model, consumption is equivalent to being better off. Here, as in real life, welfare derives from many sources, which may be negatively affected by increasing consumption. For example, an increase in productivity may reduce work satisfaction to an extent that more than outweighs any increase in income. Moreover, the effects of growth on the social and environmental fabric may both reduce welfare directly or reduce future production by depleting one or more of the capitals. The four-capital model gives a clear insight into why the use of the growth rate of GNP as a sign of being better off is probably the most misleading practice in economics today.

Substitution between capitals

The conventional economic view is that capitals can be easily substituted for each other and that it does not matter if one form of capital is depleted as long as another is built up. Using this argument, the sacrifice of the environment is unimportant provided that some other capital is developed. This view as applied to the environment is as fallacious as it is widely held. As David Pearce and his colleagues, in their book *Blueprint for a Green Economy*, have observed: "There are many types of environmental asset for which there are no substitutes." The implications of this are profound, for if capitals are not freely interchangeable, then sustainability demands that at least minimum or irreplaceable stocks must be preserved. The most important components of ecocapital, such as the tropical rainforests, cannot be traded off. They must be absolutely protected.

Measuring wealth creation

The four-capital model of wealth creation described on the previous pages may be richer and reflect more accurately the real-life economic experience than the simpler three-capital model it replaces. However, it is of limited practical use unless the quantities and qualities it describes can be measured in a meaningful way. Fortunately they can.

In the three-capital model, the measurement technique is relatively simple. Utility is held to be directly related to market-based consumption valued at market prices or, broadly, GNP less depreciation. This is not quite the whole story. GNP also includes government expenditure and some nonmarket production, but the latter is only a tiny proportion of the wealth that is actually generated by the household sector.

Nonmarket goods and services become much more important in the four-capital model for several reasons. First, utility is seen to derive from many more sources than just marketed consumption. Second, the new conceptions of capital contain important, nonmonetary elements. Third, the purpose of the measurements is to give an indication of the total economy (see pp. 38-9) rather than just the marketed portion of it.

The inadequacies of GNP as a welfare indicator have led to many attempts to reform or replace it for this purpose. Three broad approaches seem possible.

o To add to or subtract from GNP various elements to produce an Adjusted National Product (ANP) that is a better indicator of sustainable income.

o To supplement this ANP with figures for nonmarketed production and social and environmental indicators to give a broader framework within which welfare can be evaluated.

o To combine ANP with other indicators to give an overall Index of Welfare, which could replace GNP as a social welfare indicator altogether.

The approach taken on pages 64-71 develops the first two of these options, encompassing GNP and market prices, but going well beyond them. It does not seek to construct a welfare index, in agreement with Manchester University researcher Ian Miles, who has written: "Insurmountable difficulties are posed by the search for a single composite measure of welfare or quality of life. Perhaps we should be glad that human life remains too rich to be represented in one-dimensional terms."

Beyond GNP

One of the most widely used attempts to measure welfare beyond GNP was the Overseas Development Council's Physical Quality of Life Index (PQLI), which combined infant mortality, life expectancy, and literacy, with equal weights, into a single number. To take account also of respect for human rights, Professor of Economics at the University of Maine, USA, Mark Lutz, has recently combined PQLI with the human rights index produced by *The Economist* to generate an Authentic Socioeconomic Development Index (ASEDI). The United Nations Development Programme's Human Development Index (HDI) (see pp. 40-1) adjusts GNP to reflect purchasing power and then combines it with life expectancy and literacy. Far more comprehensive, and the first index here to include ecological factors, is Daly and Cobb's Index of Sustainable Economic Welfare (ISEW), which combines a figure of personal consumption with statistics on income distribution, capital growth, value of household labour, and others, including a number of environmental indicators. ISEW, which has declined from a peak in 1979, provides graphic confirmation of the way in which the welfare benefits of increasing GNP are now being offset by a variety of factors (see graph below). As Daly and Cobb say: "Economic welfare has been deteriorating for a decade, largely as a result of growing income inequality, the exhaustion of resources and the failure to invest adequately to sustain the economy of the future."

GNP and ISEW compared

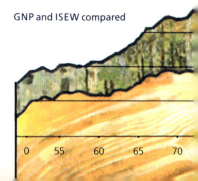

| 0 | 55 | 60 | 65 | 70 |

Out of the shopping mall

Laying the consumer mentality to rest demands an indicator framework that shows the richness and variety of life, that supplants the dominant image of the shopping mall by an organic metaphor of wealth creation. Here the economy is shown as a tree yielding four fruit. Each corresponds to different aspects of the wealth produced, and each becomes a component of the indicator framework to be developed in the following pages. There is an ecological account to show the natural capital stocks and how economic activity is drawing on them; an account of monetary production, essentially consisting of GNP with the deductions necessary to turn it into a sustainable income figure; an account of nonmonetary production, mainly comprising all the wealth produced in the household; and, finally, a set of social indicators chosen to show the most important impacts of the economy on society at large.

Per capita GNP

Inflation-
adjusted
1972
US dollars

7000

6000

5000

4000

Per capita ISEW

3000

2000

80   85

Ecological accounting

The purpose of ecological accounting is to help ensure that the environmental capital base needed for economic production and human welfare in the future is not heedlessly consumed in the present. The depletion of the UK's North Sea oil provides a clear example of this type of heedless consumption (see right).

Ecological accounting seeks to monitor the crucial economic functions of the environment: the resource inputs into the economy; the disposal of wastes from it; and the direct provision of environmental services. Wherever possible these are then related via costs and prices to the standard economic accounts. The ultimate objective is in line with the recommendation of the Brundtland Report that: "Where resources and data permit, an annual report and an audit on changes in environmental quality and in the stock of the nation's environmental resource assets are needed to complement the traditional annual fiscal budget and economic development plan."

There has been much progress in recent years with ecological accounting techniques. In Europe, Norway, France, and the Netherlands have developed sophisticated environmental databases, and more countries are planning to do so. In addition, Norway and France have both devised comprehensive accounting systems for this data. Third World countries, such as Indonesia, are also increasingly recognizing the vital importance of what remains of their natural resources, although as yet this recognition has failed to slow significantly their destruction.

Developing full ecological accounts takes time and considerable investment, as the Norwegian experience shows (see right). Such development is crucial but it should not be allowed to postpone the necessary immediate decisions on environmental protection and regeneration. There is already a clear case for a large programme for investment in ecosystem renewal, especially in desert or degraded forest areas, even where the financial return of such action is uncertain or will be delayed. As the Director of India's Centre for Science and the Environment, Anil Agarwal, says: "We cannot allow the Gross National Product to destroy the Gross Nature Product any further. Conserving and recreating nature has become our highest priority."

Natural capital losses in Indonesia

Robert Repetto of the World Resources Institute has calculated the value of the natural capital depletion in Indonesia for three key resources – oil, timber, and soil. His method is conceptually simple, if imprecise in practice: first, determine the stocks of the resources and their net rate of depletion; then put a price on this depletion. For the oil and timber, the value is simply the price times quantity depleted; for the soil, the value is the cost of soil erosion due to lowered yields and forced changes to lower value crops. Repetto found that between 1971 and 1984 Indonesian GDP increased 2.44 times, an average growth rate of 7.1%. If the loss of these three natural resources is taken into account, these figures fall to 1.68 times and 4%.

The Norwegian resource accounts

Norway was the first in the field of natural resource accounting, beginning in 1968. By the mid 70s its system was well into development. Its approach seeks to provide an integrated information system across the whole range of natural resources, monitoring in physical units changes in the stocks and flows of these resources, and, where possible, relating these to economic activity and valuation. The resources are divided into three main categories: renewable resources (solar radiation, wind, waves, tide); conditionally renewable resources (land, water, air, plants, and animals); and nonrenewable resources (minerals and fossil and nuclear fuels). As with other industrial countries, the Norwegian government has yet to commit itself wholeheartedly to ecological sustainability, and its resource accounts are underused. They will, however, prove an invaluable tool as sustainability becomes the principal imperative of public policy.

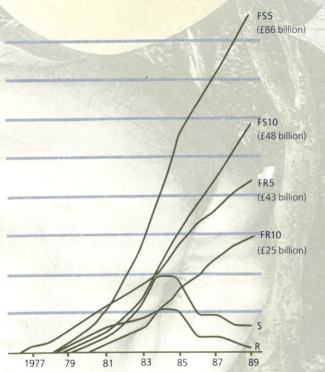

FS5
(£86 billion)

FS10
(£48 billion)

FR5
(£43 billion)

FR10
(£25 billion)

S

R

Thousand million pounds

1977   79   81   83   85   87   89

North Sea oil – a study in unsustainability

In a sense, any depletion of nonrenewable resources is unsustainable. However, if some of the receipts from the depletion are reinvested then they will yield an income even after the resource is gone. If the proportion reinvested is such as to yield a constant, permanent income both during and after depletion, then the resource can be said to have been used sustainably. World Bank economist Salah El Serafy has derived a formula to calculate this proportion of receipts from natural resource depletion that should be used as capital, relating it to the life expectancy of the resource and the discount (interest) rate. This formula has been applied to the depletion of UK North Sea oil since 1976.

The graph (lower left) shows the total proven and probable reserves of UK North Sea oil from 1976 to 1989 and the cumulative production for that period, from which the life expectancy of the resource can be calculated. The graph (upper left) shows the annual total value of sales of oil (S) and the annual royalties and taxes received by the UK government (R). El Serafy's formula has been applied at two different discount rates – 5% and 10% – to both S and R to yield the annual capital component of each. FS5, FS10, FR5, FR10 show the funds arising from the cumulative totals of these components. Assuming that the fund is invested at an interest rate equal to the discount rate, and topped up as far as possible to take account of inflation, the industry should have generated by 1989 a capital fund of £48-86 billion (FS5, FS10) to compensate future generations for the depletion of the resource. And the government should have a fund of £25-43 billion (FR5, FR10, 6-10% of UK GDP) earmarked to safeguard the energy future of coming generations. In fact, no such fund exists. The oil has simply been consumed.

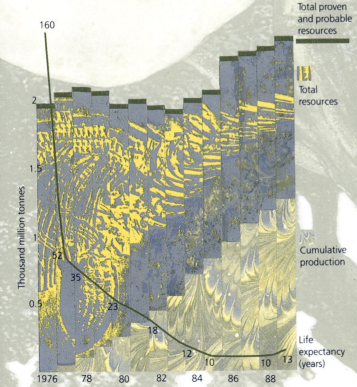

Total proven and probable resources

Total resources

Cumulative production

Life expectancy (years)

Thousand million tonnes

160

2

1.5

1

0.5

52

35

23

18

12   10   10   13

1976   78   80   82   84   86   88

Adjusted National Product

There are numerous ways in which Gross National Product (GNP) could be adjusted to become a more accurate indicator of human welfare. Unfortunately, the more you make such adjustments the less useful GNP becomes as a measure of the financial flows through the economy, which is what it was originally created to be. The identification with welfare came later.

The Adjusted National Product (ANP) recommended here is still intended to be an indicator of formal economic output: marketed production and government expenditure. Nonmonetary outputs and outcomes are dealt with on pages 68-71. Therefore, only three reforms to Net National Product (NNP), which is GNP less depreciation of human-made capital, are suggested here. These reforms relate predominantly to the environment and are intended to remove anomalies that have worried economists ever since GNP was devised in the 1930s and 40s. They would correct GNP for the depreciation of natural capital, "defensive expenditures", and the loss of sustainability (see right).

Regarding the third of these reforms, the sacrifice of sustainability can be viewed as perhaps the heaviest unpaid bill bequeathed to this and future generations by the industrial-economic process. Until that sustainability starts being restored, we are all living on our children's future, as indeed some of our own life opportunities have been pre-empted by the profligacy of earlier generations. Defining, and then achieving, the conditions for sustainability for the environment will be as tough a task as humanity has ever faced. But it is increasingly clear that the survival of what we call our "civilization", and perhaps of human life itself, demands nothing less.

The three reforms of GNP advocated here are very close to the recommendations of the economist David Pearce and others in their report to the UK Department of the Environment. These recommendations amount to replacing GNP with a figure closer to real (sustainable) income. Computing such a figure is well within the capability of two or three years' hard work by a governmental statistical office, work that is already under way in the Netherlands Central Bureau of statistics under the direction of Roefie Hueting, head of the Department of Environmental Statistics. There is perhaps no more pressing task if we are to determine whether our industrial production is making us better off or putting our future in jeopardy.

The fruit of the formal economy
NET NATIONAL PRODUCT (NNP)

Sustainable income (ANP)

Natural capital depreciation

Natural capital depreciation

The techniques for calculating natural capital depreciation have been illustrated by the previous examples of Indonesian resources and North Sea oil (see pp. 64-5). In the long term there is clearly a limit to the income that can be drawn down from the natural system for human consumption. Nature is powered by the sun; sunlight's photosynthetic product basically determines how much life can be supported and at what standard of consumption. Industrialism's relatively short bonanza of intensive fossil fuel and mineral use could have been used to reclaim Earth's barren patches and so enhance its natural productivity: a clear case of capital appreciation. But it has not been so used. Earth's productivity is nearly everywhere on the decline. That this global decline can register as global economic growth is one of the madder economic conventions.

> "We should measure income as the flow of goods and services that the economy could generate *without reducing its productive capacity – i.e. the income that it could produce indefinitely"*.
> David Pearce et al

Defensive
expenditures

Costs of unsustainability

Defensive expenditures

Industrial society's process of growth causes damage and deterioration to some conditions of life, work, and the environment. Defensive expenditures are outlays made to eliminate, mitigate, neutralize, or anticipate and avoid these effects. Christian Leipert, of Berlin's International Institute for Environment and Society has calculated these expenditures for the West German economy in six areas: the environment, including all costs and expenses associated either with environmental damage caused by the economy, or with preventing such damage from happening; transport, including the increase in commuting costs and the cost of traffic accidents; housing, principally the increased rent due to urbanization; civil security, including the extra cost of police forces, security guards, and alarm systems; health, including the costs of unhealthy environmental, living, and working conditions and unhealthy behavioural and consumption patterns; and, finally, work, mainly the costs of industrial injuries and occupational diseases. Leipert found that between 1970 and 1985, defensive expenditures in the West German economy increased by a factor of 2.6, from a ratio of 5.6% to 10% of GNP. Defensive expenditures grew nearly four times as fast as GNP itself. An increasing proportion of GNP growth is not making people better off; it is having to be applied to mitigating the problems that growth itself has caused.

Defining sustainability

Across the whole range of economic effects on the environment, the conditions for sustainability need to be defined. The conditions will come from the ecological accounts combined with scientific knowledge about the environment, based on the answers to such questions as:
○ How much carbon dioxide (and other greenhouse gases) can be emitted without triggering global warming?

○ What toxic wastes can be dumped, where and how, if the environment is to be sure to neutralize, absorb, or diffuse them harmlessly?
○ What is the minimum conservation area needed to arrest the extinction of species?
After defining the conditions, the cost of meeting them must be calculated. This is the adjustment for unsustainability that must be made to GNP.

The nonmonetary economy

"In Africa women bear exclusive responsibility for child care, cooking, cleaning, processing food, carrying water and gathering fuel; they grow 80% of the food, raise half the livestock and have 27 million babies a year." (*State of the World 1989*) Even in industrial countries, households' production has a value of 25-40 per cent of GNP. Yet in conventional economic analysis this wealth is ignored in national accounts and the women who produce it are classified as "economically inactive".

Marilyn Waring's book *If Women Counted* is a biting indictment of this nonsense of economic "science" and crass patriarchy. Waring and other economists and statisticians whom she quotes, emphasize that valuing household production would only extend procedures that are already used in calculating some nonmarket parts of GNP. Luisella Goldschmidt-Clermont of the International Labour Office has studied possible ways of doing this, concluding: "It is possible . . . to devise a combination of methods for approximating, at least in order of magnitude, the relative value of unpaid housework compared to market work. . . . If meaningful decisions are to be taken in the economic, social and manpower fields, the economic and social value of unpaid housework has to be taken into account."

If the household sector is important, no less so are the voluntary, community-based societies, organizations, and movements that also create nonmonetary wealth. It is arguable that such groups do as much for our quality of life as the formal business sector. Human rights groups safeguard our basic freedoms; peace groups confront the arms race; environmental groups work for a secure future; women's groups give gender solidarity and provide the backbone of community life in many countries. Mutual aid groups of all types, often of some of the most disadvantaged in society, bring succour and support to their members and those farther afield. Development groups either raise awareness about, and money for, Third World problems, or set about directly solving those problems.

There is no way that the wealth-creating contributions of these diverse groups can be given a financial tag. Yet for many people they are already the difference between life and death. And because they are tackling the big issues of our time – peace, human rights, environment, and development – it is possible that they will perform the same service for humanity as a whole.

What is household work?

One way of deciding what should count as household "work" is whether it is something that people can and do pay others to do on their behalf. This would exclude such activities as eating or watching television. A Chase Manhatten Bank survey in 1970 entitled "What is a wife worth?" specifically listed the functions of nursemaid, housekeeper, cook, dishwasher, laundress, food buyer, gardener, chauffeur, home maintenance, seamstress, dietitian, and practical nurse. To this list could also often be added that of teacher. The bank believed its survey demonstrated "that maintaining a household often requires as many or more skills as required in jobs outside the home".

People's movements for progress

The explosion of popular movements around the world defies measurement. In development alone, the author Bertrand Schneider estimates that developing world groups have directly benefited some 100 million rural people, helping them from destitution to self-reliance, at a cost of some $6.50 per head per year. The figures of Worldwatch Institute researcher Alan Durning are similar: "Grassroots environmental and anti-poverty groups probably number in the hundreds of thousands and their collective membership in the hundreds of millions." The map (right) identifies just a tiny proportion of these activities for a viable future.

Valuing household production

Household work accounts for about a half of all work done, even in industrial societies. In two-thirds of 75 studies of household work in these societies, its value was put at 25-40% of GNP. Such calculations can be done either by assigning equivalent wages to the time spent in household work; or by assigning equivalent market prices to its products. Goldschmidt-Clermont prefers the latter method, here illustrated for homemade yoghurt (see right). Through a questionnaire, similar to the family expenditure surveys conducted in many countries, it would be possible to value most household goods and services and construct an account for the household sector parallel to the Adjusted National Product (see pp. 66-7) accounts.

Yoghurt is tops

In 1983 a study in Stanford, California by Goldschmidt-Clermont calculated the effective wage of several household activities by comparing the output with equivalent market products, including food preparation, ironing, and knitting. Making yoghurt came out as most valuable with an hourly return of $29.83. The calculation went as follows:

Preparation time (shopping, making, cleaning)	20min
Cost of ingredients	$2.41
Price of market equivalent	$11.36
Shopping time for market equivalent	2min
Net saving	$8.95
Hourly return ($8.95 x 60/18)	$29.83

The author concludes: "Contrary to common prejudice, market production may sometimes be less efficient than household production: in such a case, the returns to household labour are high."

The fruit of household and community

Mexico 250 independent development organizations

Brazil 100,000 Christian Base communities with 3 million members

São Paulo 1300 neighbourhood associations

Burkina Faso 2500 NAAM village groups

Kenya Up to 25,000 women's development groups

Zimbabwe Small-farm groups with 276,500 family members – 2.3 million people

India 12,000 independent development organizations
Bangladesh Bangladesh Rural Advancement Committee has a membership of 350,000 organized in 5800 groups
Thailand Population and Community Development Association representatives in 16,000 villages
Philippines Up to 5000 Christian Base communities
Sri Lanka Sarvodaya Shramadana Movement reaching 3 million people in 8000 villages
Indonesia 600 independent environment/development groups

Social indicators

A social indicator (SI) is any measure that describes some aspect of society. The term itself comes from the 1960s and was expressive of a new concern to become better informed about social goals, processes, and achievements. By the end of the decade it was possible to speak of a Social Indicator Movement reflected in such pioneering publications as Britain's *Social Trends* and similar social reports from other countries.

Industrial countries, especially, now have an enormous range of social indicators from which they need to make careful choices to illustrate the desired social condition. As Ian Miles says in his book *Social Indicators for Human Development*: "It is the definition of overall social goals which determines which SIs are relevant; these SIs may then enter dialectically into the policy-making process, being used to specify concrete performance objectives around the policies".

SIs are now routinely used to supplement economic data about a country's development. For example, PQLI, HDI, ASEDI, and ISEW (see pp. 62-3) are all attempts to devise a better welfare indicator than GNP. A different approach to providing a more detailed picture is to present an array of indicators without seeking to aggregate them into a single index. This approach is adopted by UNICEF in its annual *State of the World's Children* reports and by Victor Anderson of the UK's New Economics Foundation, whose book *Alternative Economic Indicators* outlines the indicators for a new Global Report.

For the purposes of the framework being developed here, it would be desirable to construct a system of indicators to assess those aspects of the four-capital model and of the wheel of welfare (see pp. 30-1) that have not already been evaluated. The very process of elaborating such a system would be a valuable exercise in goal definition and political debate, and there is no presumption that all countries would choose the same system. Ideally, each country would, after selecting the basic indicators, concentrate on its weak spots. Thus, for health, while infant-mortality and life-expectancy rates would probably feature in the framework of all countries, some might focus on nutrition, access to clean drinking water, and the incidence of malaria and schistosomiasis, while others might concentrate on suicides, drug abuse, crime, and the "diseases of affluence", such as cancer and heart disease.

1 Montreal VG (74
27 New York G (3
28 Los Angeles G (11)
83 Mexico City P (2)
43 Lima P (30

The quality of urban life

In 1990 the Washington-based Population Crisis Committee published a ranked survey of "Life in the World's 100 Largest Metropolitan Areas" based on scores dervied from ten social indicators: murder rate, food costs, living space, access to water/electricity, communications (telephone ownership), education, infant mortality, air quality, noise pollution, and traffic congestion. The map (above) shows a sample of these cities in four categories -- very good (VG), good (G), fair (F), and poor (P) -- with their survey ranking before the name and their size ranking in brackets after it. For example: 10 Tokyo-Yokohama VG (1), means that this is the world's largest metropolitan area, in the "very good" category, with an urban quality ranking that is 10th in this survey.

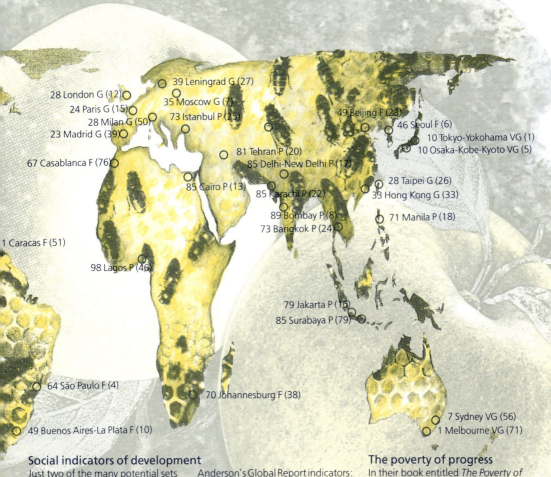

28 London G (12)
24 Paris G (15)
28 Milan G (50)
23 Madrid G (39)
39 Leningrad G (27)
35 Moscow G (7)
73 Istanbul P (25)
49 Beijing F (23)
46 Seoul F (6)
10 Tokyo-Yokohama VG (1)
10 Osaka-Kobe-Kyoto VG (5)
67 Casablanca F (76)
81 Tehran P (20)
85 Delhi-New Delhi P (17)
28 Taipei G (26)
85 Cairo P (13)
85 Karachi P (22)
33 Hong Kong G (33)
89 Bombay P (8)
73 Bangkok P (24)
71 Manila P (18)
1 Caracas F (51)
98 Lagos P (46)
79 Jakarta P (16)
85 Surabaya P (79)
64 São Paulo F (4)
70 Johannesburg F (38)
7 Sydney VG (56)
1 Melbourne VG (71)
49 Buenos Aires-La Plata F (10)

Social indicators of development

Just two of the many potential sets of social indicators of development are presented here.

UNICEF's basic indicators:
○ Mortality rates (under 5 and under 1)
○ Number of births to number of child deaths
○ Life expectancy
○ Adult literacy rates
○ Primary school enrolment
○ Share of income of the poorest 40% and richest 20%
○ Population
○ Per capita GNP
(The UNICEF reports give many further SIs under the headings nutrition, health, education, demography, economy, women, and rate of progress.)

Anderson's Global Report indicators:
○ Mortality rates (under 5 and under 1)
○ Girls' and boys' primary school enrolment
○ Male and female illiteracy rates
○ Unemployment rate
○ Ratio of income share of richest to poorest 20%
○ Telephone ownership
○ Calorie consumption compared with minimum requirements
○ Access to safe drinking water
○ Deforestation, carbon dioxide emissions
○ Rate of population increase
○ Energy intensity of GDP
○ Operable nuclear reactors
○ Ratio of wealth share of richest to poorest 20%
○ Rate of desertification
○ Rate of species extinction

The poverty of progress

In their book entitled *The Poverty of Progress*, which derives from the programme on "Goals, Processes, and Indicators of Development" of the UN University, the authors Miles and Irvine present a battery of statistics of modern life in the UK strongly descriptive of maldevelopment. They conclude: "By presenting and assessing our data in terms of the four categories of security, welfare, identity and freedom, we have been able to identify many facets of contemporary life in Britain where stagnant or deteriorating conditions, rather than improvements, are the rule." This is in stark contrast to the impression gained from the continuing growth of GDP.

Power unlimited

It has already been argued that wealth creation is the result of the judicious combination of different forms of capital (see pp. 48-9), the purpose of which is to increase people's welfare. At this point two questions arise: who decides which and how capitals are combined; and whose welfare benefits as a result? These questions take the argument into the political arena.

Wealth and politics have one great common attribute. They are both routes to power. A form of power, which both politics and wealth-as-money can deliver, is power over other people. Adam Smith (see pp. 12-13) even defined wealth as the number of people you could have working for you. The ultimate in such power – slavery – is not uncommon even today (see pp. 122-3).

The experience of power as enslavement has been a familiar enough part of the human condition for extensive thought to have been given to its prevention. The means are now well understood and can be formulated in relatively simple Principles of Power Limitation (see right). The organizational forms that are supposed to give substance to these Principles are political democracy and the market economy. For the market is a wonderfully democratic mechanism if the conditions for the "invisible hand" to work are met: all exchanges in the market must be voluntary; no producer or consumer may be large enough to have an influence over the crucial arbitrating mechanism, the price; and everybody must know what is going on.

In reality, the Principles are revealed far more often in the breach than in the observance. In the political sphere, and even in some of the advanced democracies, there are many ways in which votes can, in effect, be bought through advertising and tax breaks. In the economic sphere, subservience or impotence, enslavement in all but name, is the principal economic experience of most of the world's people. And the great, successful, centrally planned economies of our time are not the crumbling dinosaurs of socialism but the huge transnational corporations. Apart from being incompatible with democracy, these concentrations of economic power make a mockery of such economic notions as the free market, the invisible hand, or perfect competition. The maintenance and growth of such power in a competitive, unregulated environment, as the global economy largely is, leads to exploitation and coercion.

The transnational corporation (TNC)

Even Marx, as he predicted the centralization and concentration of productive capital, could not have envisaged the extent to which he would be proved correct. The 100 largest of the mighty companies have a turnover that exceeds the GDP of more than half of the world's nation-states. For example, the 91,000 employees of Korean TNC Daewoo generate as much cash income as Bangladesh's population of 116 million. The map (right) shows the distribution by country of the 100 largest corporations and the list (below) compares some of these companies' 1989 turnovers with similar-sized GDPs of various countries. The numbers in front of the company and country names give their rank. Thus General Motors is the world's largest corporation and has roughly the same income as Austria, the 21st-largest GDP.

Comparisons between countries and companies
(Figures are in US$ million)

(21) Austria **127,200**
(1) General Motors (US) **126,974**

(29) South Africa **78,970**
(4) Royal Dutch Shell (UK/Netherlands) **85,527**

(34) Yugoslavia **61,710**
(6) Toyota (Japan) **60,443**

(37) Algeria **51,900**
(10) British Petroleum (UK) **49,484**

(47) Malaysia **34,680**
(22) Siemens (Germany) **32,659**

(54) Peru **25,670**
(22) Peugeot (France) **24,090**

(62) Bangladesh **19,320**
(47) Daewoo (Korea) **19,981**

(67) Sudan **11,240**
(100) Enimont (Italy) **11,191**

Sweden 2
Belgium 1
Netherlands 2
West Germany (pre unification) 11
Switzerland 3

UK 8

France 9

Spain 1

USA 35

Korea 2

Japan 17

Kuwait 1

Mexico 1

Venezuela 1

Home countries of the 100 largest TNCs

Brazil 1

Market power
The pie charts (right) show, for different food exports from developing countries, the market share of the 15 largest transnational corporations in that market. Adam Smith, apostle of a market whose invisible hand worked through small, numerous, and consumer-led businesses, must be turning in his grave.

85-90%
Pineapples,
wheat,
coffee,
corn

80-85%
Tea,
cocoa

70-75%
Rice,
bananas

60%
Sugar

Principles of Power Limitation
○ Those who wield political power must be elected by, accountable to, and replaceable by the people over whom power is exercised. There should be sufficient central funding of political participation to ensure that the wealthy do not have a decisive advantage.
○ Everybody should possess sufficient autonomous economic power to guarantee their decent subsistence. The individual "entitlement", each person's socially guaranteed minimum, should yield both life and health. Conversely, nobody should possess so much economic power as to make possible the coercion of others. The forms of capital must not be held out of the popular reach.
○ There must be a clear barrier between economic and political power. Possession of one must not in itself permit the acquisition of the other. The powers of the visible hand of government and the invisible hand of money must be separated.

Enhancing capability

Wealth as power over people has been one of the great motivating forces in human history. It has also been responsible for much human misery. But power over others is not the only form of power wealth can bring – it can also yield power over oneself, the ability to fashion and achieve one's own fulfilment.

This is the power expressed by the word *capability*. In Green economics the whole notion of economic "development" boils down to an increase in capability of the least well-off people in society, and thus their ability to satisfy an ever-increasing number of the needs discussed on pages 30-1. Defining development in this way makes it a creative, active, subjective concept. It makes people the participatory subjects of development rather than its objects, or, worse, its victims. And it places the fruits of development unequivocally in the hands of those who have developed their new capabilities.

Power over others does not imply nor yield power over oneself. The two forms of power are not substitutable. Each, if sought, must be specifically acquired. It is clear that those who are dominated by other people are denied both types of power: they surrender their own fulfilment and their capabilities are stunted. If the increase of capabilities for all is the object of both democracy and economic development, certain conclusions are obvious.

First, political power must be insulated from economic power. Second, because this will not be entirely possible, the concentration of economic power must be prevented. Third, everybody must have effective access both to the sources and fruits of wealth creation and to political institutions. This final conclusion means that all must have access to each of the four capitals necessary for production: environmental resources, including land; human capital, through education and health rights; social and organizational capital, through the freedom to organize and agitate, and to live in communities free from disruption; and tools and machines, through co-operative ownership structures and the creation of public infrastructure (see pp. 50-9). Around the world, progressive movements are seeking to give people with few capabilities greater power over their lives by enhancing their access to these four capitals. Usually this process entails the diminution of the power of those in control, and this is a prime cause of political conflict.

Brazilian land reform

Brazil has the most unequal land distribution in the world – only 6.7% of all farms are larger than 120ha, yet these occupy 70% of the land, while 65% of all farms are less than 20ha yet occupy a mere 9.4% of the land. Of the large properties, some are very large indeed, and up to 100 million ha of land in these estates is estimated as being unproductive. Yet 5 million landless families in the countryside, and twice that number in city slums, live in abject poverty.

The Movement for Rural Landless Workers (MST) was founded in 1985 and is now organized in 19 Brazilian states. With a slogan of "Occupy, Resist, Produce", it helps people invade unproductive land, enter into settlement negotiations with the government, and set up new farms. By 1990 MST had, through 500 occupations and direct political lobbying, secured land for 100,000 families. Many MST farmers are committed to co-operative working, and the fact that all Brazilian government support for agriculture is available only to large farmers or co-operatives makes such organizations essential for the survival of small farmers.

MST is also showing increasing interest in ecological agriculture and has a co-operative centre researching into organic techniques. If MST succeeds in overcoming the political blockage to land reform, the way could at last be open to equitable, efficient, small-scale, ecologically sound co-operative farming.

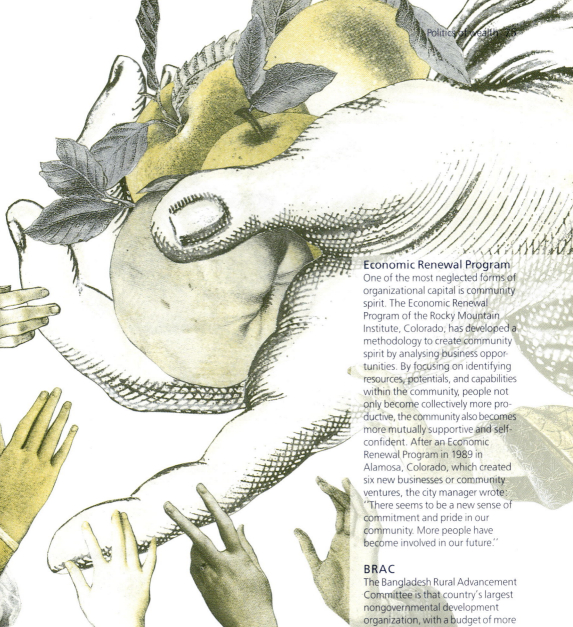

Economic Renewal Program

One of the most neglected forms of organizational capital is community spirit. The Economic Renewal Program of the Rocky Mountain Institute, Colorado, has developed a methodology to create community spirit by analysing business opportunities. By focusing on identifying resources, potentials, and capabilities within the community, people not only become collectively more productive, the community also becomes more mutually supportive and self-confident. After an Economic Renewal Program in 1989 in Alamosa, Colorado, which created six new businesses or community ventures, the city manager wrote: ''There seems to be a new sense of commitment and pride in our community. More people have become involved in our future.''

BRAC

The Bangladesh Rural Advancement Committee is that country's largest nongovernmental development organization, with a budget of more than $20 million and a membership of 350,000. It has an impressive track record across a range of concerns: health, income generation, advocacy, and, especially, education. Starting in 1985 from 22 village schools aiming to provide basic literacy, numeracy, and social awareness to children of landless workers, BRAC now runs more than 4000 such schools with over 250,000 children. The pass rate to official schools is 95%, at a cost to BRAC of $15 per pupil per year – an extraordinarily effective investment in human capital.

Charter 77 and Solidarity

The building block of organizational capital is the right to organize. In insisting on this, Solidarity in Poland and Charter 77 in Czechoslovakia laid a foundation for the peaceful revolutions that took place in Eastern Europe in 1989.

Charter 77 was founded in 1977 by dissident intellectuals. Despite repression, it established contacts with Western social movements during the 1980s, forging a common understanding on the relationship between peace and human rights.

This received an organizational form with the first Helsinki Citizens' Assembly in Prague in 1990.

Solidarity developed from the confluence of independent worker organizations, supportive middle-class intellectual ferment, and the Catholic Church, which was becoming increasingly outspoken. Following its great 1980 occupation of the Gdansk shipyard, Solidarity went on in the 1989 general election to win all but one of the seats it was allowed to contest.

Failure of capitalism and communism

Both capitalism and communism have, in different ways, diminished the capabilities of multitudes of people. Capitalism, as the dominant world economic system encompassing the First and the majority of the Third Worlds, has brought about extreme inequalities of wealth with, at the bottom end, impoverishment of hundreds of millions of people, marginalized or pauperized by "development". It has also brought humanity to the the brink of environmental bankruptcy.

Communism, in what was the Second World of the USSR and Eastern Europe, is now hopefully part of the history of oppression. But its legacy of environmental catastrophe will long outlive the oppressors. Elsewhere, totalitarian socialism is being challenged, by people who are determined to exert some influence over their political destiny.

What has become obvious is that both capitalism and communism are problematic for the decentralized, participatory enhancement of individual capabilities. Private ownership has led to great concentration of economic power in ever fewer hands, and continues to do so. Public ownership places such ownership in the hands of an all too corruptible state system. The wage relationship can lead to exploitative, alienating social relations, but allocations unrelated to effort or productivity destroy motivation and self-development. The market entails externalities and cannot address issues of distribution. Central planning is inflexible and fails to reflect individual preferences. What capability enhancement obviously requires is an appropriate mix of the two systems and new forms of worker ownership.

Brazil and China – two archetypes

Before President Gorbachev came to power, the USSR was the best example of monolithic communism. China also exhibits many features of this type of state, most notably its repression as demonstrated in Tiananmen Square in 1989 and, ongoing, against the people of Tibet. But the ordinary people of China, especially those in the countryside, are undoubtedly better off than those in the capitalist paradigm of Brazil. The indicators below tell their own story.

		Brazil	China
Population (millions)		147.4	1122.4
Adult literacy rate (%)		79	68
Population density (per 1000ha)		174	1201
Average daily calories (as % of requirements)		111	111
Life expectancy at birth (years)	1960	55	47
	1989	65	70
Deaths of children under 5 per 1000 births		85	43
Deaths of women from pregnancy-related causes per 100,000 live births		120	44
Secondary school enrolment ratio	male	32	50
	female	41	37
% of age group enrolled in primary school*		103	132
GNP per head (US$)		2160	330
Income distribution: % of national income received by	richest 20%	58	31
	poorest 20%	4	12

* A figure over 100% indicates pupils outside age group.

The growth of communism

The expropriation of resources, both land and the means of production, is here enacted by the state, total dependence on which reduces most people's autonomous capabilities to about nil. Wages bear little relation to productivity, nor is the wage relationship any more humane than under capitalism. Individual motivation is stifled by a lack of incentive. The collective is experienced as an oppressive denial of individuality rather than a celebration of community or solidarity, while autonomous popular organizations are rigorously prohibited. While education and health services may be widely available, the former tend to degenerate into propaganda and production-orientated training, while the latter are geared only to developing productive "human resources". Apart from the theoretical problems of centrally planning an economy, the power this gives to the planners inevitably leads to corruption. Politically powerful people become rich.

The growth of capitalism

In the early days of capitalist development, people are first driven off the land through Enclosure Acts, brute force, or both; or the resources on which their sustainable livelihoods depend are expropriated for unsustainable industrial activity. Health and education systems for the poor tend to be of greatly inferior quality to those of the rich. The poor are either forbidden to organize or their organizations are harassed. The private ownership of the means of production makes them dependent for their livelihoods on capitalists, who then are able to exploit them through the wage relationship – the "labour market". In other markets their minimal purchasing, and therefore bargaining, power leads to similar exploitation, while the individualistic structure of society, militating against solidarity and community, makes the exploitation far harder to overcome. Rich people become politically powerful.

Balancing the market and state

The desirability of mixing or balancing the economic functions of the market and the state is hardly a new perception. Indeed, the mixed economy that characterizes the economic systems of First World industrial countries was developed precisely from such an insight. However, the way in which the "mixing" in these systems has been accomplished has in the main failed to eliminate the shortcomings of either system.

Thus the concentration of wealth under capitalism has proceeded apace and, in countries such as the US and the UK at least, the gap between the rich and the poor has remained obstinately wide. The market "externalities" (see pp. 36-7) entailed in the destruction of the environment and community also proceed unchecked, despite widespread acceptance in political rhetoric of the "polluter pays" principle. Too often states that have tried to grapple with these and other problems have either failed to grasp the nettle or engendered new problems of their own. Thus monopoly-and-merger, or anti-trust, legislation to prevent economic concentration has been feebly enacted and enforced. State corporations have been run as inefficient, state-capitalist monopolies, rather than responsive public service-driven enterprises geared up to meeting the expressed needs of the people. In agriculture, huge subsidies from taxation, administered through such structures as the Common Agricultural Policy of the EC, have produced large and expensive surpluses of food at great, unaccounted for, environmental cost. And the military-industrial complex has exerted all too great an influence on the political system.

The very concept of the welfare state, too, has been brought into question. Partly it has been undermined by dubious criticisms concerned with the erosion of incentives and fraudulent claimants; partly it has fallen victim to inflexible or self-seeking bureaucracy that simultaneously militates against democracy, accountability, popular participation, and human dignity while failing to encourage appropriate self-help. Market failure has been compounded by government failure. The type of mixed economy to be pursued clearly needs to be redefined. On the basis of the analysis presented here, the organizing principles of a Green Mixed Economy begin to emerge.

The local state in business
Larry Agran, the mayor of Irvine, California until 1990, summed up the 1990s way for local governments to persuade outside companies to move to their area: "When a foreign firm is thinking about locating in California, I want them to look at Irvine and see five things: a responsive local government, well-educated workers, the best cultural opportunities in the region, a transportation system worthy of the 21st century, and an external environment worthy of a week-end walk . . . The old way is to cut taxes, loosen environmental restrictions and open the community up to short-term exploitation. The new way is to create a community where people want to live and work."

The organizing principles of a Green Mixed Economy

○ Universal small-scale ownership of enough of the four forms of capital to permit personal self-reliance for all. Such ownership could be personalized, or held equitably at the community level as in many preindustrial societies.

○ Co-operative work structures based either on extensive profit sharing by the workforce and industrial democracy or, better still, full worker ownership of their workplaces.

○ A vigorous, decentralized, progressive market in which consumers are informed and motivated enough to base their purchases on ethical, social, and environmental, as well as conventional consumer, criteria.

○ A state that enforces and enables. Its enforcement of the "polluter pays" principle, of anti-monopoly and anti-trust legislation, of standards of product and company information, of personal and community rights, and conditions of environmental sustainability, is crucial to preserve the efficient, externality-free workings of the market. Its safeguarding of universal access to the four capitals implies strict limits on the size of landholdings, the provision of high-quality education and health care, training and business advice, and some scheme of inalienable, universal share ownership. Its appropriate support, encouragement, and recognition of the household and voluntary economies should enable those who wish to work in these vital sectors to do so. Beyond enablement, the state should also guarantee a decent, minimum standard of living to those who, through age or disability, have special needs.

○ A concept of "the state" that embraces international and local institutions, as well as national organization, to accommodate processes of globalization and decentralization as appropriate.

Kerala – India's enabling state

Kerala state on India's southwest coast is home to 27 million people. If it were a separate country, it would in terms of per capita GNP be the ninth poorest in the world. Yet, as the comparative indicators show, the average Keralan lives longer and is healthier and far better educated than the average Indian, although the latter in terms of income has almost half as much again. In fact, Keralans compare well in terms of health and education with the average Brazilian (see pp. 76-7), who has more than ten times as much income.

Kerala's achievement is the result of sustained government action and reform at the state level, often obstructed by the central government, across the whole range of human needs. These actions and reforms include: land reform whereby 1.5 million tenants became small farmholders; price controls on food and other necessities and expanded educational services, such that primary schools and cheap food "ration" shops are within 2 kilometres of about 99% of all Kerala villages; public housing; free or inexpensive medical care; and any number of special programmes to benefit the disadvantaged, including considerable achievements in breaking down discrimination within the caste system.

All of these reforms are the result of an unrelenting popular struggle on every front, with the exception of armed revolution, over a period of decades. Kerala's lesson is clear – the enabling state becomes so only under extreme popular duress.

Indicator	Kerala	India	Low-income countries
Per capita GNP (US$)	182	290	200
Adult literacy rate (%)	78	43	–
Life expectancy (years)	68	57	52
Infant mortality (per 1000 births)	27	86	106
Birth rate (per 1000 of population)	22	32	43

Green Mixed Economies

The mixed economy described on the previous two pages would differ significantly from the mixed industrial economies of today, but it could easily grow out of them. There are many practical initiatives that show or have shown how the Green Mixed Economy could be developed, whether from the starting point of the more capitalist industrial world, from the erstwhile socialist economies of Eastern Europe and the USSR, or from the richly diverse cultures and economic traditions that still exist today in the Third World.

Nothing could be more misplaced than the triumphalism of capitalism over the peaceful revolutions in Eastern Europe and the USSR. Western capitalist economies have a huge distance to travel toward the goals of economic justice and sustainable prosperity. Nothing would be sadder than if, instead of carefully introducing the best of market liberalizations, Eastern European countries insist on rushing into a gung-ho capitalism, which will sacrifice their community integrity and further ravage their environment on the altar of inequitable consumerism. Nothing is more urgent than that Third World countries reject the Dallas-like fantasies that distort so many aspirations for "development", in favour of sound and sustainable betterment of their human conditions rooted in their own cultural traditions.

All these developments could be characterized as "Green Mixed Economies", but they would be diverse economic worlds, which must interrelate equitably and sustainably on this one Earth that must support us all.

The progressive market

The market is a marvellous institution for expressing and giving effect to individual preferences. It is often assumed that these preferences are exclusively self-orientated and related to such issues as price, quality, and safety. Indeed, consumers are not normally given any other information about products and so could not express any other preference even if they wished to. Yet many people care, often very deeply, about issues not related to their immediate self-interest. Increasingly, they are coming to realize that there is no reason in principle why they should not express these preferences too through their market choices, their everyday acts of consumption or investment. To do this effectively, they need information about the products and the companies that make them or in which they might want to invest: their impact on their employees and the natural environment; their involvement in the arms or nuclear industries; and their position on animal testing, intensive farming, or political donations, to name but a few of the issues on which it is clear that people have strong opinions. On the producers' side, the progressive market is in evidence in co-operative business or when companies commit themselves to social or environmental objectives beyond the legal minimum. If the progressive market continues to develop along recent growth paths, it is set to become a major influence on business before the end of the decade.

Community Land Trusts – USA

In recent years the increase in land values in the US and other industrial countries has driven farmland and housing beyond the purchasing power of many low-income groups and those without capital. The Community Land Trust (CLT) movement in the US seeks to take land into community ownership, to promote its socially and ecologically beneficial use. The land is leased only, not sold, to farming tenants or low-income residents, though they may buy the houses or other buildings on the land and benefit on resale of property from any improvements made. In the last ten years, CLTs have mushroomed across the US, and there are now 125 in operation or development nationwide. Their growth is nurtured by the Institute for Community Economics in Massachusetts, whose revolving Loan Fund manages more than $10 million, having made 256 loans to borrowers totalling more than $17 million since it was established.

The Co-operative Movement

The broader socioeconomic analysis of wealth creation that has been presented here has to some extent been prefigured in both theory and practice by the Co-operative Movement. This is the largest voluntary socioeconomic movement in the world, in the sense that each member has positively chosen this means of association with others for the mutual benefit of all. In the mid-1980s the International Co-operative Alliance had an aggregate membership of 500 million people in 70 countries, who had come together for a diverse range of purposes, of which co-operative consumption, production, housing, agriculture, and the provision of credit are probably the most important.

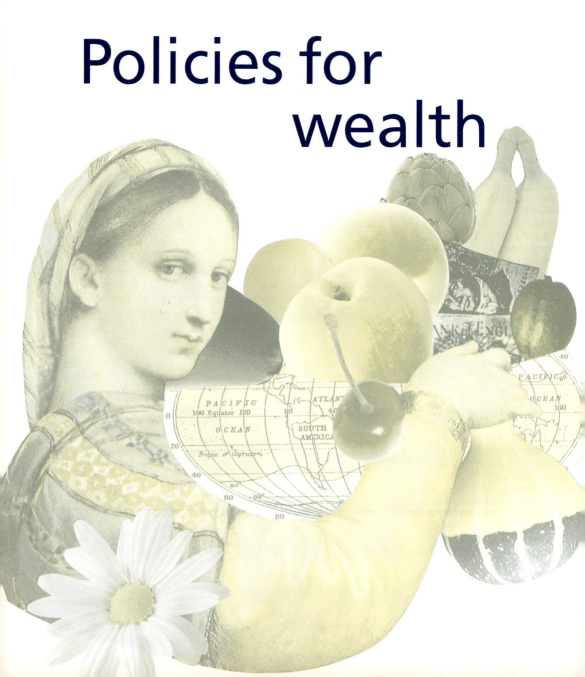

Part three

Policies for wealth

Ela Bhatt is the founder and General secretary of India's Self-Employed Women's Association. She was also a Member of the Upper House of India's Parliament and, until January 1991, was a Member of the Union Planning Commission, India's highest body concerned with economic planning. She has also served as the Chair of India's National Commission on Self-Employed Women. Internationally, she is the Chair of Women's World Banking, an international banking and financial network of and for women in 50 different countries.

SEWA

The Self-Employed Women's Association was founded in 1972 as a trade union for self-employed women working as small-scale workers, home-based producers, or labourers. Such women in India are usually greatly exploited in terms of both pay and working conditions, to combat which SEWA adopted a twin policy of struggle and self-development. Through struggle, exploiters are resisted, exposed, and forced to change. Self-development is fostered by awareness-raising, training and education, organization into co-operatives, the provision of credit through the SEWA Bank and elsewhere, and the provision of such services as childcare, healthcare, maternity benefits, water and sanitation, housing, life insurance, and legal aid. SEWA has 100,000 members organized in branches throughout India; the SEWA Bank has 25,000 members.

My experience as an activist and of organizing poor, self-employed women workers in India has shown me that all human activity, economic and noneconomic, is subject to a variety of motivations and considerations. Any action that compartmentalized human activity was divorced from reality and a poor guide to policy. Policy making is largely determined by the distribution of political and economic power, but the cohesive power of the state or the money power of the individual are not the only forces at work. Moral principles also have to be considered because they are an essential part of all human activity. Distinguishing between what is wrong or right, immoral or moral, material or spiritual is an important aspect of human nature.

Modern economic policies promote economism, where conflicts, wars, exploitation, and disparities become natural. In a new economics, there has to be scope for the elements of voluntarism and strong values that undermine the force of economism.

Historical experience suggests that the systems of capitalism, socialism, communism, or mixed economies alienate people from people, people from nature, and people from production. The alternative is to create a nonviolent and nonexploitative property relationship, with theories, policies, and practices of need-based production, equitable distribution, and social justice. Policies toward people's participation, such as decentralized power centres, social accountability, simplicity, and maintaining ecological balance, have to gain ground step by step.

For us, this means starting from the village, the most fundamental reality of Indian life, which symbolizes the continuity of India's cultural tradition through the ages. The village has been an autonomous and self-reliant unit in most aspects of human life, an organic whole. It must, therefore, remain the foundation on which our country has to be reconstituted. The alternative to private ownership is not state ownership – the alternative is village ownership.

A further answer lies in people's organizations, through which people develop their own body of knowledge and their own meaning of development. I also believe that in building a society based on equity and social justice, women will be the natural leaders – Gandhi called women the vanguard of social change.

Ela Bhatt
Self-Employed Women's Association (SEWA)

Policies in perspective

So far the exposition of Green economics has necessarily been fairly general and theoretical. The rest of the book seeks to apply the principles discussed to specific economic sectors and policy areas in order to gain a more detailed grasp of their implications.

Using the four-capital framework developed in the previous part of the book, topics have been grouped under the form of capital that seems most appropriate, either to the topic itself or to a problem associated with it. However, all capitals are likely to be relevant to all topics, so that the grouping reflects the desired present emphasis rather than any hard-and-fast division. For each topic some of the main trends in operation today are identified, with their possible future implications. Where these seem likely to be negative – ethically, socially, or environmentally – alternatives are suggested in line with the theoretical approach of Part Two.

Green economics does not pretend to be value-free and, in fact, three core assumptions underlie all the policy approaches that are suggested. The first is the absolute imperative of ecological sustainability. Industrial countries, in particular, have hardly begun to consider the implications of this imperative for every aspect of their way of life. Second, human beings are assumed to have intrinsic worth, their fulfilment is the objective, the purpose of economic development. Third, therefore, human fulfilment must also be the *means* of economic development for, as is apparent with the market and the shopping mall (see pp. 28-9), means largely dictate ends. The only way people can be fulfilled through the process of economic development, as opposed to mere consumers of its end products, is for them to participate in all aspects of it that affect their lives.

These three assumptions add up to a radically different perception of value. Conventional economics seeks to give value for money, addressing the question as to how goods and services of the highest possible quality are to be produced at the lowest possible cost. Green economics seeks to subordinate this still important consideration to three greater values: value for nature, leading to sustainability; value for people, based on fulfilment and social justice; and value for human relationships, through participation. These are the guiding principles from which the policy approaches in this part of the book have been derived.

Value for people

A people-valuing approach to economics has been developed in considerable detail by what Mark Lutz and Ken Lux call Humanistic Economics, which is also the title of their book. The idea that the economy is there to serve people, rather than people being inputs into the economy, has a distinguished pedigree. The concept of "disposable people" (see pp. 22-3), prevalent in present development practice, is simply not one that can morally be entertained.

Value for relationships

Development is often seen as something done *to* people, while the welfare state is perceived as delivering services to passive clients. People's participation in these crucial arenas of their lives should be regarded as central to the process. Robert Adams of the British Association of Social Workers put the issue well in the social work context: "Self-help . . . points to means by which people can have a greater say in the nature and delivery of their services, either independently of, enabled by or in partnership with social workers." Precisely the same emphasis on enabled self-help applies to participation in development and the role of development professionals.

Value for nature

There is near universal agreement that nature has been perhaps catastrophically undervalued by economic activity. The revaluation that is necessary was admirably delineated by the Dutch National Environmental Policy Plan, published in 1988-89, which concentrates on three basic policy dimensions: targets, timescales for their achievement, and financial implications. The targets and timescales are ambitious, and the net annual costs until 2010 will be 37 billion guilder (about £12 billion), 4% of Dutch GDP. The seriousness of the approach contrasts starkly with the UK government's environment White Paper of September 1990, which relegated economics to an Annex, and which was described by *The Financial Times* as "a compendium of muted declarations of hesitant intent".

Introduction: ecocapital

In the terminology pioneered by Dutch economist Roefie Hueting, the environment performs many "functions" for humanity in the way of providing resources, absorbing and neutralizing wastes, and yielding such "services" as climatic stability, the ozone layer, and the beauty of scenery. The scale and form of human activity has resulted in competition between these functions, which in turn has triggered the environmental crisis. The ozone layer can serve as a dumping ground for CFCs or as a shield against UV radiation, but not both; tropical forests can provide a temporary source of hardwoods or act as carbon sinks and climatic stabilizers, but not both.

In this context, human prosperity and, perhaps, survival depend on the preservation of essential environmental resources. These imperatives lead to the conditions of sustainability set out on the right.

Biologists Paul and Anne Ehrlich have related environmental impact (I) to three variables – human population (P), the consumption of resources per head (C), and the environmental sophistication of the technology through which that consumption is delivered (T). Assuming a linear relationship between the variables, the Ehrlich equation is $I = PCT$. Rough as it is, this equation does indicate that the scale of the challenge is enormous. With the expected doubling of population in the next 50 years (see pp. 108-9), and assuming a 3 per cent annual growth rate in consumption per head leading to a quadrupling of output per head over 50 years, to achieve the objective of halving the environmental impact, technology is left with the task of reducing environmental impact per unit of output by some 93 per cent over that same period. Only an ultra-optimist could believe this to be realistic. If it is not, then those in industrialized countries, the ones consuming most, surely have an obligation to reduce their environmental impacts and to forego some of their consumption that is adding to those impacts.

A strategy for sustainability will need to penetrate all economic sectors, the government, and other institutional structures. Most profoundly affected by the implementation of such a strategy will be those sectors with the greatest environmental impact, including energy, industry, transport, agriculture, and tourism (see pp. 180-1).

"It is inherent in the methodology of economics to ignore man's dependence on the natural world." Fritz Schumacher

Reinhabiting the Earth

Two hundred years into industrialism it is not easy to imagine a sustainable postindustrial way of life. We have much to learn from preindustrial societies, such as Native Californians, whose 500 separate tribal republics lived side by side without serious hostility or adverse ecological impact for 15,000 years. Historian Jack Forbes has described their world-view: "They perceived themselves as being deeply bound together with other people, and with the surrounding non-human forms of life in a complex, interconnected web of life, a true community . . ." There is now a movement to recover that sort of vision through the concept of a *bioregion*, defined by writer Kirkpatrick Sale as "part of the earth's surface whose rough boundaries are determined by natural rather than human dictates, distinguished from other areas by attributes of flora, fauna, water, climate, soils and land-forms, and the human settlements and cultures those attributes have given rise to" Although bioregionalism now has a sophisticated theoretical base, consistently promoted by the San Francisco-based Planet Drum Foundation, its proponents view it primarily as a practical policy for "reinhabiting the Earth", for people to become aware again, and a constructive part, of the natural cycles and processes of the places where they live. There are now bioregional groups throughout North America and a growing interest in the concept elsewhere.

Sustainability conditions

○ Destabilization of such global features as climate and the ozone layer must be prevented.

○ Important ecosystems must be protected to preserve biodiversity.

○ Renewable resources must be renewed through sustainable harvesting and the maintenance of soil fertility, hydrobiological cycles, and necessary vegetative cover.

○ Nonrenewable resources must be used intensively through durable design, repair, reconditioning, reuse, and recycling.

○ At a minimum level of reserves, consumption of nonrenewables should be matched by new discoveries of the resource. Such consumption should also involve a contribution to a capital fund to finance research for alternatives.

○ Emissions into air, soil, and water must not exceed the capability of the planet to absorb, neutralize and recycle them.

○ Risks of life-damaging events from human activity must be kept low. Technologies threatening long-lasting ecosystem damage, such as nuclear power, should be foregone.

Energy

Typically, energy-policy decisions worldwide have made six assumptions: that demand for fossil fuels (coal, oil, and gas) must be matched by supply; that growth in demand will continue into the foreseeable future because unit costs will not significantly rise; that fuels can effectively be taken as unlimitedly available or substitutable, one for another; that more sources will always be found; that the environmental damage created by their combustion can be held at "acceptable" levels; and, finally, that new technologies will continue to improve fuel efficiency.

Indeed, international comparisons of per capita consumption are used as a measure of relative affluence. Thus growth in demand for fuel and its satisfaction by energy producers and suppliers are interpreted as reflecting improvements in living standards. At the same time, governments have invested heavily in the energy industries, especially in nuclear power, to ensure that future demand is met.

It is becoming increasingly clear that the conventional assumptions are seriously flawed and that current patterns of fuel use have many adverse effects and raise worrying questions about the future:
o The impacts on environmental quality of fuel extraction and energy generation industries.
o The quantity of greenhouse gases produced in energy generation.
o The limits on the availability of fossil fuels and uranium.
o The claims of future generations on these resources.
o Dependence on imports from countries that have, or could have, unstable governments.
o Resources may be found to have more essential and different uses in the future.

It must be borne in mind, however, that lowering consumption can generally be a realistic goal only for people in affluent countries. Those in the developing world cannot be expected to reduce their growth in demand unless the wealthy are seen to be implementing policies of dramatic reductions in their relatively high consumption (see pp. 32-3).

Proven reserves of fossil fuels

In the map below, the dominant position of different areas of the world in terms of proven reserves of fossil fuels can be seen. In the case of oil, the dominant region is the Middle East, especially Saudi Arabia; in the case of gas, it is the USSR and, again, the Middle East; and in the case of coal, it is the USA and the USSR.

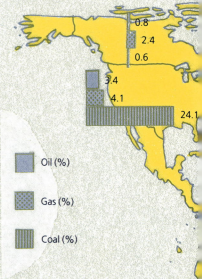

0.8
2.4
0.6
3.4
4.1
24.1

Oil (%)

Gas (%)

Coal (%)

Global CO₂ emissions

Given the ecological imperative of curbing CO_2 emissions, each region of the world faces a daunting task: affluent countries because of their high per capita emissions; poorer industrialized countries because of their excessive and inefficient use of low-grade coal; and developing countries because of burgeoning populations and massive pent-up energy demands.

The end of nuclear power

The problems of nuclear power rule it out as a solution to those associated with fossil fuels. No safe means have been found for disposing of or managing the radioactive wastes for the tens of thousands of years that are required for their decay. The predicted cost of nuclear power has proved to be grossly inaccurate. Far from being "too cheap to meter" as originally forecast, nuclear power is so uneconomic that it proved impossible to sell to the private sector as part of the UK privatization of electricity in 1990/1, even with a hefty government subsidy. Because of the unacceptable costs and risks, no new nuclear power station has been ordered since 1978 in the US, where investment in new renewable energy supply has outpaced investment in nonrenewables since 1979. Nuclear power also costs much more than investment in energy-conservation measures aimed at reducing energy demand. Only secretive, centralized, and nuclear-obsessed energy authorities now promote nuclear power to their consumers' cost.

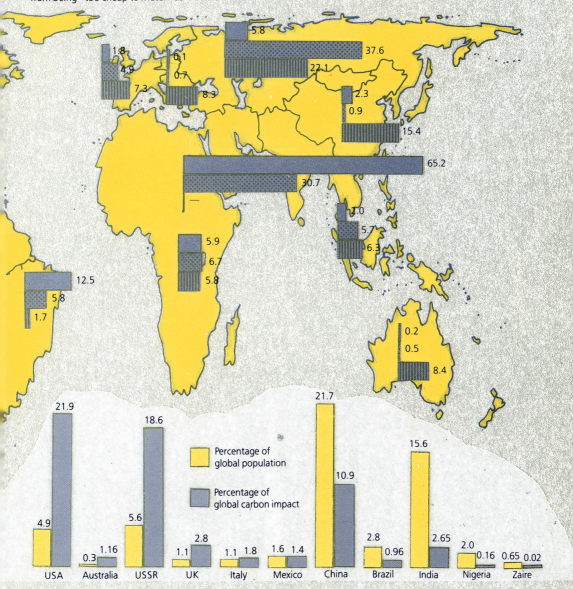

A wealth of energy

Considerations of ecology, economics, and equity point clearly to where wealth creation lies in energy policy. First, global use of fossil fuels must be reduced. Second, more dependence must be placed on those fuels that produce less environmentally harmful emissions. Third, renewable energy sources must be developed to replace fossil fuels. Fourth, whatever energy is used must be used as efficiently as possible. To abate global warming, countries will have to, in this decade, enter into international agreements to achieve national quotas of CO_2 emissions based on these four policies.

Fuel consumption in itself does not necessarily lead to improved living standards. Fuel is used to provide comfort and the mechanical power to minimize physical effort. Looked at in this way, lower fuel consumption can yield reasonable levels of comfort if, for example, building insulation is improved; and reasonable levels of lighting obtained if better use of natural daylight is made; and higher levels of nonmotorized access to people and places achieved if housing, services, and recreation are not so centralized.

With this perspective, the wealthy are not necessarily those who have full central heating or air conditioning and can afford to run it. Rather it is those whose homes are so well insulated and orientated that they need only modest amounts of fuel to be comfortable. The wealthy are not necessarily those who have cars for long-distance commuting, but those who are able to walk or cycle to their place of work or entertainment. Energy policy must be revised in accordance with these considerations of real wealth creation. If reduction of the need for finite fuels were not so strongly opposed by vested energy interests, principally the oil companies and the nuclear industry, few problems of supply would exist.

Governments have a variety of means at their disposal for reducing the use of fossil fuels or substituting for them more benign forms of energy – some combination of prices and regulation, for example, or rationing and carbon/environmental taxes. The taxation could yield significant revenue, allowing for considerable reductions in other taxes, perhaps income tax, if this were considered desirable.

Insulation

On the domestic front, new buildings can take advantage of designs for passive solar energy. At little or no extra cost, homes can be orientated and fenestrated so that there are large windows (or conservatories) on the sunny elevations, and only small windows on the shaded elevations. And it is now possible to construct efficiently insulated buildings that keep occupants comfortably warm using only a tenth of the fuel for space heating used in traditionally built homes. Some countries have already turned to legislation to get the point across: in Denmark, building regulations stipulate that the energy needed to heat new buildings must be reduced by 25% by 1993 and by 50% of current levels by 2005.

Geographic dispersal

The increase in car ownership, especially in the affluent West, has led to patterns of daily activity that rely solely on motorized transport. Giant out-of-town shopping malls (see pp. 28-9); enormous supermarkets on city ringroads; centralized hospital and medical-care facilities; centralized educational establishments – all are located to be easily accessible only by car. New-town development on formerly greenbelt land also throws tens of thousands of extra cars daily on to the roads. In contrast, the town of Davis, California, increased housing densities and protected surrounding farmland while planting trees, providing allotments, and fostering local markets. The town's 40,000 bicycles now outnumber cars by more than 4 to 1.

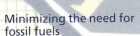

Increasing energy wealth

Everyone can help to lower the burden of pollution on the planet and conserve energy in order to increase energy wealth.

○ Practise conservation, such as roof insulation.
○ Avoid energy-intensive and geographically dispersed patterns of activity, such as car commuting.
○ Wherever possible, use sweaters, clothes' lines, windows, and bicycles rather than domestic heating, tumble dryers, air conditioning, and cars.
○ Switch to more fuel-efficient products and appliances.
○ Use less-harmful fossil fuels, such as gas instead of coal.

Minimizing the need for fossil fuels

There are many ways the need for fossil fuels can be minimized. In the transport sphere, research and development teams have designed and produced cars that run for 35km on just one litre of fuel, and further improvements are expected by the end of the 1990s. Even more significant reductions could be achieved if governments were to enforce lower speed limits that better reflect economical driving patterns. And raising the cost of fuel would spur industry to produce, and consumers to demand, cars that are more energy-efficient. In time, this policy would lead to a reduction in the distance people travelled and, where appropriate, to an increase in the use of bicycles and public transport.

Energy-efficient products

In the US since 1979 conservation and efficiency have saved seven times as much energy as all net increases in energy supplies. Full use of the best technologies available would save about 75% of total US energy consumption with no loss of service. Compact fluorescent lights, for example, last up to ten times as long as incandescent types and use only 20% of the power for the same light output. Refrigerators and freezers already on the market use less than 25% of the energy of traditional models. Many US electricity and gas utilities will install low-energy lighting, heating appliances, and insulation for their customers, recovering their cost through the billing procedure.

Percentage of electricity generated by:

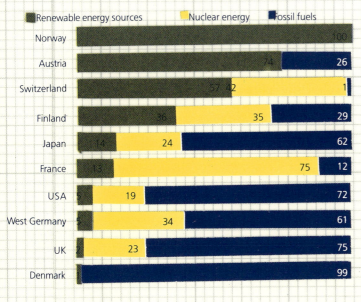

	Renewable energy sources	Nuclear energy	Fossil fuels
Norway	100		
Austria	74		26
Switzerland	57	42	1
Finland	36	35	29
Japan	14	24	62
France	13	75	12
USA	5	19	72
West Germany	5	34	61
UK	2	23	75
Denmark	1		99

Renewable electricity

Wind power is currently one of the most cost-effective means of generating electricity. Denmark and Holland are planning to generate 10% of their electricity from wind turbines by the end of the century, and the potential of offshore U K wind farms has been estimated at about 50% of its current electricity needs. Water power extracted from waves, tides, and rivers is another growing source of renewable electricity. Small hydropower schemes using modern materials and techniques are now efficient and relatively cheap to install in some locations for domestic and commercial uses. Biogas from landfill sites is also used to generate electricity in 20 countries. District heating schemes can be a valuable byproduct from any heat-based electricity source not contaminated by radiation.

Industry

The development of industry, and its social causes and consequences, have been both a blessing and a curse. On the one hand there has been an explosion of consumer goods, the satisfaction of wants previously undreamed of, and, in some countries, a generally high level of material affluence. On the other, industrial society has exacted its price in terms of environmental destruction and cultural and spiritual impoverishment. That this price will be high and is still largely unpaid is becoming increasingly clear.

Despite the cornucopia of industrial products, the accompanying environmental destruction, depletion, and pollution give rise to doubts as to whether industry's present activity creates or destroys wealth. Yet it is clearly in industry's own interests that its resource base should be sustainably used. On current trends, the only rational strategic plan for the tropical hardwoods industry, for example, is to move into a different line of business in the next 20 years, once it has liquidated its basic raw material. Similarly, the global environmental changes now in prospect threaten widespread social disruption that will be bad for all business.

Industry needs to confound its critics and use its powers of organization and leadership to become an environmental protector rather than exploiter. A large number of companies have shown through their own initiatives just how much individual businesses can achieve in terms of "greening" production. Collectively, industry needs to show that it has learned from the bad experiences of such bodies as the International Tropical Timber Organization (see right). It urgently needs new international associations, whether organized by industry, such as the ITTO, or more broadly, such as the Business Council for Sustainable Development (see right) to provide their members with environmental encouragement and information, as well as to police their own performance. Furthermore, rather than lobbying governments on the basis of outdated attitudes and practices, industry should be pressing for tougher regulations against environmentally irresponsible companies, and for incentives to enable the establishment of new, environmentally sound practices and products. "Sustainability" for industry means that good business stays in business, unambiguously creating wealth for itself and for society as a whole.

Rainforests' requiem?

When the International Tropical Timber Organization (ITTO) was formed in 1985, many environmentalists welcomed it in the hope that it would self-regulate an industry that had proved uncontrollable by any other means. Unfortunately ITTO's structure gives more weight to the promotion of the trade in tropical timber than to its conservation and sustainable use. The result, according to Marcus Colchester of the World Rainforest Movement, is that "the organization is little more than a lobbying group for timber interests", which has totally failed either to define or secure the significant practice anywhere in the world of the "sustainable logging" on which it originally set its sights. Concerned nongovernmental organizations, noting at the ITTO's 1989 meeting that during 15 years of failure in tropical forest negotiations "163 million hectares of tropical forest have been destroyed", are increasingly calling for a total consumer boycott of and trade ban on tropical hardwoods.

Greening production

Companies can decide to reduce their environmental impact for many reasons: a commitment at top management level to a clean, sustainable future; the avoidance of financial penalties and bad publicity; a perceived competitive advantage; to save money by using resources more efficiently and reducing wastes; to respond to pressure group and public opinion; to keep ahead of legislation; to be good corporate citizens; or the belief that good management includes good environmental management. This variety of motivations explains the recent growth of environmental awareness and activity in many businesses, which are exemplified by the 3P Programme and the Winter model, described in detail on page 95.

Industry and sustainable development

"Sustainable development" is a phrase popularized in 1987 by the report of the World Commission on Environment and Development, *Our Common Future*, which defined it as "development that meets the needs of the present without compromising the ability of future generations to meet their own needs". The phrase won universal political support, nobody ever having been in favour of "unsustainable development", but has been quickly emptied of meaning by repeated redefinitions. The Pearce Report, *Blueprint for a Green Economy*, even gives a "gallery of definitions" at the end. A typical example of the corruption of the term emerged at the launch in 1991 of the Business Council for Sustainable Development (BCSD), a high-level business advisory group. At the launch of BCSD, its chairman, Swiss industrialist Stephan Schmidheiny, spoke of sustainable development as "nothing more than a simple combination of growth and environmental protection". He went on to say: "I do not believe that we have to make sacrifices in the sense of abstinence. We must however keep our consumption within bounds." Such incoherence in the definition of its aims augurs ill for BCSD's environmental effectiveness.

The greening of industry

To move toward sustainability, industry will need government push, consumer pull, and management will. Government will have to adopt a mix of regulations, price-based mechanisms, and strategic support for emerging environmental technologies in order to push industry toward sustainability targets. Consumers will need to demand and use information on companies' environmental performance, whether through government-backed schemes, such as Germany's Blue Angel (see far right), or through private companies, such as New Consumer and CEP (see pp. 144-7).

In responding to these two pressures, management will need to give real thought to the cradle-to-grave environmental impact of their products, as well as to their environmental policies overall, which both influence Green consumers. Environmental audits (see pp. 144-5) and product analysis will have to become as important management tools for improving company performance as the half-yearly profit statements. Just as national economies are going to have to become more circular than linear in terms of their resource flows (see pp. 50-1), individual industries are going to have to become similarly organic in form, using renewable resources and either reclaiming wastes or passing them on as useful inputs to another process.

These exhortations are falling on increasingly receptive ears. National industry/environment organizations are attracting increasing business interest and support. Internationally, 1991 saw the launch of both the Business Council for Sustainable Development (BCSD, see p. 93) and the International Chamber of Commerce's "Business Charter for Sustainable Development" at its Second World Industry Conference on Environmental Management (WICEM) in Rotterdam. While the ICC's notion of sustainable development is flawed similarly to the BCSD's, its charter embodies 16 key Principles of Environmental Management, with the objective "that the widest range of enterprises commit themselves to improving their environmental performance in accordance with these Principles, to having in place management practices to effect such improvement, to measuring their progress, and to reporting this progress as appropriate internally and externally." This is an important initiative, which could provide a first basis for global environmental responsibility and accountability in business.

Zero pollution

All human activity – even breathing – produces emissions, but pollution occurs only when these emissions rise above the level at which the environment can safely disperse, neutralize, or transform them. Sustainability demands zero pollution. This is increasingly being treated as a realistic industrial goal. Axel Iveroth, former Director-General of the Federation of Swedish Industries, told the Ecology '89 congress in Gothenburg that Swedish industry was prepared to reduce pollution almost to zero by the end of the century. The electronics company Philips is moving toward zero emissions of heavy metals; Volvo is looking to eliminate hazardous emissions entirely; Dow's "Waste Reduction Always Pays" (WRAP) Programme is making zero emissions seem a realistic target; Dupont's waste is already 99.5% internalized and a further 35% reduction is planned by the year 2000; for Hercules BV in the Netherlands, "a problem" as far as environmental impact is concerned "is seen as anything above zero".

The Winter model

Georg Winter of the medium-sized German diamond tools manufacturer Winter & Sohn has pioneered a complete "integrated system of environmental business management". The Winter model goes well beyond the quest for competitive advantage and includes changing employee attitudes; enhanced personnel management; improving products, processes, and working conditions; environmentally orientated purchasing policies; and support for environmental organizations. Many of the resulting improvements have also saved the company money. Employees receive one-third of the savings that result from their suggestions: one saves the company DM60,000 annually for an initial cost of DM24,000. Winter was also active in the creation of the German Environmentalist Management Society, BAUM (meaning tree), which aims to promote environmental collaboration between businesses. BAUM now also has branches in Austria and Sweden.

3M's 3P Programme

When the US multinational computer and computer services corporation 3M introduced its 3P (Pollution Prevention Pays) Programme in 1975, it was the first major corporation to link environmental performance and competitive advantage. Through product reformulation, process modification, equipment redesign, and resource (waste) recovery, 3P had, by 1990, achieved worldwide savings of more than $482 million, cutting air pollutants by 122,000 tonnes, water pollutants by 16,000 tonnes, solid wastes by 400,000 tonnes, and waste water by 7.27 billion litres. 3M's new Pollution Prevention Plus Programme aims to cut air pollutants by 90% during the 1990s.

Blue Angel

The German government, at state and local levels, was the first to respond to increasing consumer desire for environmental information about products when it introduced the Blue Angel labelling scheme in 1977. The scheme is intended to identify products "characterized by a particularly high degree of environmental soundness" when compared with other products serving a similar function. A 1989 poll showed that 75% of German consumers preferred Blue Angel products, of which by 1990 there were more than 3000 in 54 categories, including retreaded tyres, asbestos-free floor coverings, low-noise lawnmowers, and recycled wallpapers. The Nordic countries have now launched their own label and Denmark, the Netherlands, and France are considering following suit, while the EC is planning a label for the single European market.

Product lifecycle analysis

Increasingly consumers are demanding to know about, and companies being expected to take responsibility for, a product's environmental impact over its entire lifecycle—from the raw materials and their extraction, through the manufacturing process, the packaging and distribution of the product, to its use and final disposal. At each stage, consideration needs to be given to the implications for sustainability of the resources used, renewable and nonrenewable; the emission of wastes and pollution caused; the impact on "global services", such as climate and the ozone layer, or wildlife, biodiversity and ecosystems; and on the health, beauty, and amenity of the local environment. Aggregated across industry as a whole, these impacts must be brought within clear sustainability standards covering the entire range of environmental functions, formulated by applying the precautionary principle (see pp. 154-5) to the best available scientific knowledge.

Transport and accessibility

Cars and air travel are seen as barometers of modern living standards; trucks have become the dominant method of freight transport. So it is not surprising that road and air are the principal perceived means of meeting future transport requirements. The conventional way of measuring progress in this sphere is through the annual rise in car ownership, miles travelled by road and air, and the number of freight-tonne kilometres carried on the roads.

Viewing increases in these indicators as signs of affluence makes it logical to devote a larger share of the public purse to expanding the transport infrastructure. However, rather than reflecting *wealth creation*, rising vehicle ownership and growing dependence on motor-orientated lifestyles can be viewed as *wealth consumption*. The cost of traffic accidents and injuries, of increasing commuting and other travel, of the destruction by roads of communities and the environment – all are routinely ignored or downplayed by decision makers. This biases transport patterns in favour of cars, heavy trucks, and air travel. Taking account of the full range of the external costs these impose could mean that increased wealth actually lies in minimizing the demand for motorized mileage rather than the reverse.

Many institutions encourage the process of motorization. First, there is a powerful coalition of motor manufacturers, the petroleum industry, and road builders, which exerts considerable influence on political decisions. Second, there are the providers of public and commercial facilities, such as schools, hospitals, and shopping centres, who achieve internal economies of scale and offer better services by ignoring the access costs imposed on users and the environmental costs borne by those living along the access routes. Third, there are the transport professionals who believe that the primary purpose of planning is to accommodate future demand determined by projecting past trends. Finally, and not least, the process has been encouraged by that section of the population – those with optional use of cars – who derive most of the benefit and impose on others most of the costs of a motorized society.

Traffic generation

The distances travelled by car in the European Community from 1968 to 1988 rose by 99% in the UK, 118% in West Germany, 148% in France, 293% in Italy, and 322% in Spain. Maximum truck weights in the UK increased from 24 to 38 tonnes from 1955 to 1983. The intention of the single market is to remove barriers to trade and reduce direct costs of serving distant markets. As a result, more industries are becoming multinational and specialized, and are being rationalized in order to serve larger populations in more member states. By the year 2000 this will lead in Germany to a 70% growth from 1987 levels in road freight-tonne km, with a resulting increase in road deaths, road damage, and ill-health on busy routes.

Environmental impacts of selected travel methods

	Transport method					
	Walk	Cycle	Bus	Rail	Car	Air
Land usage	○	•	●	●	●	●
Population dispersal	○	○	•	●	•	●
Provision costs	○	•	●	●	●	●
Fuel usage	○	○	•	●	•	●
Reduced amenity	○	○	•	●	●	●
Damage to health	○	○	•	•	●	●
Cause of fear	○	○	○	○	●	•
Cause of death	○	○	○	○	●	○

○ very low • fairly low ● average ● fairly high ● very high

Car km per head 1968 to 1988

Country	Car km per head (1988)	% increase (1968-88)
Japan	2539	434
Spain	1907	322
Italy	4181	293
France	5396	148
Netherlands	5170	134
FRG	6160	118
United Kingdom	5185	99
USA	9024	77

■ Car km per head (1988)

▦ % increase (1968-88)

Wealth consumption

The price for car travel can be high (see also pp. 34-5):

○ High public expenditure on infrastructure.

○ Large-scale death and injury (more than 5000 people killed annually in the UK alone).

○ Out-of-town facilities and low-density housing fuel the need for car transport.

○ Heightened fear for safety, especially of children.

The costs of air travel include:

○ Exhaust gases damaging the atmosphere.

○ Mass tourism destroying local cultures.

Problems common to both include:

○ Countryside ruined by roads, parking lots, and runways.

○ Environmental degradation through noise and pollution.

○ High rate of fuel consumption.

Transport wealth

True wealth creation with regard to transport lies in being economical in the use of finite resources, improving amenity by reducing pollution from traffic, minimizing danger, promoting health, lowering the financial costs of meeting transport needs, and enabling those needs to be met so that the convenience of some users is not achieved at the expense of others. This means reducing the need, and charging far more, for motorized travel.

To encourage this process, access to amenities has to be increased. For a start, we need to consider the provision of basic facilities – schools, shops, parks – that are easily reached on foot or by bicycle, or, if a longer journey is required, by public transport rather than by private car. Contradictory as it may initially sound, transport-wealthy communities are ones in which motorized traffic is minimized because amenities are readily accessible and there is greater self-sufficiency in jobs and services. The potential for this type of transition exists in many industrialized countries, with the modern technology of computer-based systems and telecommunications opening up increased possibilities for home-based employment, thereby avoiding all the costs of commuting.

To generate this type of wealth requires *planning* to ensure that the need for motorized travel is minimized in all areas of work and leisure; it needs public *investment* in transport to be prioritized according to its social, environmental, and economic impacts; and it requires a more effective *taxation* of personal travel according to distance travelled, of road freight according to weight distance, and of both according to the external costs incurred (see p. 97).

Individuals, organizations, and companies can help by reducing their dependence on motorized transport, and by paying more regard to the travel impacts both on themselves and on the community when they make decisions about the physical relationship between home and job, and their patterns of travel for shopping and leisure activities.

Traffic calming

Excellent examples of priority on road space being given to pedestrians can be found in Germany. Streets have been redesigned to slow down traffic, in extreme cases down to walking pace. The technique, known as traffic calming, relies on physical measures, such as widening footpaths, constructing speed humps, staggering traffic lanes, and road resurfacing. It was first applied to residential areas but is now being extended to whole cities and, more recently, incorporates the greening of residential areas with trees and shrubs to combat air and noise pollution. Not only has there been a marked reduction in the severity of pedestrian injuries (and often their number), it has also allowed public spaces outside the home, which had been progressively colonized by the car, to be returned once more for social and recreational use, especially by children and the elderly.

In collisions with cars, 15% of pedestrian injuries are fatal or serious at 20kph; 74% at 40kph; and more than 95% at 60kph.

Car emission controls

California is a world leader in air-quality protection. Limits on the emissions of hydrocarbons, carbon monoxide, and nitrogen oxides for new cars are far tougher than those planned for the EC. And 50% cuts in even these limits are proposed throughout the US for new models toward the end of the decade, with a further 50% cut in the first decade of the 21st century.

The role of cycling

The number of cars per capita in the UK and the Netherlands is almost identical. In the UK, however, 2% of all journeys are made by bicycle whereas in the Netherlands the figure is 28%, including 60% of the journeys made by young teenagers and 25% of those of pensioners. The Netherlands' government has long recognized the environmental impacts of the growth in car usage. Under its National Environment Policy Plan, it intends to bring about a further increase in the number of personal journeys made by bicycle, especially over distances of 5-10km. To achieve this, it is implementing a strategy to improve cycle routes in and around towns, notably in commuter corridors and on routes to and from stations. Capital expenditure on this programme has been set at 10% of the total allocated to transport purposes.

Food and agriculture

Between 1950 and 1984 the world output of grain increased 2.6 times, due to the combination of increased areas under cultivation and three powerful technological processes: *mechanization*, the use of larger, more specialized machines; *intensification*, the increasing use of irrigation and chemical inputs; and *specialization*, the concentration on single crops, or even single varieties, in place of traditional mixed farming. World population over the same period increased 1.9 times. Basically there was enough food to go around if it could have been distributed to those who needed it.

While these technological developments have done much to increase productivity per hectare, whether through the so-called Green Revolution in the South or through such agricultural support policies as Europe's Common Agricultural Policy (CAP), other effects on the environment and social fabric of rural areas have been far less benign. In fact it has become clear that industrial agriculture as it has developed over the last four decades is literally unsustainable. Its reform has become a necessity.

Perhaps the single most counterproductive and perverse example of misguided agricultural policy is the CAP. With its guaranteed intervention prices the CAP is hugely expensive, costing EC governments 28 billion ecu (about £19 billion) in 1989. Yet only about half of this goes to support farmers; the other half is swallowed up in storing the massive surpluses resulting from over-production and in export subsidies. In 1984 EC taxpayers and consumers paid nearly 14 billion ecu more in costs than the benefits received by EC producers. CAP price support and capital grants have also increased land prices, decreased farm employment, favoured large farmers over small, and inflicted enormous environmental damage.

The environmental costs take many forms: destruction of landscape, loss of recreation and amenity, erosion of the soil, decrease or extinction of flora and fauna (70-80 species per year in Europe), pollution of people, food, air, soil, and water by pesticides and fertilizers, and depletion of fossil fuels. These costs reveal the extent to which traditional farming systems produced, in addition to food, a wide range of vital environmental goods. It is only by recognizing and rewarding this that farm policy can begin to move agriculture toward sustainability.

Costs of the Green Revolution

The Green Revolution in South Asia and elsewhere has undoubtedly increased crop yields. According to the Indian scientist Vandana Shiva it has also led to: "reduced genetic diversity, increased vulnerability to pests, soil erosion, water shortages, . . . soil contamination, reduced availability of nutritious food crops for the local population, the displacement of vast numbers of small farmers from their land, rural impoverishment and increased tensions and conflicts. The beneficiaries have been the agrochemical industry, large petrochemical companies, manufacturers of agricultural machinery, dam builders and large landowners." Shiva identifies these as the interests that overturned India's original post independence agricultural policy "based on strengthening the ecological base of agriculture and the self-reliance of peasants". Production growth under this policy, Shiva claims, exceeded that following the Green Revolution.

Farming blocks GATT

The General Agreement on Trade and Tariffs (GATT) is a forum involving 102 countries that seeks the progressive liberalization of world trade. In early 1991 its current round of negotiations was frustrated by the refusal of the EC to agree to US demands for drastic reductions in export subsidies. The US was not prepared in return to accept anything like the same cuts in its own system of farm-support. While the Western dumping of food on world markets has undoubtedly hurt Third World farmers, GATT-type liberalization would bring more benefits to Northern food multinationals than the South. Countries should be stopped from flooding markets with subsidized surpluses, but there needs to be recognition that countries have a right to protect their own farmers' ability to produce for their home market.

Mechanized agriculture

Modern mechanized agriculture not only replaces animals by machines, it treats all animals, indeed all living things that are the inputs to its processes, as machines. Thus chickens are egg or meat machines and sows are piglet machines. And as machines they are treated with unrelenting cruelty.

Biotechnology has extended this outlook to the fundamentals of life itself, genetically engineering seeds and hormones today, and new animals tomorrow (see p. 169). Moreover, these new life forms can be patented as the property of their inventor. "Playing god" has acquired a more literal meaning in the factory farm of the 1990s.

Safeguarding future harvests

With future food security uncertain at best, total reliance for food supplies on the world market would seem a very risky national agricultural strategy. In Japan, the Network for Safe and Secure Food and Environment (NESSFE), a coalition of farmers', consumers', and environmental organizations and individuals, is urging the government to hold firm to its policy of national self-reliance in rice in the face of strong US pressure through GATT (see p. 100) to open up its rice market.

Maintaining national self-determination in food by keeping domestic agriculture economically viable and moving it toward ecological sustainability must be a top priority of any responsible government. This requires a policy that recognizes that food is just one of the products of a healthy agriculture that also generates social, cultural, and environmental wealth, such as cohesive rural communities and biodiversity. These are positive externalities of many traditional farming systems. Industrial agriculture, which is heavily subsidized, instead generates large negative externalities, such as pollution and rural depopulation. An analysis that included social and environmental costs would reveal it as uneconomic compared with available alternatives.

The alternatives include organic and biodynamic farming, integrated pest management, and low-input approaches, which seek to substitute mixed farming, biodiversity, crop rotation, intercropping, agroforestry, and minimum tillage for monocultures; animal and green manures for chemical fertilizers; nontoxic biological control of weeds and pests for pesticides and herbicides; and an emphasis on soil health and fertility for crop output. Techniques vary, but many of them have proved their viability and only await a policy framework for their large-scale introduction.

Such a framework will also vary widely between countries, but it is likely to contain the following components: land reform to make land available to small farmers; income support to farmers in relation to the environmental goods they produce; taxes on and regulation of socially and environmentally damaging farming practices; financial support for the conversion of chemical-intensive farms to low-input agriculture; research, development, and extension services for ecologically sound agriculture; and the protection of agriculture from the uncertainties of climate and the world market in favour of long-term food security.

Food insecurity

In recent years the growth of the global grain harvest has come to a halt. Although from 1984 to 1989 fertilizer use increased by 14%, grain production remained about the same, except in 1988 when for the first time in history, US grain production fell below US consumption. Greater food production is being constrained by a scarcity of new cropland, water, and by environmental degradation. Given the present population increases of more than 90 million annually, world food output needs to grow by 28 million tonnes a year just to maintain the often inadequate per capita consumption. Another poor 1988-style US harvest before stocks are rebuilt would set the hundred countries that import US grain scouring the world market for scarce surpluses. Unless rich nations diverted into food aid some of the 600 million tonnes of grain currently fed to livestock, mass starvation would be inevitable.

The map (right) shows for cereals, net imports (exports) per head (in kg) and receipts (donations) per head (in kg) of food aid for major regions for 1975-77 and 1985-87, together with regional populations in millions for 1975 and 1987.

Sustainable agriculture

A recent book, *After the Green Revolution*, produced by the International Institute of Environment and Development says of the problems of the Green Revolution: "These are not . . . capable of being solved by further technical adjustments." It advocates "sustainable agriculture", characterized by ecologically sound agriculture and five criteria: political will; proper economic analysis of environmental impacts; appropriate incentives, such as prices, share rights, and effective participation; institutional flexibility; and complementary infrastructure, such as transport, storage, credit, and research.

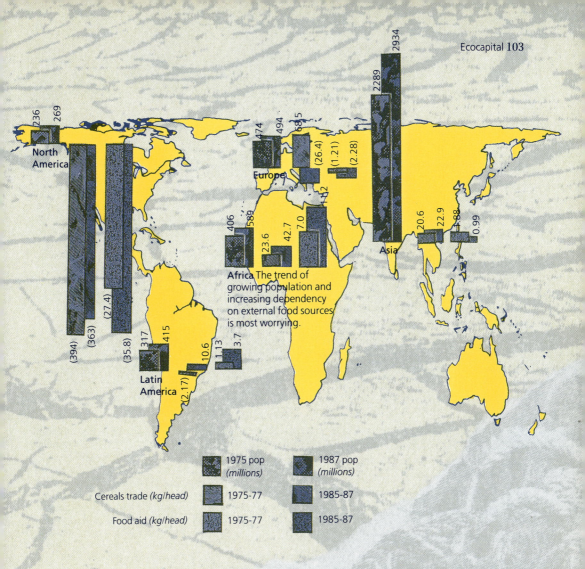

North America
236 269
(394) (363) (27.4) (35.8)

Europe
474 494 68.5 (26.4) (1.21) (2.28)

Asia
2289 2934
20.6 22.9 1.88 0.99

Africa
406 589 23.6 42.7 7.0

Latin America
317 415 10.6 1.13 3.7 (2.17)

The trend of growing population and increasing dependency on external food sources is most worrying.

	1975 pop (millions)	1987 pop (millions)
Cereals trade (kg/head)	1975-77	1985-87
Food aid (kg/head)	1975-77	1985-87

The future is organic

Alternatives to chemical-intensive agriculture work. The Worldwatch Institute's Sandra Postel has given examples of highly successful applications of biological control and integrated pest management in Brazil, China, India, Africa, Central America, Indonesia, the US, and elsewhere. A US National Academy of Sciences' report concluded: "Well-managed alternative farms use less synthetic chemical fertilizers, pesticides and antibiotics without necessarily decreasing – and in some cases increasing – per acre crop yields and the productivity of livestock systems." As well, it noted "greater economic benefits to farmers and environmental gains to the nation". One of the most promising forms of alternative agriculture is organic farming, which emphasizes the need to produce high-quality food by working with rather than against natural processes, concentrates on enhancing soil fertility, and promotes biodiversity, animal welfare, and a healthy nonpolluted environment. In consequence, it avoids the use of artificial fertilizers, pesticides, growth regulators, and livestock feed additives.

Organic farming will become widespread because consumers want it. A study by consultants Coopers & Lybrand Deloitte of the UK organics market, foresees it growing from £40 million in 1988 to £1-2.5 billion in the year 2000. Other forecasts of growth in Europe and the US are comparable. The strict standards for organic products, refined over the years by such bodies as the UK's Soil Association, and the associated symbols they award, now recognized by consumers, give a clear marketing advantage over hybrid "low-input" farming systems. For reasons of environmental conservation, sustainability, and consumer recognition, organic farming is, as Nicholas Lampkin says in his landmark study, "an agriculture for the future".

Introduction: human capital

People and their fulfilment are both the objectives of development and the means to that development. In this respect human capital differs from the other forms of capital because, insofar as health, skills, education, and motivation yield people satisfaction, their attainment can be regarded as an end in itself, irrespective of any productivity they may engender.

There is another important difference: people have fundamental rights as universally agreed in the UN Declaration of Human Rights. This greatly limits the use to which human capital can be put, ruling out exploitation as incompatible with those rights. It also affects the ways human capital can be owned. With slavery prohibited, ownership of human capital must remain vested in the individual concerned.

There are two groups of people, comprising well over half of humanity, for whom the three imperatives of human capital formation – fulfilment, productivity, and justice – are regularly denied. They are the great majority of the world's women and children. Janet Momsen's study *Women and Development in the Third World* found that: "economic development has been shown to have a different impact on men and women and the impact on women has, with few exceptions, generally been negative. . . . The costs of ignoring the needs of women are many: uncontrolled population growth, high infant and child mortality, a weakened economy, ineffective agriculture, a deteriorating environment, a divided society and a poorer life for all." For children, the human capital of the future, the effects of discrimination against women are severe. Mothers tend to be far more responsible for children's development, particularly in the early years, than fathers.

Countering the process of maldevelopment, especially that oppresses women, must be the first priority of human capital formation, especially but not only in the Third World. Bertrand Schneider in his report for the Club of Rome called this task "tackling the factors of impoverishment": militarism, indebtedness, repression, the misuse of land and natural resources, displacement by "development". Only then can fruit be expected from "the factors of development": land reform, education, health care, community organization, credit. For these development factors to yield the greatest human capital return they must start from where women are, with what they need, and what they know.

Views on human capital
The difference of emphasis between Green and conventional economics is apparent from their treatments of human capital. For Green economics the issue of human capital is inextricably related to justice and human fulfilment as well as to productivity. Conventionally, as in the *Palgrave Dictionary of Economics*, it is regarded as "the productive capacities of human beings as income-producing agents in the economy", one result of which is that human capital theory has been based largely on the assumption that the only purpose of education is to increase future income. From *Palgrave* again: "Rational agents pursue investments (in education) up to the point where the marginal rate of return equals the opportunity cost of funds." This illustrates the distinction between the *income-production* focus of conventional economics and the Green emphasis on *wealth creation*.

The promise to childhood

One Sunday in September 1990 a million people around the world lit candles in witness to the World Summit for Children in New York. There, 71 presidents and prime ministers and other representatives from a total of 159 countries pledged to the children of the 21st century that "the quiet catastrophe" decimating the children of the 1990s – "the 40,000 deaths each day from ordinary malnutrition and disease, the 150 million children who live on with ill-health and poor health, the 100 million 6-11 year olds who are not in school" (UNICEF) – will by then have been brought to an end. The cost of achieving this goal – $20 billion a year over the present decade – is equivalent to just ten days' military expenditure per year.

Muslim women's liberation

From the general oppression of women there stand out the hardships of the 500 million women living under Muslim laws. These laws have been used recently to justify the 1990 proclamation in Iraq that "any Iraqi who kills . . . his own mother, daughter, sister, aunt, niece or cousin for adultery will not be brought to justice". In Pakistan the Hudood Ordinance has been used to convict raped women of fornication and whip and imprison them. The international network Women Living Under Muslim Laws provides information, support, and solidarity for women in such countries. Its researches show that these laws, which vary greatly from country to country, derive more from patriarchy and political power than from a "correct" interpretation of the Koran.

Spiritual resources

Most people instinctively believe that there is more to life than the material world, even if precisely what this is cannot be fully comprehended. At the same time, the horrendous environmental destruction can be seen as expressions of the inner turmoil of the human species.

The fundamental changes needed to avoid an accelerating process of ecological breakdown will only come about through a widespread acceptance of a new set of values. And some of the most basic changes will need to come through a new emphasis on philosophical questions, on the human relationship with the whole of creation rather than the immediate external world. In his book *A Continuous Harmony*, Wendell Berry gives a historical perspective to our dilemmas: "Perhaps the greatest disaster of human history is one that happened to religion, that is the division between the holy and the world, the taking out of the Creator from creation." He goes on to argue that without God in the world, the world is a place of inferior importance, leaving those disposed to exploit it free to do so. "A man could aspire to heaven with his mind and his heart while destroying the earth and his fellow man with his hands."

This removal of the Creator from creation has been part of the compartmentalization of life that has been going on for hundreds of years. The life of the Spirit is sometimes spoken of as if it, too, belonged to its own sphere. But if there is a life of the Spirit, as most people believe, then it is that aspect of life that is central and all pervading.

Religion reconnects humanity with reality, whether this reality be called God, Truth, Allah, or Nirvana. Developing our spiritual resources rests on the quest to get away from what Fritz Schumacher called "the little, egocentric 'I' ", and to awaken to a deeper reality. Spiritual resources beyond measure are part of that wealth that is beyond measure. Although it is possible to have a spiritual life without practising any religion, religions are important because they reaffirm the sanctity of life; they attempt to affirm human beings in the lives that they lead; they offer consolation and healing; they give people their own personal sense of the totality or the interrelated oneness of the universe. Thus spiritual development should increase our reverence for the natural world just as it has tended to increase our regard for our fellow humans.

Wealth and the faiths

It is clear that the economic views of the world's great religions differ greatly from those underlying modern economics and the world economy, giving far greater emphasis to generosity and charity, the dignity and importance of work, and the care by the state for its citizens and the environment.

In 1986 the World Wide Fund for Nature (WWF) launched at Assisi in Italy the International Network on Conservation and Religion, now involving the Baha'i, Buddhist, Christian, Hindu, Islamic, Jain, Jewish, and Sikh faiths and environmental groups. A similar network on economics and religion is planned to be launched in 1993 by the International Consultancy on Religion, Education and Culture (ICOREC) and the UK New Economics Foundation, with WWF backing, who have already prepared a schools' educational package, *A Wealth of Faiths*.

Creation spirituality

Unlike much Christianity, which is based on the essential sinfulness of human beings, the tradition of creation spirituality as described by Matthew Fox starts from the premise that human beings are born blessed and that creation is good. Fox, an American Dominican priest, believes that an emphasis on sin in both its religious and secular forms has always strengthened those in power by allowing them to define the powerless as sinful. By contrast, he celebrates the joy and beauty that everyone can find in relationships with each other and with nature. It is a deeply political spirituality in which compassion is seen mainly as a search for justice.

Spiritual wealth in South Asia

The Swadhyaha philosophy in India, with 3 million adherents, is based on a commitment to the service of God and love for one's fellow human beings. It has been the motivation for the creation of 3500 "farms for God", which generate food that is distributed to the needy. Also in India, the Chipko movement is working for the conservation and regeneration of the forests from an attitude of reverence for nature rather than a desire for its exploit-ation. Its motive force, according to Sunderlal Bahuguna, one of the movement's leaders, is love and affection: "This is our capital." Sri Lanka's Sarvodaya Shramadana Movement, which is active in a third of the country's villages, describes its work as: "creating a mass of spiritual consciousness which brings about a humanizing and liberating impact on social, political and economic institutions that have enslaved us for decades."

Population

The extent to which environmental destruction is the result of the increase in human numbers is a matter of controversy. For HRH the Duke of Edinburgh, International President of the World Wide Fund for Nature, the "human population explosion" is "the root cause of the degradation of the natural environment".

It is clear that the number of people the Earth can sustainably support has a limit and that, in a situation where people's lifestyles are damaging the environment, more people with similar lifestyles will increase the damage. But these premises are far from bearing out the "root cause" assertion, especially as applied to Third World population growth. Analysis by the ecologist Barry Commoner has shown that industrial countries, with less than a quarter of the world's population, and long-standing stable or declining populations, are responsible for more than 75 per cent of global waste, a major cause of environmental degradation, while polluting technology has more than twice the environmental impact of population.

It is still environmentally desirable to stabilize world population. There is in fact an established pattern of declining fertility rates as countries industrialize, known as the "demographic transition" (see right). Almost all societies have passed through transition I and populations in many countries are rapidly increasing. Transition II depends crucially on these countries reaching a level of socioeconomic development that assures parents that a high proportion of their children will reach maturity, and that they will not be totally dependent on them in old age; and that gives to women the opportunities for fulfilling activity outside the home.

The demographic transition can be and is being hastened by family planning. Women nearly everywhere are having fewer children and, in the Third World, want still smaller families. Providing the necessary contraception would cost, according to UNFPA, $9 billion a year by 2000 – double present allocations but "far smaller than the cost of failure". Half of these resources will need to come from rich countries as extra aid. These same countries will also have to relieve the poverty-inducing Third World debt burden. As Lester Brown said in *State of the World 1990*: "Unless debt can be reduced to the point where social progress resumes, the needed decline in fertility may not materialise."

Population problem

Paul Shaw, a senior economist at the UN Population Fund, attributed a tiny share of environmental degradation to population growth when compared with other factors (see pie chart). It is clear that the environment's principal population problem is not just people, but too many high-consuming, high-polluting, industrialized people.

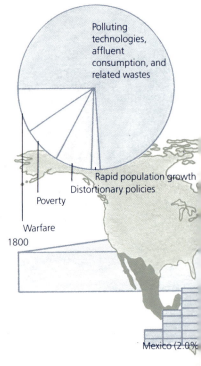

Polluting technologies, affluent consumption, and related wastes

Rapid population growth

Distortionary policies

Poverty

Warfare

1800

Mexico (2.0%

Peru (2.4%

These bar charts plot the populations of the different countries (in millions) in 1960, 1990 and projected figures for 2025. Each division represents 20 million people. Bracketed figures represent population growth rates for selected countries.

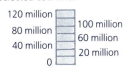

120 million		100 million
80 million		60 million
40 million		20 million
0		

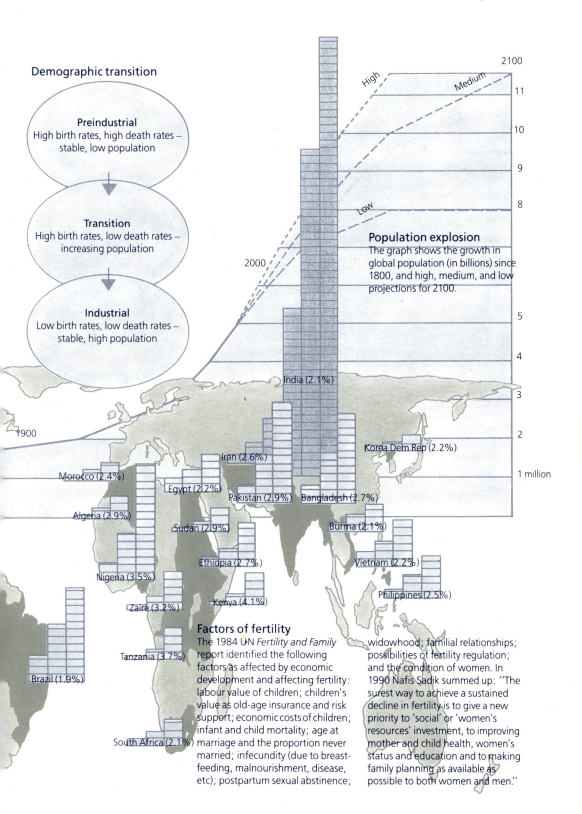

Demographic transition

Preindustrial
High birth rates, high death rates – stable, low population

Transition
High birth rates, low death rates – increasing population

Industrial
Low birth rates, low death rates – stable, high population

2100

High

Medium

Low

2000

Population explosion
The graph shows the growth in global population (in billions) since 1800, and high, medium, and low projections for 2100.

India (2.1%)

Korea Dem Rep (2.2%)

1 million

Iran (2.6%)

Morocco (2.4%)

Egypt (2.2%)

Pakistan (2.9%) Bangladesh (2.7%)

Algeria (2.9%)

Sudan (2.9%)

Burma (2.1%)

1900

Ethiopia (2.7%)

Vietnam (2.2%)

Nigeria (3.5%)

Kenya (4.1%)

Philippines (2.5%)

Zaire (3.2%)

Tanzania (3.7%)

Brazil (1.9%)

Factors of fertility
The 1984 UN *Fertility and Family* report identified the following factors as affected by economic development and affecting fertility: labour value of children; children's value as old-age insurance and risk support; economic costs of children; infant and child mortality; age at South Africa (2.1%) marriage and the proportion never married; infecundity (due to breast-feeding, malnourishment, disease, etc); postpartum sexual abstinence; widowhood; familial relationships; possibilities of fertility regulation; and the condition of women. In 1990 Nafis Sadik summed up: "The surest way to achieve a sustained decline in fertility is to give a new priority to 'social' or 'women's resources' investment, to improving mother and child health, women's status and education and to making family planning as available as possible to both women and men."

Sickness and health services

A high level of expenditure devoted to health services, reflected in such figures as the number of doctors and hospital beds available per thousand head of population, is often taken as the key indicator of public health-care commitment. But there are problems with this approach. First, it directs investment to treat illness rather than to prevent it. This is reinforced by the fact that high treatment levels yield more political advantages than low admissions, which could, in any case, be seen to be due to inadequate service provision rather than reduced need. Second, there appears to be no end to the demand for resources for the treatment of illness. This leaves little room for health promotion and prevention, and leads to the dominance of high-profile diagnostic procedures and hospital-based surgical and pharmaceutical treatments. Such methods derive, too, from modern medicine's mechanistic and interventionist approach to health care (see right), which, through such slogans as "a pill for every ill", excludes holistic approaches and takes away the sense of personal responsibility for health.

More recently, greater attention has been given to preventative medical care, concentrating on immunization, vaccination, cancer screening, antenatal care, and family planning. However, treating illness remains the main function of health services worldwide.

In the South, spending on such things as clean water and sanitation has led to significant reductions in some diseases; but problems remain acute, exacerbated by an international economic system that drains the South of resources (see pp. 164-5). In the North, the main preventable causes of death are now cardiovascular diseases, cancer, and traffic accidents, which are variously and clearly linked to smoking, drug abuse, fat-rich diets, bad housing and education, poverty, environmental pollution, lack of exercise, occupational hazards, and car usage. There is, however, no strong link between medical expenditure and longevity. The explanation is that longevity is heavily influenced by policies and practices beyond the immediate control of medical authorities.

"The poorest and most vulnerable children have paid the Third World debt with their health." UNICEF 1990

Health file
"The progress and potential of immunization, oral rehydration, antibiotics, breast-feeding, birth-spacing, and strategies for improving nutritional health show that effective solutions to the most important causes of illness, malnutrition, and death among the children of the 1990s are available and affordable today." UNICEF 1990

○ 14 million children die each year in developing countries because of tainted drinking water, poor sanitation, pollution, common diseases, and malnutrition.

○ Nearly one person in ten now suffers from tropical diseases, the most common being malaria and schistosomiasis. Malaria kills 2 million people a year.

○ In Third World conditions a bottle-fed baby is 25 times more likely to die than a breast-fed one.

○ Cigarette smoking is responsible for more than 1 million premature deaths each year. Multinational tobacco companies are especially targeting women in developing countries. China's cigarette consumption has trebled within the last decade and lung cancer rates are rising sharply.

○ There are about 1 million unintentional poisonings and 2 million suicide attempts with pesticides each year, resulting in more than 200,000 deaths.

○ 1.5 million women, a million of them in Africa, are HIV positive. Their children have a 25-40% chance of contracting AIDS before or during birth and of dying before the age of five.

○ From 1984 to 1989 Latin America trained 200,000 doctors, many of whom are now unemployed. For the same resources it could have had 150,000 doctors and in addition both trained and paid a decent wage to half a million primary health workers.

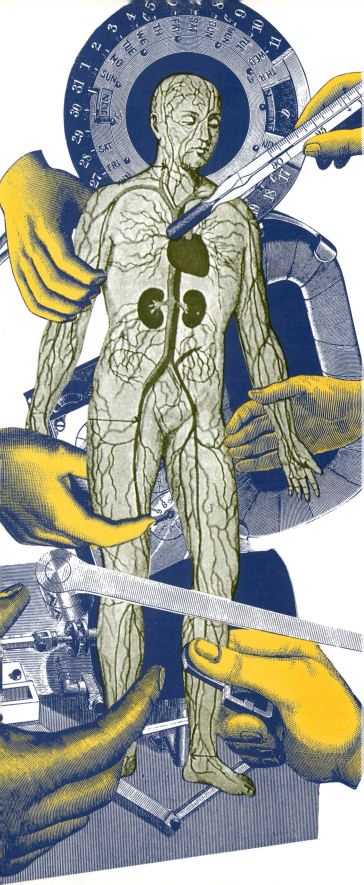

Economic growth and life expectancy

It is often thought that healthy longevity results from higher material living standards. But this is not necessarily true. In spite of the considerable disparity in income per capita between the US, UK, Sri Lanka, and China, longevity in these four countries is very similar. Moreover, changes in life expectancy at birth in the UK and Japan during this century show that the greatest increase occurred during the austerity years of wartime and postwar reconstruction—years of high employment, equitable food rationing, and support given to health maintenance.

Traffic impacts on health

Air pollution from motor vehicles aggravates medical conditions such as heart and respiratory disease. Physical fitness becomes more problematical as current patterns of traffic and planning have diminished the attractions of walking and cycling as a means of transport and regular exercise. Psychologically, distress and bereavement result from road accidents, but the mere risk of this happening causes fear and anxiety. A substantial proportion of children have diminished opportunity to lead lives that do not depend on being escorted to and from their desired destinations. Socially, the growth of traffic is increasingly destroying the traditional function of the street as a place for social contact and community life.

Health as wealth

Authorities need to place the prevention of disease and the promotion of health at the heart of policy planning. Mental health and harmony are also important since the quality of life is intrinsically bound up with such factors as self-esteem, the ability to socialize, and the degree to which people are free to make their own decisions.

Such an approach creates "wealth" in two senses. First, it increases welfare by enabling people to live longer and enjoy their natural life span as free as possible from physical disability. Second, since health promotion is far cheaper than medical intervention, it reduces the need for high levels of investment for patients suffering from preventable disease. More resources are thus available for areas of the economy that are associated with improved wellbeing, and that also have a causal relationship with healthy longevity.

What is needed is a shift of emphasis from the provision of medical services to collaboration among agencies whose activities directly affect the following:
○ availability of safe drinking water;
○ provision of adequate, well-insulated houses;
○ promotion of a healthy diet with local, fresh food if possible;
○ reduced alcohol abuse and tobacco and drug addiction;
○ generation of jobs with a wide range of skill requirements to lower unemployment;
○ creation of a safe, clean, and quiet environment;
○ redistribution of income and opportunities through taxation and international economic reform;
○ institution of systems of education on health care, including community involvement and public information;
○ emphasizing primary health care for all.

Progress in all these areas could be monitored by the development of indices and the setting of targets. A nation's health would then be judged not by the size of its "health" services but by the health of its people. For the medicine-intensive systems of the North, every hospital ward closure, redundant doctor or dentist, or fall in drug company's sales would then be indicative of a healthier society.

Global health targets
The following indicators have been proposed by Denmark.
○ Equitable distribution of resources.
○ Minimum health expenditure of 5% of GNP.
○ Safe water within a 15-minute walk, and adequate sanitary facilities in the home.
○ Immunization against infectious diseases.
○ Minimum of 20 essential drugs within an hour's walk.
○ Trained personnel attending childbirth.
○ Life expectancy at birth of at least 60 years.
○ Targets for lowering infant and maternity mortality rates.

Primary health care in operation
Community health in developing countries can depend crucially on the availability of clean water, good sanitation, and adequate food supplies. In rural south India, malnutrition and contaminated water are key causes of illness. Lack of transport to distant medical facilities and the loss of a day's wages travelling to them are also an impediment to good health. Credit programmes are boosting food production, and "barefoot" clinics are being established as a highly cost-effective way of providing care. A medical van, run by one or two trained village "paramedics" who can carry out basic tests for diagnosis and the treatment of simple conditions, tours rural areas on a regular timetable. The paramedics take patients with more complex conditions to the nearest centre for specialized attention.

Health promotion works

Just two examples highlight the potential benefits of positively promoting health. Premature death from heart disease has been halved in the last 25 years by reductions in smoking and saturated fat intake, and lowered blood pressure. Regular exercise for 20-30 minutes a few times a week can reverse conditions of angina and narrowing arteries.

Cycling for health

The provision of urban cycle networks can create a health-enhancing spiral. Bicycles promote physical fitness and thereby reduce the incidence of heart and respiratory disease. And where the effect is to bring about a transfer from motorized travel, cycling removes the previously generated costs of traffic – danger, pollution, and noise.

Rational drugs policy

Medicinal drugs can be a mixed blessing, especially in the South. Useless or dangerous drugs are common and their ill-effects can be compounded by ignorance among consumers, dispensers, and prescribers. Bangladesh was the first to tackle this issue through the organization Gonoshasthaya Kendra, founded by Dr Zafrullah Chowdhury. As well as setting up a pharmaceuticals factory to produce essential drugs, Chowdhury was a key government adviser in 1982 in the formation of a policy based on 16 criteria of usefulness, effectiveness, and harmfulness that generated an essential drugs list that banned 1700 drugs. Similar schemes are now in place in more than 100 countries, including the UK, Germany, and France.

Knowledge

Knowledge is a vital source of human capital. The 20th century has seen a knowledge explosion, but the way humankind has been treating its own life-support systems suggests that we are perilously short of wisdom. For wisdom is knowledge in perspective, just as knowledge is information placed in an appropriate framework.

Perhaps the deepest bias of Western life – and a primary source of our current ills – lies in the mechanistic worldview. For four hundred years up to the start of the present century, the world came to be seen as a machine composed of elemental building blocks. Mind and matter were strictly separated. This approach, deriving from Descartes and Newton, pervaded all areas of knowledge. Such a strategy for explanation has been allied with a belief in continual progress and growth, and an implicit assumption that we learn in order to control and manipulate.

Over the last two hundred years this approach has bequeathed to humanity the mixed "blessing" of modern science: medical advances that have increased healthy longevity, along with space vehicles, nuclear power, computers and telecommunications, and weapons of mass destruction. At the same time, the triumph of science has become clouded by growing difficulties in providing for the simple necessities of life for billions of people. Today, we are suffering from centuries of the misapplication of knowledge and of the misdirection of technology, both of which have been harnessed too narrowly, to serve only the cause of output, production, and money.

Technologically the world has changed at a great pace. By 1800 the sum total of human knowledge was doubling every 50 years; by 1950 every 10 years; in 1990, in the midst of the computer revolution, the timescale might be only months. But meanwhile the gap between the information-rich and the information-poor countries continues to grow. Since the start of the imperial phase of its history, the West has been tightening its grip on information. And we can expect to see greater enhancement of information technology in general and computer power in particular in the next decade or two. Some of the biggest impacts are likely to be in artificial intelligence and scientific modelling, including that needed to enhance our understanding of global systems.

World's biggest information systems companies 1988
(turnover in $ millions)

1	IBM (US)	55,003
2	Digital Equipment (US)	12,285
3	Fujitsu (Japan)	10,999
4	NEC (Japan)	10,476
5	Unisys (US)	9100
6	Hitachi (Japan)	8248
7	Hewlett-Packard (US)	6300
8	Siemens (FRG)	5951
9	Olivetti (Italy)	5428
10	NCR (US)	5324
11	Groupe Bull (France)	5297
12	Apple (US)	4434
13	Toshiba (Japan)	4227
14	Matsushita (Japan)	3441
15	Canon (Japan)	3392
16	Control data (US)	3254
17	Wang (US)	3074
18	Nixdorf (FRG)	3045
19	NV Philips (Netherlands)	2795
20	Xerox (US)	2650
21	AT&T (US)	2445
22	STC (UK)	2425
23	Memorex Telex (Netherlands)	2078
24	Compaq (US)	2066
25	Nihon Unisys (Japan)	2058

Knowledge is power

The power and danger of knowledge have long been recognized. The chief adviser to the first emperor of China, for example, ordered all books other than agriculture and medicine texts to be burned, and the emperor ordered 460 scholars to be buried alive. "Those that take power by force have usually acted on the principle that you can't make a revolution without breaking egg-heads . . ." Maurice Line, to the UK Library Association, 1990

The knowledge industry

In his book published thirty years ago, *The Production and Distribution of Knowledge in the United States*, Fritz Machlup identified five main components of the knowledge industry: education, research and development, the media of communication, computers, and special-ist information services. But the growth of one of these components, computer power, has been simply phenomenal. If the cost/performance ratio of cars since 1970 had

increased by as much, Rolls Royces would be doing 2 million miles to the litre and selling for a price of $2.50. First World domination of the information services industry is total, as the map below showing the largest companies and their annual turnovers illustrates. It is, however, less dominated by the US than it once was, as Japanese and European companies have captured a growing market share.

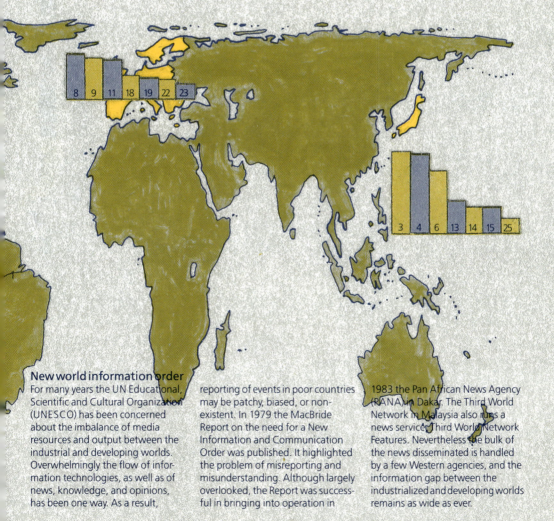

New world information order

For many years the UN Educational, Scientific and Cultural Organization (UNESCO) has been concerned about the imbalance of media resources and output between the industrial and developing worlds. Overwhelmingly the flow of infor-mation technologies, as well as of news, knowledge, and opinions, has been one way. As a result,

reporting of events in poor countries may be patchy, biased, or non-existent. In 1979 the MacBride Report on the need for a New Information and Communication Order was published. It highlighted the problem of misreporting and misunderstanding. Although largely overlooked, the Report was success-ful in bringing into operation in

1983 the Pan African News Agency (PANA) in Dakar. The Third World Network in Malaysia also runs a news service, Third World Network Features. Nevertheless the bulk of the news disseminated is handled by a few Western agencies, and the information gap between the industrialized and developing worlds remains as wide as ever.

The route to wisdom

Our productive and technological capacities have run far ahead of our social capacities, our ethical norms, our knowledge of how to manage innovation, of how to advance just political systems, and of how to humanize science. The definition of wealth used in this book puts much emphasis on the personal development of individuals, their capacity to exercise and enhance skills of all kinds, and their abilities and opportunities to express and exercise their power. In parallel with this emphasis on empowering, four key policy directions emerge.

First, there is a need to move beyond the mechanistic worldview of Cartesian-Newtonian science to an approach that emphasizes the fundamental interdependence of all phenomena, one that acknowledges the significance of imprecision, risk, uncertainty, ignorance, and indeterminacy. As part of this shift we need to enquire into the limits of our understanding of the natural and social sciences, and the ways in which scientific knowledge not only achieves social and political authority but how it is applied in practice.

Second, as our understanding of the social construction of knowledge changes, so must we pay more attention to the possible impacts of new technologies. The increasing number of ethical issues raised by scientific and technological advances – for example, pre-embryo research and genetic engineering – represent a crucial interface between knowledge and wisdom. "The only wisdom that we can hope to obtain is the wisdom of humility." (T S Eliot)

Third, we need to develop freedom-of-information policies. Secretiveness and the trend toward the privatization of knowledge, whereby information becomes a commodity available only to those who can pay, are threats to that flow of knowledge that is a prerequisite to building the shared understanding essential in complex, sustainable societies. The right to know must become a universal human right.

Finally, information systems cannot be concentrated in the hands of a few. In recent years the mass media have become increasingly commercialized and their ownership increasingly concentrated. As a first step toward the devolution of media power, there is a need to build up regional news and data services, and the capacity to exploit them fully.

The right to know

In any democracy, the "right to know" must be a fundamental right. One expression of a citizen's right to know is Freedom of Information (FOI) legislation, which puts into law the presumption that the public has the right to official information unless the government can show that disclosure – of, for example, military or trade secrets – would be harmful. About a dozen countries, including the US, Canada, and Australia, have already adopted such legislation. One celebrated disclosure under the Australian law forced the cancellation of an expensive military project for the establishment of a tank training area after internal documents revealed that the site was totally unsuitable for the purpose. The amount saved represented nearly 40 times the annual cost of implementing the Australian FOI law.

"Wisdom is nothing more and nothing less than inspired selectivity, the power to sense what is beautiful, right and good."
George Stapledon

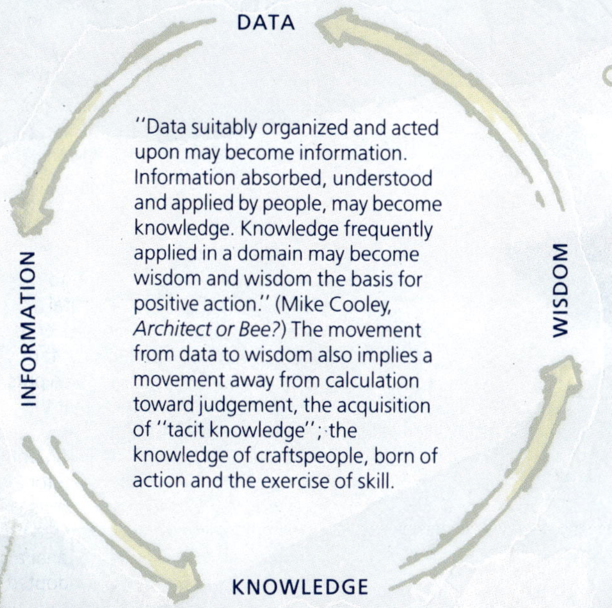

DATA

INFORMATION

WISDOM

"Data suitably organized and acted upon may become information. Information absorbed, understood and applied by people, may become knowledge. Knowledge frequently applied in a domain may become wisdom and wisdom the basis for positive action." (Mike Cooley, *Architect or Bee?*) The movement from data to wisdom also implies a movement away from calculation toward judgement, the acquisition of "tacit knowledge"; the knowledge of craftspeople, born of action and the exercise of skill.

KNOWLEDGE

Indigenous knowledge

Knowledge systems throughout the planet are disappearing. As explained by Darrell Posey in *Anthropology Today* in 1990: "For many years there have been warnings of the impending destruction of indigenous cultures and the implication of those losses for all of humanity ... Medicinal plants, natural insecticides and repellents, fertility regulating drugs, edible plants, animal behaviour, climatic and ecological seasonality, soils, forests and savannah management, skin and body treatments — these are just some of the categories of knowledge that can contribute to new strategies for ecologically and socially sound sustained development." The annual market value for medicines derived from medicinal plants discovered from indigenous peoples is $43 billion: less than one-hundredth of one per cent of the profits derived from those sources has ever been returned to those peoples.

Education and training

There have been two powerful traditions in education theory and practice. The first derives from Plato, who placed the supremacy of reason above all other human attributes. Plato argued that it was through reason alone that people could attain knowledge and establish truth in all areas of life, and he saw education as the transmission of the knowledge and culture of the adult world to the young. The second main tradition is the child-centred approach coming to us from Rousseau, Froebel, Pestalozzi, and Montessori, all of whom saw self-activity as the central feature in child education.

Overlaying the contest between knowledge- and child-centred education has been the long history of education to meet the perceived needs of particular social classes. In China 3000 years ago there were schools for the sons of the nobility, the curriculum of which consisted of rituals, music, archery, charioteering, writing, and mathematics. In the France of Louis XIV the academies for nobles taught deportment, modern languages, fencing, and riding.

In many countries it is only recently that education, or rather schooling, for all has come to be seen as a duty of government. Schooling often provides a telling reflection of the norms and values of a society. In Japan, for example, following a highly competitive examination at age 15, most pupils go on to high schools clearly organized on a hierarchical basis. Throughout Japanese education a huge emphasis is placed on effort, and the entire system can be seen as a preparation for employment in sharply hierarchical companies and organizations.

Globally there have been pressures to expand the number of children in full-time education. On the one hand there has been the democratic pressure for greater social justice, with schools seen as a way of righting inequality and social injustice. On the other, education is seen as a worthwhile investment both by individuals and nations. Nevertheless, illiteracy remains a major global problem. Countries with over 50 per cent illiteracy rates have a total population of more than 1.4 billion people.

Education in turmoil

International economic competition and rapid technological development are placing unprecedented pressures on the education systems of the industrialized world. Academic institutions are being pressed to become parodies of industry, with profit centres, "products" (students or publications), and "employees" (lecturers). Increasingly, education is being treated as a commodity, and the possibility of providing a rich, broad-based learning process for the majority of pupils in some countries is being put at risk by curbs on public expenditure. In many developing countries there is a struggle to meet rising expectations and to provide a basic education for all. Against the longer-term trend of increasing enrolment, since 1980 spending per student on primary education has declined in two out of three developing countries, resulting in the first increase in 40 years in the number of primary-aged children not attending school.

The enrolment explosion

The last 25 years have witnessed an enrolment explosion throughout the world. In 1990 there were twice as many children in school as in 1965. UNESCO has published the figures for enrolment at the second level, shown in the chart (see right). Education at the second level is based on at least four previous years of instruction at first level, and consists of school-based general or specialized instruction or both. The enrolment percentages are arrived at by dividing the total enrolment for this level of education (regardless of age) by the population of the age group that, according to national regulations, should be enrolled at this level.

The enrolment explosion

		Male	Female	
World	54	31	24	43
Africa	39	7	3	23
Asia	49	26	15	35
Europe (including USSR)	89	56	53	90
Oceania	80	56	53	82
North America	100 / 87		88	100
Latin America & Caribbean	52	15	14	56
Developed countries	91	62	60	92
Developing countries	47	20	11	33

1960   1987

Education for capability

Education needs to cater for people's creative and spiritual development as well as their physical and intellectual needs. Education should encourage people to think independently, to work co-operatively, and to make a constructive contribution to their community. As Patrick van Rensburg of the Foundation for Education with Production has argued: "In this new conception of education people should develop themselves naturally as fully as they can, have all modern knowledge available to them, but also have technical skills." Today modern knowledge should include environmental education and a real understanding of the global situation.

After a professional life in primary education, Norman Kirby, the author of *Personal Values and Primary Education*, is convinced that no matter what the content of school curricula, no matter how technically proficient teachers are, no matter how good the parent contact, there is no "good" school unless the relationships between those who work within schools, pupils and teachers, is such that people draw strength, satisfaction, and happiness from them. For Kirby a good school is about being "good" with and to people.

Among policies likely to improve the quality of education in all countries are those designed to increase the status of teachers, not least through better pay and conditions; those that realize the importance of offering opportunities for lifelong education; and those that emphasize the significance of "education for capability" – the concept that embodies the principle that education must concern itself with motivation, feelings, citizenship, and social and practical skills, as well as developing the capacities to think logically and critically.

Within this envisaged system, special emphasis needs to be given to preschool education. It is here that an early identification of any problems can be recognized, and help given to overcome or at least minimize them. Preschool is also a valuable preparation for subsequent schooling, providing an all-round development of the child's personality. And by involving adults outside of the home, children are helped to develop confidence and social skills. The significance of these factors for mobilizing human resources cannot be overstated.

Distorted values
In most societies the more important the teacher, the lower the status, and remuneration, of that person. The parent at home – almost certainly the mother – is the most important teacher of all. It is in what are termed the preschool years that children are most open to acquiring learning skills and basic aptitudes; an ability (represented by head size in the illustration above) that declines as the child grows and matures. A UNESCO study indicates that 50% of aptitudes are fixed at age four, and 80% by age eight.

Pedagogy of the oppressed

Paulo Freire was born in Recife, Brazil in 1921. As a student he developed an educational method aimed at not only widespread literacy but also the freeing of the people from their material poverty and political marginalization. Through consciousness raising it encourages victims of injustice to recognize themselves as such and to take action against the oppressive elements. His approach was widely adopted in literacy campaigns throughout the northeast of Brazil, and has been very influential in other countries. In 1975, for example, the Catholic diocese of Machakos, Kenya initiated a Freirian literacy programme that was so successful that by 1984 it involved some 60,000 participants. Freire is currently Education Secretary in São Paulo.

Education with Production

Education with Production is an officially sponsored approach in Zimbabwe, where more than 75% of children now complete primary school. Its techniques are not traditional. At one school, pupils dug a fishpond in the shape of a world map, thus learning not only about fish farming, but also about geography, building techniques, food and nutrition, the environment, and the control of water-related diseases. All schools now have fruit and vegetable gardens, and some grow trees for firewood and to protect against erosion.

Training

A skilled workforce that trains and retrains regularly is increasingly being regarded as the key to industrial success. Germany and Japan, for example, have managed to embed a commitment to training deep into their corporate cultures. Employers devote resources to apprenticeship schemes in the knowledge that others will do the same and a higher general level of skills results. Another approach, as in France, is based on vocational training in educational colleges. A less successful approach, evident in the US and, to some extent, in the UK, relies on on-the-job training. A 1989 Massachusetts Institute of Technology Commission report on the US system described it as little more than "following Joe around". Highlighting the sharp differences in the success rates in Europe, a 1990 European Commission Labour Market survey gave these figures for the percentages of the workforces in various countries classified as skilled: France 80%; Italy 79%; Holland 76%; Germany 67%; Belgium 62%; Denmark 62%; Ireland 59%; Spain 56%; Portugal 50%; and the UK 38%.

Work and employment

Work can be any activity, remunerated or not, that produces goods and services. From history it is possible to discern four main modes of organizing work: slavery, whereby the worker was physically owned by another person; serfdom, an unequal worker-master relationship based on domination and open to exploitation but with theoretical reciprocal responsibilities; employment, or wage-labour, a system in which labour-time is exchanged for income; and what James Robertson, the author of *Future Work*, calls ownwork, defined as "activity which is purposeful and important and which people control for themselves".

Slavery is supposedly outlawed but is still widespread around the world. Serfdom is still common in rural areas of nonindustrialized countries. Employment is the dominant work relationship of industrialism – a relationship that has frequently involved exploitation, to protect workers from which the trade union movement was established. Ownwork exists in a variety of forms in all economies: the self-employed, co-operators, small-holders, housewives are all ownworkers.

Only in societies where work is based on employment are people who wish to work sometimes prevented from doing so, creating the condition known as unemployment. This is not only wasteful of the health, skills, and motivation – the human capital – they embody and wish to use productively, it is also a great human tragedy. In industrial society, a job is far more than livelihood, important though this is: a job gives self-respect, identity, and a sense of social purpose. One of the great political regressions of the 1980s was the progressive public acceptance in many countries of high levels of unemployment (see right). A dual society has emerged. In one, people have jobs and relative affluence; in the other, people are either unemployed, on "welfare", or marginalized in the low-wage or "informal" sectors.

It is arguable whether most people have ever enjoyed the work they do. What is indubitable is that those who do enjoy their work regard it as one of life's greatest satisfactions. There is in principle no reason why a primary economic objective should not be to give everybody the opportunity to do fulfilling work. But in practice improving the quality of work is nearly always subordinated to increasing labour productivity. Promoting work satisfaction remains a marginal consideration in employment policy.

Slavery in the 1990s

There are millions more slaves in the world today than there were at the time of the antislavery campaigner William Wilberforce in the 18th century. Chattel slavery, the absolute ownership of other people, still exists: Anti-Slavery International estimates there are 100,000 in Mauritania alone. Children are openly sold in Thailand and the practice has recently reappeared in Sudan. Far more common than chattel slavery is debt bondage, whereby an unspecified amount of labour is pledged for an unspecified time in repayment of a loan. At the wages paid, if any, the debt is often irredeemable, and so children born to such a family are born into slavery. According to the 1981 landmark study *Bonded Labour in India* by Sarna Marla, India has a minimum of 5 million bonded labourers, of whom 500,000 are slave children.

Of the 100,000 young boys working in the carpet-making industry of Uttar Pradesh, many are effectively slaves, sleeping on the premises, terrorized by the loom owners, working 15 hours a day, seven days a week in dark, airless, and extremely hot mudbrick huts with no real meal breaks and minimal or no wages. In April 1984 *The Times of India* headlined one such workplace as "The Torture Camp of Mirzapur". And the fruits of their labour can fetch thousands of dollars in the exclusive stores of the West. More than 200 million children worldwide work in similar conditions in different industries.

78 79 80 81 82 83 84 85 86 87 88

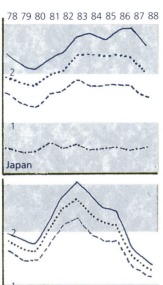

Japan

"Without work all life goes rotten, but when work is soulless, all life stifles and dies."
Albert Camus

The tragedy of unemployment

Research quoted by Peter Warr of the University of Sheffield has established a number of likely effects of unemployment: loss of income, variety in life, social contact, status, self-esteem, skills and security; and psychological stress. It is thus unsurprising that the unemployed show significantly higher levels of depression, alienation, ill-health, and suicide than society at large.

—— Total unemployed

········ Unemployed for less than 12 months

– – – Unemployed for less than 6 months

·–·–· Unemployed for less than 1 month

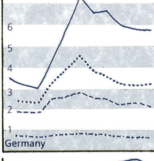

Sweden

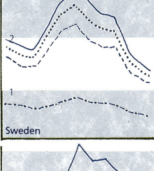

Germany

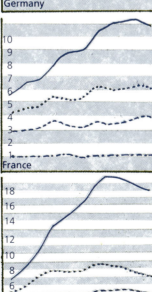

France

Spain

78 79 80 81 82 83 84 85 86 87 88

Trade unions: achievements and challenges

Trade unions have played a vital role in the evolution of a more humane capitalist society, and continue to do so. Moreover, it is trade union pressure on the political process, through their support for or organization into political parties, that has yielded the formation of comprehensive welfare states in many countries of the industrial world. All citizens in these countries have a deep cause for gratitude to trade union activity, the more so since these achievements are won at considerable personal risk and cost: in 1991 the Independent Confederation of Free Trade Unions reported union rights abuses in 72 countries, with more than 250 unionists killed and thousands tortured over a 15-month period.

However, despite their achievements, unions run an ever present risk of degenerating into mere powerful organs for promoting their members' interests. Where one or a few large unions are organized in monopolistic industries crucial to society's operation, such as transport or energy supply, there is always a danger that relatively advantaged labour forces will seek to exploit their powerful position at the expense of the wider society.

A climate of persistent industrial conflict is a lose-lose-lose situation: businesses lose, trade union members lose, and so does society at large. Successful industrial economies, such as those of the former West Germany, Japan, and Scandinavia, have all evolved systems of negotiation between workers, management, and government that promote a perception of common interest rather than mutual competition. Worse-performing economies of the capitalist world would do well to follow suit, as would the economies of Eastern Europe and the USSR as they evolve their own market structures.

A mix of options

Green economic policy on work needs to address the maldistribution of work between men and women, and that between the employed and the unemployed. The gender differences need continually to be diminished by policies of equal opportunities and equal pay for equal work, the provision of parental leave and childcare services (see pp. 132-5), and an attack on sexual stereotyping. With regard to employment policy, Professor Charles Handy of the London Business School wrote bluntly in 1984: "If jobs for all means full-time, lifelong jobs for all who want them at good rates of pay, then full-time employment is not feasible in the foreseeable future." The intervening years have proved him right. Handy's remedy is to promote as the dominant working strategy of the future the concept of a "portfolio of work", whereby people work fewer hours at full-time paid jobs, starting later in life and ending earlier, working shorter weeks, and taking more time off; and they supplement this work with part-time work, self-employment, sabbaticals, parenting, volunteering, and other ownwork.

For all to have such a portfolio, skill levels must be raised so that everyone has a chance of securing one of these shorter-working-life jobs. Further, governments can help to increase the number of jobs by investing in essential, noninflationary, nonimport-intensive public infrastructure, such as housing, energy conservation, and environmental improvements of all kinds. And, if ownwork is to become an attractive option, governments will need to increase its status and rewards.

Since 1960 annual working hours worked per person have in fact dropped in all OECD countries except Japan, falling in Germany, for example, from 2081 to 1622 between 1960 and 1988. They need to fall to 1430 to give a 50,000 hour, 35-year life in full-time employment. At the same time, the most vigorous "active labour market" policies, especially of education and training, need to be followed to draw into employment the millions who want jobs but are still excluded from them. Furthermore, the jobs must be such, as the thrust of German co-determination has sought to ensure (see right), as to be fit for people rather than machines.

An important approach for generating economic development, especially in depressed or disadvantaged areas, is the *local* development strategy, which focuses

German co-determination

In 1972 the German Works Constitution Act instituted what has come to be known as co-determination in German companies. It established works councils representing all employees, elected members from which sit on a supervisory board whose function is to monitor the company's executive board. The works councils are given "the right of co-determination" in a number of areas, including working hours, work breaks, temporary short-time working, overtime, annual leave, principles and methods of remuneration, job and bonus rates, vocational training, occupational health and safety, housing and welfare services, and the impacts on employees of technical change. Following a debate concerning the "humanization" of work organization, the unions came to place increasing importance on working conditions and job security. By 1983, management had largely accepted that new technologies should be introduced without dismissals, loss of skills, and wage reduction and, according to a recent OECD paper, with "the imperative to organize work so that it is fit to be carried out by human beings". The same paper reported on some 1988 research that concluded: "The worker is regarded by management today as a person who is equipped with complex abilities and with potential for diverse development, which will be used most efficiently when that potential is made fully functional." (West) Germany's economy is probably the most successful in Europe.

Allowances for enterprise

Moving from unemployment to successful self-employment is an enormous step. Would-be entrepreneurs must not only gain access to the four capitals (see pp. 60-1), they might also risk losing their entitlement to unemployment benefits. It was to make self-employment easier in the UK that the Enterprise Allowance Scheme (EAS) was established in 1983. EAS provides an allowance of £40 per week for a year, plus free counselling and advice, to those who have £1000 to invest in their own business. Since its launch more than half a million people have benefited. Of those who complete their first year in business, 65% are still going after three, and overall they have generated another 114 jobs per 100 successful businesses.

LEDA

Local Employment Development Action was founded in 1986 and is targeted on 24 disadvantaged areas, with more to be added, in 11 EC countries. Two such areas are in each of the Republic of Ireland, the UK, Portugal, Spain, Italy, Greece, Belgium, the Netherlands, and Denmark, and three each in France and Germany. LEDA proceeds through two key concepts: the building of partnerships at the local level between business, local government, agencies of central government, labour organizations, and voluntary and community groups; and the building of local capacity through these partnerships, to understand local problems and conditions, work out solutions, and mobilize and administer the necessary resources to achieve them. LEDA is not just about employment. As Portuguese Professor Alberto Melo said at a recent LEDA conference, it is about "social, cultural, political and economic development": in other words, the regeneration of community.

specifically on local resources and local opportunities for the purpose of meeting local needs. The EC, for example, has put considerable resources from its Structural Funds behind a programme of Local Employment Development Action (LEDA – see left), of which the EC's John Morley, who oversees LEDA's funding, has said: "Motivating, mobilizing, educating and training people is as important as the accompanying physical investments."

The enabling of ownwork is similarly a process of ensuring that people have access to each of the four types of capital (see pp. 60-1) that all work needs in order to be productive: land, skills and motivation, supporting organizations, and tools/machines or the finance to buy them. One successful ownwork initiative is the UK Enterprise Allowance Scheme (see left), which has itself proved to be an effective piece of "organizational capital". Another is the Trickle-Up Program, based in New York City, which provides grants of $100 to start up businesses. In 11 years it has supported in this way more than 18,000 businesses, principally in the Third World. Its 1990 Annual Report indicated that nearly 120,000 people had benefited from these businesses, generating $6.8 million in sales and an estimated profit of nearly $2.5 million. This indicates the real economic vitality in Third World countries, which requires few financial resources, but the right approach, to be released.

Whether work is organized as employment or ownwork, it should be good work, which, as Handy puts it: ". . . allows us to express ourselves, which provides an outlet for our creative energies, our ability to work with and relate to others, work which is under our control, not in control of us." If lifetime hours in employment continue to fall; if programmes of training, education, enablement, and local development are imaginatively executed; if female participation in employment continues to increase and to be conducted on more equal terms with men; and if men begin to take more responsibility for domestic work; then it is possible that working lifestyles will converge to a fairer, more balanced, more satisfying mix of paid and unpaid work, employment, ownwork, and leisure.

Social security

Most people today live in chronic economic insecurity. In the Third World supportive families are the principal form of social security, which provides a powerful motivation for their enlargement. In the book *The Greening of Aid* Robert Chambers advocates a strategy of "sustainable livelihood security" (SLS) for the Third World poor. "Livelihood is defined as adequate stocks and flows of food and cash to meet basic needs. Security refers to secure ownership of, or access to, resources and income-earning activities . . . Sustainable refers to the maintenance or enhancement of resource productivity on a long-term basis." Enhancing the SLS of the poor should become the principal objective of aid and development programmes.

In most industrialized countries since the end of World War II social security has been, to a lesser or greater extent, provided by "the welfare state", which seeks to ensure universal access on the basis of need to some or all of the fundamental components of life. The achievements of the welfare state, in acting as a safety net for the disadvantaged, have been generally impressive and humane. There can be no doubt that those on lower incomes in countries such as Sweden have a far higher quality of life than the poor in, for example, the US, where, of all industrialized countries, the safety net is most badly holed.

The welfare state tended to be based on an implicit assumption of continuing economic growth and full employment – conditions that in the 1970s ceased to pertain. At the same time, government expenditure rose dramatically, surpassing 50 per cent of GNP in a number of European countries. To fund this expenditure taxation levels rose – personal income tax in Sweden topped 60 per cent for the average waged worker. The welfare state was criticized from all sides. Conservatives attacked it as demotivating and an economic burden. Supporters in countries such as the UK realized with dismay that it had not even brought about greater economic equality. People generally have often experienced the administration of the system as demeaning and inflexible, with services not reflecting their perceived needs. Moreover, benefits systems have tended to create "traps" of poverty and unemployment, due to the withdrawal of benefits as people begin to earn, which destroy the incentive to work and can make it uneconomic to work at all.

Public action works
The way in which concerted public action benefits the disadvantaged is most clearly shown by Sweden's commitment to social welfare. The Black Report, *Inequalities in Health*, compared the decline in infant mortality from 1920 to 1960 for five Swedish counties of widely differing incomes. In 1920 infant mortality rates in the richest and poorest were 60 and 96 per 1000 respectively; by 1960 they were 15 and 19. Sweden has also eliminated socioeconomic differences in the height and age of maturity of children, of which social class remains an important determinant in, for example, England and Scotland.

Sustainable livelihood security

To promote sustainable livelihoods in the Third World, Robert Chambers advocates five priorities: flexibility to learn from experience; putting people's needs above those of bureaucrats; giving people secure rights; encouraging sustainability; and having staff of high calibre and commitment.

Restructuring in Europe

The moves to a single European market significantly undermine the national autonomy that has produced the welfare state. For example, Swedish business, in anticipation of EC membership, has increased investments in EC countries and lost domestic commitment. It intends to withdraw from the business-government-union negotiating forums that have been the basis of the social consensus underlying Sweden's welfare state. Such loss of national political coherence has built support for welfare-state-like institutions at the European level, notably the Structural Funds and the EC Social Charter. The Funds, used to promote development in deprived areas, will have their 1987 resources doubled by 1993; the Charter, adopted in 1989 by all EC members except the UK, contains a commitment to "social protection".

Access to land

That the drastic poverty in rural Brazil could be ameliorated by land reform was shown by a World Bank project at Piaui. The project bought 200,000 hectares over five years and distributed it to nearly 3500 families, and regularized tenure for 1500 more. The income of 7800 farmers in the area subsequently increased by 240-295%. A clear title to land was the key to self-reliant development.

Moving toward equality

Only the insensitive or inhumane advocate the abolition of the welfare state as a solution to the crisis it faces. But its operation and rationale clearly need to be rethought. The classic distinction with regard to state benefits is between selectivity and universality. Universal benefits are paid to all people in a certain group, as, for example, child benefits in the UK are paid to all parents. Such benefits have the advantage of avoiding means tests and the poverty and unemployment traps. Their disadvantage is their cost. Selective benefits are supposed to be able to target the needy and so use available resources more efficiently than a universal approach. However, they involve means tests and the traps of withdrawal as people cease to qualify for them. Generally favoured by more conservative governments, selective benefits have tended to result in the stigmatization of recipients, low take-up of benefits and a lower overall commitment of resources. The most comprehensive approach to universal benefits is the proposal to pay a Basic Income (BI) as of right to all citizens (see right).

At the heart of the debate about the level, and degree of selectivity or universality of benefits, lie the fundamental issues of liberty, equality, and justice. Malcolm Wicks in his book *A Future For All* rejects any trade-off between these concepts, regarding a just society as one that is equal enough for *everybody* to experience freedom. Wicks' recipe for short-term social security priorities for such a society include reductions in taxation for the low paid, a guaranteed, non-means-tested minimum income for those not working, a minimum wage, and enlarged child-support and home-care allowances. The BI could easily fit into such a scheme, the aim of which goes well beyond equality of opportunity. Its goal is the equality of citizenship, whereby all can participate in the mainstream life of society.

The emphasis given here to the welfare state must not obscure the other sources of social security: families, above all, and also communities and employers, as in the Japanese system of lifetime employment (see right). For the welfare system to work, as is the case with these other social security systems, mutual commitment rather than one-way dependency must become the dominant feature. The BI is not a "free income", and will be politically infeasible if it is regarded as such. It is a cost embraced by those on higher-than-average incomes as an expression of commitment to the wider health of their

Employment for life

In Japan a major element of social security comes from companies through the lifetime employment system, which is essentially a commitment by the company that its workers will not be laid-off except in the direst emergency. The eminent Japan specialist Professor Ronald Dore describes such a company as "primarily a community of people rather than a piece of property belonging to shareholders . . . The sense of community is consciously valued as a precondition for high work morale . . . One precondition for maintaining this sense of community is guaranteed security of membership . . . Hence, having to declare involuntary redundancies is seen as a more serious sign of management failure than failure to pay dividends for two or three years." The lifetime employment system increasingly covers more workers and more small and medium as well as large companies. The system is built on rights and responsibilities on both sides. As Akio Morita, founder of Sony, said: "We have a long-time commitment to our employees and they have a commitment to us." One of the problems of the welfare state is that too often the commitments are designed only to be one way.

society. In return, those whose BI is greater than their tax payments must express their commitment and make a contribution to their society in other ways. Self-help to the limit of personal ability, and participation by beneficiaries both in social services themselves and in society at large are the new ingredients needed to revitalize the welfare state. Such participation is anything but automatic in industrial societies. It needs to be fostered and institutionalized, and made transparent and accountable. The welfare state will not be sustainable – politically, socially, or financially – until it becomes a real welfare community of mutual rights and responsibilities.

The Basic Income (BI)

The key element of a BI as defined by the UK-based Basic Income Research Group (BIRG) is that it is a universal, unconditional, individual entitlement to income, subject only to citizenship or legal residence.

The benefits of a BI payment are many. Such an income entitlement would: diminish the poverty and unemployment traps; give an independent income to homemakers and other unpaid carers; provide income support for adult education and training; widen employment options; and enable the tax-benefit system to be much simplified.

The extent to which these benefits are achieved depends on the level at which the BI is paid. Costings for the UK indicate that a Full Basic Income (FBI) at a level enabling subsistence would require a 70% income tax rate. A Partial Basic Income (PBI) at half subsistence could be financed by a 35% tax rate, a £20 per week tax allowance,

and the abolition of National Insurance and existing tax reliefs on pensions and mortgages. This is comparable to existing UK taxes on income. The first step toward PBI and FBI might be a transitional BI at 40% of PBI to get the system established. Both this and PBI would require other income-support benefits for those with special needs.

Thus a PBI is financially feasible. It would yield in significant measure the advantages mentioned above. In societies that cannot deliver full employment, in which people are working more and more flexibly, the old social security safety net is hopelessly holed. Add to that the urgent need to give recognition, status, and encouragement to unpaid household and caring work, and the gradual but determined introduction of a PBI becomes both a social and a moral imperative.

Introduction: organizational capital

If human capital formation is the principal means through which human welfare can be achieved, such capital will be more productive if it is appropriately organized. This insight goes back at least to Adam Smith (see pp. 12-13), one of whose great contributions to economic theory was an analysis of the division of labour, whereby people by co-operating in a task and each concentrating on a small part of it are able to be more productive than if each individual performed the whole task alone. However, the division of labour is not the reason that social and organizational capital has acquired a new significance in these latter decades of the 20th century: the reason resides in the modern imperative of evolving effective structures of posing and making *collective choices*.

One of the most challenging features of the present time is that none of the major, global, economic problems, nor an increasing proportion of local ones, can be solved through the market alone. The market is a valuable piece of social capital that can be constructed only with difficulty, as the East Europeans are discovering. But its operation, involving millions of individually marginal choices with a significant aggregate impact, can only contribute to social "ill-fare" unless it is guided and checked by a collective process of decision making.

There are several reasons for this. One is the problem of negative externalities (see pp. 34-5), which can be internalized or regulated only by a collective process. Such a process is also required to redress the current imbalance between rich and poor, both within and between countries, which has become an environmental as well as a moral imperative. Finally, only a collective process can ameliorate the problems of "positional goods" (see right).

The world of the coming decades will not be ordered by anything resembling a "free market". The dominant forces will be organizations, either those of the powerful acting in their own self-interest, and possibly against the public good; or those of government, at many levels, which at least have the chance of being participatory, or representative and accountable, and democratic; or the self-helping, mutually co-operative initiatives of the civil society. People and their relationships will have value only if democratic government and civil society are in the ascendant.

Positional goods

Economist Fred Hirsch's concept of positional goods in the economy is a key insight of great relevance to a number of modern problems. These goods are those that are in fixed supply, including: historical artefacts such as period houses, antiques, or works by dead artists; the top positions in hierarchical organizations; and many categories of environmental goods such as rainforests, the ozone layer, scenery, or road space in city centres. As societies become more mobile, educated, and affluent, more people aspire to these goods (or to other products that negatively affect them), but their quantity remains the same, or can be reduced. Either the relative price of these goods will rise or their quality will be degraded, or both. Such phenomena are commonplace in the modern world, with increasingly serious effects. The market by itself is powerless to address these because they are actually caused by decentralized individual decisions in the marketplace. As Hirsch puts it: "Individual behaviour on the basis of given preferences produces a chain of reactions that works itself out only after culminating in a pattern that no single individual would choose." Polluted and congested city streets exhibit just such a pattern. Only a collective decision-making process that guides or limits the market can resolve these problems, requiring, again, the formation and operation of organizational capital.

The neo-liberal paradox

The Reagan-Thatcher neo-liberalism of the 1980s has bequeathed a tragic paradox. An important part of their message was the inherent ineffectiveness, or worse, of government. Despite the fact that during their terms of office their governments either amassed unheard-of budget deficits (the US) or became unprecedentedly centralized and authoritarian (the UK), they both dismantled important parts of the public sector in the name of "the market". Their project could not have exerted such influence had it not contained a grain of truth. Government failure was common; markets were in places undervalued. But their remedies for these failings worsened both problems. Markets were further concentrated by business mergers and takeovers and the ongoing globalization of the economy. And government, far from being reformed, was undermined. Its failure has been compounded by intensified market failure as the environment and social quality of life continue their decline; and its ability to govern is being diminished by the growing power of non-democratic, unaccountable, centrally planned corporations.

Families

There are huge differences in the forms taken by "the family" within and between different countries. At the same time, everywhere the family is the basic unit of social organization and, in many places, the basis of economic activity. Even in industrialized societies, with their often attenuated family functions, families produce goods and services of equivalent value to 25-40 per cent of GDP (see pp. 68-9).

Families are governed by detailed customs and rules that can be thought of as enduring and deep-rooted social or cultural capital, transmitted from generation to generation. In many societies these rules are profoundly patriarchal, with practices including female circumcision, arranged marriages, dowry deaths (the "accidental" deaths of wives whose dowries have not been forth-coming), forced sexual submission, and wife battering. The basic wealth of societies that families, and predominantly women within them, create is all too often produced in conditions that Marilyn Waring, in her book *If Women Counted*, describes as slavery (see pp. 18-19). Even where these conditions do not prevail, the unwillingness of men to share the burdens of housework and childcare, and of states and employers to support parents, means that children and family entail for women an enormous economic cost in terms of foregone income and career fulfilment.

As with the environment, the family's economic contribution can be analysed in terms of the functions it performs. Most important among these are the birth, nurturing, and socialization of children; the provision of services and goods for household use and for the market; the provision of social security in sickness and old age; and the principal building block of community. The importance of these functions makes the decline of family life, a phenomenon apparent in most countries, a matter of grave concern. The reasons are complex: the individualistic, market-oriented ethic of the Western consumer society; the refusal of women to submit any longer to discrimination; the mobility of industrial societies; the mass rural-to-urban migrations, or move-ments of individuals abroad; the disruptions of desperate poverty, ecological degradation, repression, and war. The results are loneliness and institutionalization of the old, delinquency and alienation of the young (see pp. 20-1), general stress and trauma, and a profound tearing of the social fabric.

The diversity of family

It is the nature of the relationships involved in the family, and of the transitions from one stage of the human life cycle to the next, that gives families their variety in different societies. They may have many children or few. Children may remain in full time education and economic dependence until their 20s, or they may be earning from age seven. Marriage and child-bearing may be early or late. Different generations may form an extended family with a key role for older members; or adults may have quite separate households – the old living and dying in institutions or alone. Statistics can only give some idea of the diversity involved (see right). On the principal trends of family structure, the 1984 UN *Fertility and Family* report concluded that the process of modernization as experienced by "the more advanced countries" involved a change "from family-oriented to highly individualized societies".

Street children

Millions of the world's children spend their childhood in city streets. Estimates as to numbers vary wildly. In 1984 the Inter-American Parlia-mentary Group on Population in Development put the figure at 60-70 million, with more than half in Latin America. Anthropologists Judith Ennew and Brian Milne estimate 30 million on the basis of 1981 figures of population, urban-ization, and economic activity. The street-children phenomenon has existed in all industrial and indus-trializing societies, a desperately rational family response to acute poverty in an urban setting. Increas-ingly frequently, however, the poverty breaks the family apart and the child is abandoned. Perhaps one-third of all street children have no home but the street and no "families" but their fellow street children.

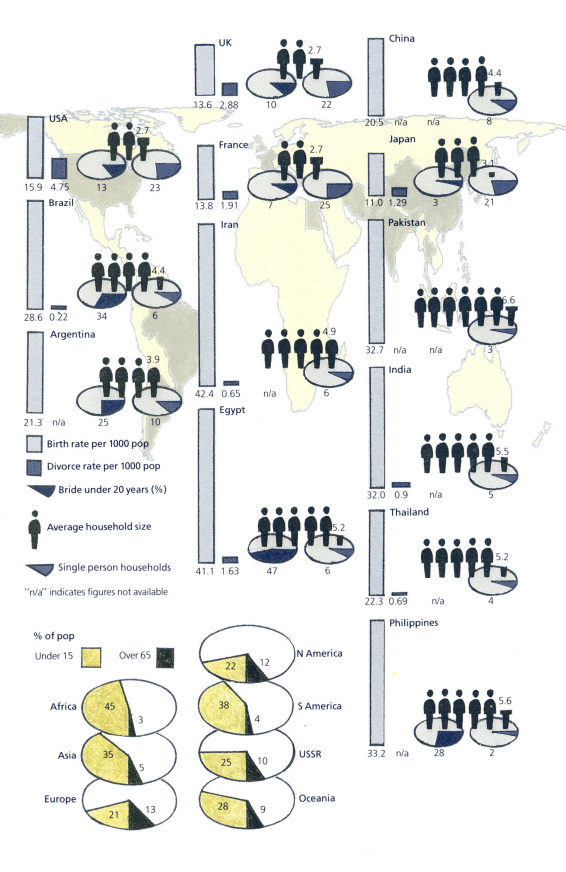

UK
2.7
13.6 2.88 10 22

China
4.4
20.5 n/a n/a 8

USA
2.7
15.9 4.75 13 23

France
2.7
13.8 1.91 7 25

Japan
3.1
11.0 1.29 3 21

Brazil
4.4
28.6 0.22 34 6

Iran
4.9
42.4 0.65 n/a 6

Pakistan
6.6
32.7 n/a n/a 3

Argentina
3.9
21.3 n/a 25 10

India
5.5
32.0 0.9 n/a 5

Egypt
5.2
41.1 1.63 47 6

Thailand
5.2
22.3 0.69 n/a 4

Philippines
5.6
33.2 n/a 28 2

Birth rate per 1000 pop

Divorce rate per 1000 pop

Bride under 20 years (%)

Average household size

Single person households

"n/a" indicates figures not available

% of pop
Under 15   Over 65

N America
22 12

Africa
45 3

S America
38 4

Asia
35 5

USSR
25 10

Europe
21 13

Oceania
28 9

Life stages

Within the family are enacted the most intimate dramas of the generational life cycle: birth and dependent childhood, adolescence and the challenges of the new independence of early adulthood; courtship, marriage, and the responsibilities of full maturity; followed by the decline of physical powers, renewed dependence on others, and, finally, death. People in the different stages of the life cycle are net producers and consumers of four different types of wealth: recreation (or pleasure), care, other household services and goods, and income.

The diversity of the family situation in different cultures makes it difficult to specify general public policy in this area, but it is possible to spell out some broad principles. The first is that public policy must start from the reality of the family rather than some idealized conception of it. Woman-headed households will not be helped by policies specifying male breadwinners. Subsistence-farming workshops for men will not increase food production if women are the ones growing the crops. Second, parents may need support that does not undermine their self-reliance. Where there is an extended family, this need may be minimal; where wages are low or in the case of lone parents, the need may be substantial. Third, the principle of supporting family carers should include those who look after the elderly or disabled as well as those who care for the young. Fourth, direct support to the elderly or disabled should enable them to maintain their independence and activity in the community for as long as possible.

In countries with a welfare state these principles can be converted into policies: provisions for childcare and parental support; payment of a child benefit or carer's allowance, either universally or according to income; payment of income support to the low paid or those unable to work; and provision for special facilities to those in need, such as special or sheltered housing for the elderly, or training for the disabled and unemployed to increase their chance for self-reliance.

The EC study *Families and Policies* warned: "Continued economic progress must not bring about the gradual disintegration of the family structure." This disintegration is now well underway. Reversing the trend will take not only sensitive public policy but a substitution of the now triumphant individualism with a new sense of familial commitment, rooted in gender equality.

"The issues of single-child families, of dissolving family and neighbourhood networks, and of hostile and dangerous environments for children, make access to children's groups important for all children."
Childcare and Equality of Opportunity

Safe motherhood

Each year 500,000 women die from causes related to pregnancy or in childbirth, leaving behind 1 million motherless children. In the poorest countries the death rate is 150 times that in industrial countries. Of this total number of deaths, 200,000 are from illegal abortions, reflecting the fact that one-third of the more than 150,000 million pregnancies in the South each year are unwanted. UNICEF's "Safe Motherhood" campaign stresses the dangers of four "toos": too many children, too close together, to mothers who are too young or too old. Spacing births by at least two years and not having children below the age of 18 or above 35 would reduce maternal deaths by 25%. The universal availability of family planning aids would produce an even larger fall. Contraception facilities are essential to female, and therefore family, health, and a stable population.

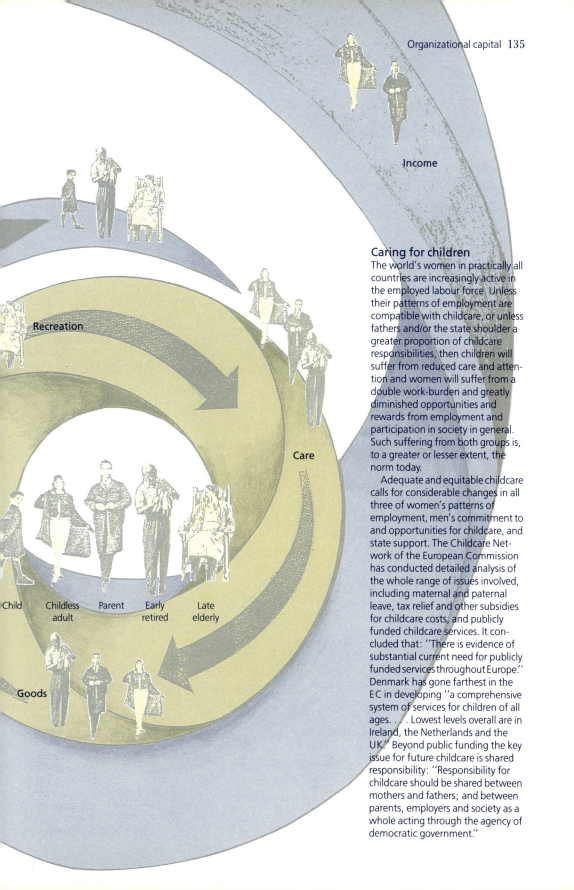

Income

Recreation

Care

Child   Childless   Parent   Early   Late
         adult   retired   elderly

Goods

Caring for children

The world's women in practically all
countries are increasingly active in
the employed labour force. Unless
their patterns of employment are
compatible with childcare, or unless
fathers and/or the state shoulder a
greater proportion of childcare
responsibilities, then children will
suffer from reduced care and attention and women will suffer from a
double work-burden and greatly
diminished opportunities and
rewards from employment and
participation in society in general.
Such suffering from both groups is,
to a greater or lesser extent, the
norm today.

   Adequate and equitable childcare
calls for considerable changes in all
three of women's patterns of
employment, men's commitment to
and opportunities for childcare, and
state support. The Childcare Network of the European Commission
has conducted detailed analysis of
the whole range of issues involved,
including maternal and paternal
leave, tax relief and other subsidies
for childcare costs, and publicly
funded childcare services. It concluded that: "There is evidence of
substantial current need for publicly
funded services throughout Europe."
Denmark has gone farthest in the
EC in developing "a comprehensive
system of services for children of all
ages. . . . Lowest levels overall are in
Ireland, the Netherlands and the
UK." Beyond public funding the key
issue for future childcare is shared
responsibility: "Responsibility for
childcare should be shared between
mothers and fathers; and between
parents, employers and society as a
whole acting through the agency of
democratic government."

Networks and community

All over the world societies are becoming more urban and more mobile. In the US, families move house every three years on average. In most cities private affluence and public squalor coexist. In the industrial world, the growth of suburbia, car ownership, and speed of change in industrial life have all served to undermine the close-knit communities of previous years and engender more loneliness and anonymity in city life. The social consequences of the decline of numerous "19th-century" industries and of the mobility of capital – with transnational companies opening or closing sites solely to maximize economic advantage – often become fully visible only when it is too late. Yet we need to guard against a nostalgic romanticizing of the past. Close-knit communities, for all their human warmth and mutual support, can be parochial, authoritarian, and emotionally suffocating.

It is useful to distinguish between communities of interest (networks) and those based on territory (neighbourhoods). The rise of social networks based on interests has meant that local attachments now constitute a relatively small part of social life for many. In industrial countries most citizens look beyond their local community for many social relationships. Many people choose to have little or nothing to do with those living nearby or with local politics or issues. The general lack of popular involvement in local decision making has tended to induce a type of "learned helplessness" in which local problems are often seen as matters for "the authorities", rather than as issues for community action.

But many local problems in industrial countries are trivial compared with the daily struggle for survival in the Third World, where the major cities are growing too fast for the services and support systems needed for healthy living to develop. There are now more urban dwellers in the Third World than in Japan, Europe, and North America combined. Most live in overcrowded conditions and many in illegal or informal settlements, built at low monetary cost and with scarce resources. The immediate problems for these people are the absence of piped water, health services, paved roads, drains, and sewers. Even where a community organization seeks to provide some of these facilities, their efforts are often undermined by the hostility of public authorities to the settlements' very existence.

The Amish: the other Americans

The US consumer society has triumphed around the world, but not with one group of its own citizens – the Amish. The Amish are a strict Protestant sect, an offshoot of the Mennonites, who came to America from Switzerland in the 18th and 19th centuries. The distinctive ethical feature of the sect is a strict interpretation of St Paul's injunction "be not conformed to this world" (Romans 12:2). Their response is to subject all the innovations of "the world" to rigorous scrutiny and, as a result, they generally make do without tractors, cars, telephones, and electrical appliances. Cultural criteria overrule economic ones. To them, consumption means fulfilment of needs rather than wants.

The Amish clearly express the self-discipline necessary to preserve communities based on contrary values to consumerism. Although their lives may seem laborious and austere, they have a sense of community purpose and meaning and a social stability that are conspicuously absent in mainstream America. They are, in essence, a unique example of successful cultural resistance.

Networks of interest

Networks can be organized inter-nationally, nationally, regionally, or locally – many operate at all four levels. Networks operate within neighbourhoods, but our communi-cation systems also make possible a type of unity over great distances in networks of kinship, friendship, work, leisure, and so on. Public policies in the West have actively encouraged space-extensive activi-ties so that, in general, people travel longer distances to work, shop, or play. Most of the dispersed-interest networks are fairly loose groupings; levels of participation fluctuate and continuing contact is lacking. Professional and kinship networks tend to be more stable and enjoy greater continuity.

World Rainforest Movement (WRM)

WRM was founded in 1986 at a meeting in Penang, Malaysia of groups and individuals from many countries concerned about the destruction of tropical forests. Its activities now include research, documentation, publication, educa-tion, campaigning, lobbying, and networking. It is a prime example of the new type of networks springing up in response to global problems, which also tend to exhibit some of WRM's distinctive characteristics:
○ It is South-led. Its international secretariat is in Malaysia and is run in co-ordination with the Third World Network and the Asia Pacific People's Environment Network.
○ It is concerned to act with and directly support affected peoples in their struggle for survival, rather than speak, plan, and act for them.
○ It is truly global, with groups from Brazil, India, Malaysia, Thailand, Indonesia, and the Philippines, as well as Europe, the US, Canada, Japan, and Australia.
○ It has informal membership and no formal constitution and procedures, thus promoting flexibility, rapid response, and action.
○ It has extensive grassroots linkages. One WRM participant, the Rain-forest Action Network, works through more than 200 local, autonomous Rainforest Action Groups in North America, Europe, Australia, and Japan – thus combining rapid global communication with effective grassroots action.

Action for community

The hundreds of thousands of citizen action groups throughout the world are in the front line of the effort to end material poverty and environmental decline. Falling into two main types, there are the grassroots initiatives often targeted on preserving or enhancing local facilities, and the nationally or internationally organized pressure groups fighting for major causes.

Poverty often creates fatalism with the result that organizing comes more easily to the fortunate than to the dispossessed. Nevertheless, the failure of Third World governments to respond adequately to the needs of their own poor has given rise to self-help groups of many types in every Third World country (see pp. 56-7 and 68-9). India's self-help movement has grown out of Gandhi's advocacy of self-contained villages. The Sarvodaya Shramadana movement in Sri Lanka combines Gandhian teachings with the social-action tenets of Theravada Buddhism. Shramadana means "gift of labour" and Sarvodaya "village awakening". In giving of their labour, people awaken the talents within their village and set it on a course of self-development.

In Latin America, after the 1968 conference of Catholic bishops, the church fundamentally reorientated its social mission toward improving the lot of the poor; in Brazil, for example, the 100,000 Christian Base Communities play an important role in peace and human rights issues. In most African countries tribal loyalties, though still powerful, are weakening as more Africans move into towns and cities. New loyalties to a variety of communities of interest, concerned with religion, education, housing, business, and women's issues, are growing. In its original conception in the 1960s, the main idea behind the Ujamaa village movement in Tanzania was to encourage voluntary collective action, not just in agricultural production, but also in the provision of health, education, and other services.

National governments and international agencies have too often failed to recognize that everybody is potentially an expert on the place where they live. They must learn to work with and defer to citizens' organizations rather than ignore or seek to control them. A sustainable society requires an enabling government that acknowledges the importance of voluntary effort and grassroots' initiative and provides the resources for them to achieve their full wealth-creating potential.

Superbarrio

The masked figure of Superbarrio (Superslum), resplendent in yellow cloak and red tights (see right), has become a heroic symbol of radical community action and political change in the slums of Mexico City. Superbarrio was the product of the Asamblea de Barrios, the mass movement of the slum dwellers that was born after the great earthquake in Mexico City in 1985. The Asamblea achieved its original goal of winning the right of the slum dwellers to be rehoused in their old quarters in the centre of Mexico City rather than on the outskirts, but remained organized to fight for poor people's housing rights. At the Asamblea's behest, Superbarrio appeared on the scene in 1987 to confront evicting bailiffs and police, to publicize their actions and to demand and lead negotiations with public housing authorities. Because of his successes, Superbarrio's popularity is enormous. He and the Asamblea are open political supporters of the main Mexican opposition party, PRD, which took 49% of Mexico City's votes at the last presidential election, as against 38% for the ruling PRI. So worried has the PRI become over the Superbarrio phenomenon that in 1989 it created its own masked figure, Super Pueblo (Super People), who has not however, made much of an impact.

Community action for housing and health

The shanty towns of the Quilmes district of Buenos Aires, Argentina provide a good example of a long history of community action. Local people have worked together both to lobby government and organize for themselves such facilities as nursery and childcare centres and first-aid centres. It was the church-based community organizations in Quilmes that gave people the confidence to invade undeveloped private land and, at great personal risk, create desperately needed new developments there.

Community building in Finland

"We believe that an effective way to attack poverty is through economic and human development programs that are small in scale, locally based and orientated towards empowering the poor to become self-sufficient."
US Bishops' Pastoral Letter on Catholic Social Teaching and the US Economy, 1986

In the 1960s and early 70s Finland experienced a trend common to all industrializing societies – massive rural depopulation. In response, a spontaneous self-mobilization of villages occurred. This was soon picked up by the media and publicized throughout the country, resulting by 1988 in the formation of Village Committees in 2300 villages – 66% of the total. The committees organize projects in such areas as culture, leisure, communications, services, housing, and economic development, and have in many cases reversed the rural decline.

The committees are elected by the whole village and have had a profound impact on the quality of Finnish public life, as reported by researcher Pirjo Siiskonen: "Planning is changing from being dominated by experts, with the emphasis on big units and directed from the top downward, to a new humanism that stresses the value of the individual and small, loosely organized units in which confidence is placed in the competence and resources of local people."

Culture

Culture should be seen broadly as the whole way of life of a society. The human world is rich in diverse cultures, though some remarkable ones, such as those of the American Indians, have been largely or completely extinguished, and many others are under threat from homogenization and the economic drive of the multi-national corporations. Within each culture, counter-cultures and sub-cultures have developed – either in opposition to the dominant one or as the articulation of a particular set of interests.

For many people, singing and dancing are almost second nature, though these basic, human expressive arts are repressed in many cultures and sub-cultures. Dancing was a passion for all the Californian Indians, including the Ohlone people, who spent days or even weeks performing dances suited to all occasions and moods. It is still possible to find beauty and ritual as an integral part of cultures that regard themselves as sophisticated. But two trends have been accelerated by the processes of industrialization. First, artists have had an unceasing struggle not to be pushed to the margins of the materialistic cultures, regarded merely as skilled workers producing some type of marginal commodity. Second, the arts have been locked into a symbiotic relationship with the mass media – particularly television.

This industrialization of culture has had two main consequences. In the Western world images are offered in such profusion, especially through TV, that everything runs the risk of trivialization. In many ways, "more" has proved to be "less". The second consequence has been the use of the mass media as agents of cultural imperialism. It is television imagery originating in the US and, to a lesser extent, Europe, that is increasingly to be found in the developing world, purveying the burger-cola culture identified as "the American way of life".

Cultural imperialism always involves some degree of subjugation. While the Western world has a culture of abundance, but displays only limited ability to distinguish between cultural wheat and chaff, in many developing countries a culture of imposition gathers strength alongside the rich and varied forms of traditional cultures. It is not necessary to romanticize the qualities of traditional cultures to appreciate that a very heavy price is being paid for the technological wizardry emanating from the West.

Turning on is a turn off

"When it comes to it, what does television provide? One of the most debilitating forms of narcotic addiction yet devised. A daily dose of hypnosis . . . a parade of stereotypes . . . An endless course of desensitization to violence and anti-social behaviour of all kinds . . . A substitute for real experience that promises everything and delivers

Canada 634

USA 732

Mexico 157

Jamaica 19

Ecuador 78

Cultural imperialism

This map shows each country where one or more films or programmes made in the US were showing on broadcast television at 2115 hours (local time) on 18 October 1989, as identified by the International Institute of Communications. The figures indicate the numbers of television sets (per thousand population) for each country at that date.

nothing but transitory entertainment that evaporates in the night . . . A mass conditioning machine . . . an artificial substitute for everything real . . . The most pernicious and pervasive of all threats to the environment." Guy Lyon Playfair, *The Evil Eye*

(right) Cultural imperialism via TV

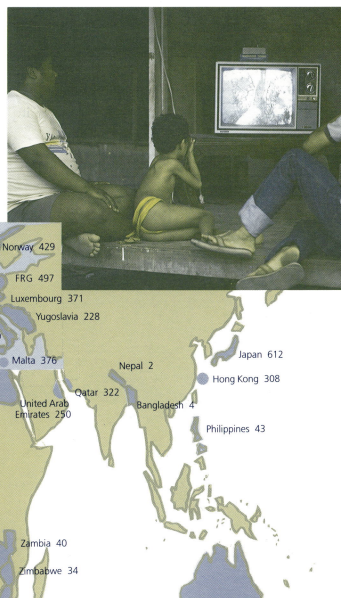

Iceland 323

Norway 429

UK 613

Ireland 282

FRG 497

Luxembourg 371

France 403

Yugoslavia 228

Italy 609

Malta 376

Nepal 2

Japan 612

Bermuda 860

Hong Kong 308

ahamas 347

Qatar 322

Egypt 116

Bangladesh 4

St Kitts and Nevis 729

United Arab Emirates 250

Windward Islands 356

Philippines 43

Grenada n/a

Barbados 70

Trinidad and Tobago 282

Guyana 49

Zambia 40

Zimbabwe 34

Chile 194

South Africa 118

Australia 454

What price "civilization"?

"Why do people think that tribal peoples' cultures are inferior? In the Third World there is a truly startling paradox when these peoples are compared with most others. In Amazonia, for example, traditional Indians live in comfortable dwellings – warm at night and cool in the day. They eat well – a varied and healthy diet. They live in a close community where loneliness is unknown, and they do it all on three or four hours work a day, leaving plenty of time for playing with their children, for contemplating philosophy, cosmology, and religion, and for external-izing whatever answers they find through profound rituals that make many of our own seem shallow and meaningless.

Compare this life with that of the Third World poor who supposedly benefit from 'civilization', and who are, by and large, growing poorer daily in spite of the billions in aid. Their children work 15-16 hours a day; they are badly nourished; serious disease is rife, infant mortality high, life expectancy low, alcohol and drug abuse common. Social breakdown is often the norm in the shanty towns where life comes and goes on the cheap." Stephen Corry, Survival International

The inimitability of the arts

The arts are forms of communication that cannot be expressed in any other way. No matter how they are practised, the arts have been both central and durable aspects of most cultures throughout history.

Art takes place at the intersection of a vertical line, representing eternal human questions, and a horizontal line, representing our lives in particular societies at particular times. The Austrian critic Ernst Fischer has argued that, in its origins, art was a magic aid toward mastering a real but unexplored world: "This magic role of art has progressively given way to the role of illuminating social relationships . . . of helping people to recognize and change social reality . . . Either of the two elements of art may predominate at a particular time, depending on the stage of society reached – sometimes the magically suggestive, at other times the rational and enlightening; sometimes dreamlike intuition, at other times the desire to sharpen perception."

The arts are important as inspiration and celebration; they point to a world of possibility beyond that which we know. They are also important as criticisms, often challenging the assumptions and complacency of the prevailing order.

It was the arts and crafts movement a hundred years ago that stressed that the quality and products of human labour ought to be the central question in any discussion of individual or social wellbeing. W R Lethaby, an influential follower of William Morris, argued that historically "the word Art meant work, production, making, doing . . . Art is the humanity put into workmanship, the rest is slavery."

The arts are skills, but they are also much more; they are disciplined forms of inquiry and expression through which to organize feelings and ideas about experience. As the source of some of our deepest insights, the arts must be protected in consumer societies from being reduced to vehicles for commerce or advertising. The cultural wellbeing of nations faces similar threats of pollution and destruction as the natural environment. Third World cultures are at risk from the combined influences of the international media (see pp. 114-17), tourism, and the misapplication of new technologies. The arts, and the arts in education, need to be nurtured with generous and intelligent political and public support.

The Kecak of Bali

"The Balinese language has no words for 'art' and 'artist'. In former times there had been no need for such definitions. Art was never a conscious production for its own sake. Rather, it was regarded as a collective obligation to make things beautiful: food exquisitely presented as an offering; a cloth wrap of gold brocade; motion in the pattern of a dance; sound in a musical rhythm." Of all the Balinese dances, none is so unnerving as the amazing Kecak (right): "one hundred and fifty men, who by a regimented counter-play of sounds, simulate the orchestration of the gamelan . . . by a choreography ingeniously simple, chorus is transfigured into ecstasy." *Bali*, Insight Guides

Popular arts

"Every real work of art, even the humblest, is inimitable. I am most sure that all the heaped up knowledge of modern science, all the energy of modern commerce, all the depth and spirituality of modern thought cannot reproduce so much as the handicraft of an ignorant superstitious Berkshire peasant of the fourteenth century; nay, of a wandering Kurdish shepherd, or of a skin-and-bone oppressed Indian ryot. This, I say, I am sure of; and to me the certainty is not depressing, but inspiring, for it bids us remember that the world has been noteworthy for more than one century, and one place, a fact which we are pretty much apt to forget . . ." From a lecture delivered in 1881 entitled "Some Hints on Pattern Designing", by William Morris

Carnival time

Artistry of many kinds is evident in the carnivals of the Caribbean and Brazil. Each has its own history and ritual, and immense care and ingenuity are invested in the carnival costumes and music. But carnival is about pleasure and liberation. Emancipated slaves in the West Indies a hundred and fifty years ago literally crashed into carnival entertainment, from which they were formerly excluded. In societies that consistently threaten or diminish black efforts, carnival has become an occasion for self-assertion, as well as for collective celebration. The music, the rhythms, and the costumes, copied from the 18th-century plantation owners, provide colourful and exciting dimensions of theatre and spectacle to the entire entertainment.

The business company

Contrary to the pure theory of Adam Smith's "invisible hand" (see pp. 12-13), pervasive externalities have meant that the self-interest of private companies has never been identical to the social interest. The economic size, power, and influence of such companies in the modern world make it imperative that public policy aligns these interests for the social good.

What is the business company for? The conventional answer is: making money for the shareholders. Therein lies the root cause of many of the company's negative effects on its employees, local community, and the environment, care for and protection of which can be perceived as being at the expense of profit maximization.

Green economics proposes another possible answer to the question of company purpose: it is to generate satisfying livelihoods for those who work in the company and value for society at large. This has two implications. First, the members (or owners) of the company should be those who work in it and not those who have lent it the necessary capital for its operation. Second, the managers of the company should be accountable to all its "stakeholders", which include those who are affected by its social and environmental impacts; to its employees, suppliers, and community, as well as to its conventional shareholders; and more broadly, to society at large and future generations for its treatment of the environment.

This broadening of accountability is by no means a revolutionary suggestion. The stakeholder theory of business has a long history, especially in the US, and many companies have explicit declarations of responsibility other than to their shareholders' wallets. The problem is that fulfilling such responsibility in a profit-maximizing business environment can put companies at a competitive disadvantage. In such an environment, even companies with objectives of wealth creation for society generally will be constrained in pursuing them, and so such companies will only ever be a minority. Industrial co-operatives are one such minority, the principles of which already show a broad social commitment. To enable such companies to compete effectively, and to encourage others to follow their lead, will require far-reaching changes in company law.

Management commitment

A clear example of management commitment that goes well beyond shareholders is that of Japan's NEC Corporation, which explicitly declares itself committed to:

○ Giving top priority to customer satisfaction through relentless efforts to provide better products and better services.

○ Creating value and usefulness for society through the active exploration of new frontiers in the areas of science and technology.

○ Tapping the individual uniqueness of each employee and realizing his or her fullest potential.

○ Fostering the autonomous spirit of each group and affiliate, which adds to the integrated strength of the organization as a whole.

○ Fulfilling its responsibilities as a corporate citizen.

○ Increasing profitability to facilitate dynamic growth internally and to contribute to society at large.

If all businesses lived up to this type of commitment, they would indeed be engines of wealth creation.

"The purpose of a business firm is not simply to make a profit . . . other human and moral factors must be considered which are at least equally important in the life of business." Pope John Paul II

Co-operative Principles

The Principles of Co-operation evolved from co-operative experiments well before Charles Fourier in France and Robert Owen and the Rochdale Pioneers in the UK laid the foundations for what has since become the modern Co-operative Movement (see pp. 80-1). These Principles lead to the Rules and ethics described below that give the Movement its specific character.

○ Association or Unity – membership shall be open, voluntary, and nondiscriminatory. Co-operation must take place between Co-operative organizations as well as between individual members.

○ Economy – the provision of economic benefit to Co-operators is the principal motive for and value of Co-operation.

○ Democracy – societies shall be run on the basis of one member, one vote, and federations of societies shall be administered democratically.

○ Equity – the interest on share capital must be limited and any surplus derived from Co-operation distributed fairly to Co-operators.

○ Liberty – entry to and exit from societies is voluntary and without political or religious conditions. Co-operation requires the right of free association of individuals in society as a whole.

○ Responsibility – a personal commitment to act in the spirit of the Principles and abide by the Rules so that Co-operation may be effectively exercised.

○ Education – Co-operative societies shall educate their members and the wider public in the principles and techniques of Co-operation.

Company accountability

The reforms in company law that are necessary to harmonize company practice unambiguously with the social interest are twofold. First, companies should have a legal obligation to report on the measures they have taken to safeguard and promote the interests of all their stakeholders. Initially, such a requirement need be no more than a mandatory report on measures in the company annual reports. Businesses wishing to establish themselves in the progressive market (see pp. 80-1) would soon evolve procedures of social and environmental audit that enabled them to give detailed accounts of their broad impacts in these fields. Good performances in these audits, as even the limited experience of Green consumerism has shown, could soon become an area of keen intercompany rivalry. As companies gained experience of these types of audit, it would become apparent whether more detailed statutory requirements in social and environmental matters, comparable with the rigours of financial accounts, were both feasible and desirable. At the same time, consumer-information companies, such as CEP or New Consumer (see right), would seek to make widely available information on companies' performance in these areas.

The second requisite reform in company law is the progressive transformation of companies from shareholder- to worker-owned enterprises. Such a reform would have two aspects: incentives to encourage new enterprises to incorporate themselves as industrial co-operatives; and incentives to existing companies to transform themselves in this direction. Legislation covering this second aspect already exists to some extent, especially in the US, where encouragement of ESOPs (see right) has brought about considerable changes. In the UK the success of such partnership companies as the retailing John Lewis Partnership (32,000 employees and 1989 sales of more than £2 billion), the Scott Bader plastics company (a 1989 turnover of £65 million), and Baxi Heating, whose 1000 employees all became partners in 1986, show that large-scale worker ownership can be commercially successful.

Worker-ownership enterprises do not experience the inflammatory division between capital and labour that has historically resulted in so much conflict and loss of production. While this division persists, trade unions will remain essential in order to promote workers' legitimate interests (see pp. 122-3).

US ESOPs

While worker co-operatives are one route to workforce democracy, another is the transfer of the share ownership of a corporation to its employees. In the US this has been widely effected by Employee Stock Ownership Plans (ESOPs), which, though a variety of legislation since 1974, have attracted significant tax concessions. By 1990 it was estimated that some 10,000 companies throughout the US had established ESOPs through which 10 million workers, nearly 10% of the workforce, had become stockholders in their companies.

While ESOPs have succeeded in spreading capital ownership more widely, only a small minority of plans have linked that ownership with giving the workers concerned a voice in running the business. This has made ESOPs controversial as a means of worker empowerment. However, where employee share ownership is allied to employee influence in management, ESOPs have led some companies to outstanding performance. Reviewing the evidence in 1987, consultant Robert Oakeshott concluded that "employee ownership works best and can work really well if it is coupled with effective schemes of nonfinancial participation" to which management is fully committed. One such company is the Weirton Steel Corporation in West Virginia, which was bought out by its 6500 employees in 1984 as an alternative to closure. In 1988 it was employing 8300 people and the year before its accounts had shown a surplus of $80.6 million.

Mondragon Co-operative Group

Mondragon is a town in Spain's Basque country. In 1959 five young entrepreneurs, under the guidance of an idealistic but pragmatic Catholic priest, Don José Arizmendiarreta, converted their cookers and stoves company, ULGOR, to an employee-owned co-operative. Also in 1959, the same group of people set up a co-operative bank, the Caja Laboral, to finance the envisaged expansion of ULGOR and other co-operatives that had sprung up nearby. The Mondragon Group now consists of about 120 co-operatives employing 22,000 people with annual sales of nearly 300 billion pesetas (about £1.7 billion). During the 1980s recession, when local unemployment rose to 30%, the Group managed to maintain employment. A hundred of the Mondragon co-operatives are in manufacturing, the rest are in the agricultural, retailing, and financial services sectors, with associated housing and school co-operatives. The success of the Group can be attributed to five factors: quality of leadership and willingness to organize innovatively; emphasis on technical competence and training; commitment of members deriving from their capital stakes in the business; the mutual support provided by the Group's social security system; and the bank Caja Laboral.

Extending the audit

Any audit can have two distinct purposes: to provide feedback on performance to those in charge of the organization being audited; and to inform outsiders about that performance. Outsiders have a right to this information wherever their lives are affected by the organization.

The main problem posed by large corporations is achieving their accountability to those affected by their activities and providing for redress where necessary. Central to accountability is the provision of precise information. Just as investors have a right to know about the financial performance of a company, so other affected parties are entitled to what Dundee University Professor Rob Gray calls "an ethical audit" addressing where the company stands "with respect to its financial markets, its customers, its suppliers, its employees, its local communities, future generations and . . . all forms of life, human and non-human".

With regard to the environment, increasingly stringent legislation backed up, in the US at least, by heavy fines and even imprisonment, means that environmental "compliance audits" are a necessity for companies working in an environmentally sensitive area. But the best companies are going well beyond this minimum requirement, setting ambitious targets, putting appropriate management and monitoring structures in place, stimulating commitment from all employees, and developing reporting procedures.

The full environmental audit includes analysis not just of product lifecycles but also of the company's own policies and performance with regard to land sites, buildings, vehicles, machinery, recycling, energy, emissions, and the local community. The Californian Elmwood Institute calls this approach "eco-auditing", in which "the company is understood as a living system", and systems theory is used to describe the various flows, causes, and effects.

Shopping for a better world

The New York-based Council on Economic Priorities (CEP), founded in 1969, has pioneered a new mode of consumer information and action. In 1986 its book *Rating America's Corporate Conscience* rated 130 major US corporations across eight social and ethical criteria. In 1988 the supermarket shopping guide to 1300 common brand-names, *Shopping for a Better World*, was published. In three years a million copies were sold and 80% of respondents to a survey claimed it had influenced their shopping behaviour. CEP also bestows annual Corporate Conscience Awards for outstanding performance in environmental responsibility, community action, charitable donations, employer responsiveness, and equal opportunities. The CEP approach is now spreading to Japan and the UK, where New Consumer's 1991 publishing programme included its major reference work, *Changing Corporate Values*, on 128 consumer-goods companies in the UK market, its own *Shopping for a Better World*, and a Third World shopping guide entitled *The Global Consumer*.

Finance

The money systems of the world are in trouble on a number of counts: irresponsible creation of credit; indebtedness in the West and Third World countries; foreign exchange speculation; and mergers and take-overs (see pp. 24-5). Reforming this situation may be beyond the democratic process, for the purveyors of finance have great power, with a grip on government and economic performance that may prevent the necessary radical reforms. In which case, the best hope for change may be the establishment of popular viable alternatives to the present financial system.

In the Third World, the process of "development banking" is already far advanced in remedying the failure of the regular banking system to make available appropriate credit to the poor (see right). There are also "development banks" in the First World. Conventional financial rules and attitudes are also being changed by social concern, as shown by the growth of socially responsible investing (see right), the investment element of the progressive market (see pp. 80-1), whereby investors consider social and environmental factors, as well as prospective financial return.

Too much credit, especially consumer credit, which amounts to spending future income, is bound to cause pressure on prices and the balance of payments, and can play havoc with economic stability. In these times of deregulated financial markets, it is fashionable to say that nothing can be done to curtail credit creation. However, it is surely possible to distinguish between producer and consumer credit; and, where necessary, as Will Hutton of the London *Guardian* newspaper has argued, to maintain high central bank interest rates and a strict system of cash reserve requirements, for the banks, and restrict second mortgages. On consumer credit, Jon Shields in the UK *National Institute Economic Review* proposed controls on the terms of new loans, especially those secured against housing, and a tax on new debt or interest payments. Where consumer credit, especially for poor people, is essential for day-to-day survival, it is best provided by credit unions – essentially savings-and-loans co-operatives run by and for their depositors. Their interest rates can be as little as one-tenth of the 120 per cent annual percentage rate (APR) commonly charged by loan sharks. Credit unions can also offer members social cohesion and financial counselling on how to escape indebtedness.

Development banking

Credit schemes in the Third World are providing a low-cost, highly effective way for the poor to move toward self-reliance. The Grameen Bank (see pp. 36-7) newsletter regularly gives examples, such as Amanah Ikthiar Malaysia, which began in 1986 and by 1990 had 1600 members, 94% of them women, and had lent nearly Mal$700,000. Social rather than profit-led investment also exists in industrial countries. South Shore Bank in Chicago was taken over in 1973 by banker Ronald Grzywinski who wanted to prove that the poor were bankable and that a commercial bank linked to other trading and development companies could be used to regenerate a community. The Bank's success has been striking: by the end of 1989 more than $130 million had been lent to 7000 local businesspeople with a repayment rate of 98%. Other Bank companies had trained 2200 people and found jobs for 2700, built nearly 9000 housing units, and disbursed $1 million in low-interest energy-conservation loans. In Frankfurt, Germany, Okobank specializes in loans to self-managed businesses and energy-conservation projects, the majority of which must be in the local region. It provides normal banking services and 18 months after its launch in 1988 had 22,000 customers and provided loans of DM5 million. Such initiatives provide the practical basis for what should become a key goal of public policy: the creation of a community-based banking system accessible to the poor.

"Money now plays the central role in late industrial society that religion played in the late Middle Ages. . . . The centres of medieval cities were dominated by cathedrals; today's cities are dominated by the tower blocks of international banks."
Future Wealth, James Robertson

Socially responsible investment (SRI)

Peter Webster of the UK Ethical Investment Research Service (EIRIS) identifies three components of SRI: ethical funds, shareholder action, and alternative investments. Ethical funds took off in the US in the 1970s and now the Social Investment Forum has more than 750 members of institutional and individual socially responsible investment professionals. About $625 billion is now subject to ethical screening of some type. One of the Forum's recent projects, CERES, seeks to persuade companies to sign the Valdez Principles of corporate environmental responsibility. In 1991, 54 shareholder resolutions on the Principles appeared on the AGM agendas of large companies. In the UK there are 20 ethical unit trusts, as well as the Ecology Building Society, offering a full range of personal investment services. Their average financial performance has been comparable to the performance of the market as a whole. Examples of alternative investments are share issues with an ethical component. Recent such issues in the UK from Traidcraft, the alternative trade company, and the Centre for Alternative Technology in Wales, have met with good investor response. In all these ways SRI is gaining financial strength.

Currency reform

One of the key functions of money is as a means of exchange. Where this function is either interfered with, as with foreign-exchange speculation, or absent altogether, as in poor communities suffering with a chronic shortage of money, economic activity becomes more difficult.

Currencies are no longer commodities, yet their continued use as such by foreign exchange speculators can be profoundly disruptive of real trade and domestic economic policy. Yale economist James Tobin believes the essential problem to be "the excessive international – or better, intercurrency – mobility of private financial capital". He has explored various measures of international monetary reform (see right). All of them involve a high degree of international agreement, which is bound to make their realization difficult.

To tackle the problem of low local liquidity, the local currency LETSystem (see below) has now been introduced by groups of people in several countries. While experience with LETS is still limited, it does conform to theoretical expectations: such systems do enable people with relatively little money to expand their economic activity. Their principal problems are that the communities that could most benefit from LETS often do not have the skills to set them up; that there is difficulty in winning the confidence of local traders whose validation would greatly increase their usefulness; and that their status vis à vis taxation and benefit systems is far from clear. Local authority involvement in local currency schemes could greatly help to overcome these problems.

International monetary reform

James Tobin sees two possible routes for reform of the international monetary system: making currency transactions more costly to reduce capital mobility and speculative exchange rate pressures; and greater world economic integration, implying eventual monetary union and a World Central Bank. He favours the first route and advocates "an internationally uniform tax on all spot conversions of one currency into another, proportional to the size of the transaction", with a tax rate of perhaps 1%. US policy analysts Makhijani and Browne go the other route, proposing an International Currency Unit, to be administered by a World Central Bank, the value of which would be an equivalent "basket" of goods in each country. The value of these "baskets" in domestic currency would determine relative exchange rates, which would therefore depend on real domestic economic conditions rather than short-term currency movements.

LETS galore

Money is a means of exchange, a unit of value, a store of worth, a form of organization, and a relationship of trust: all these features are exhibited by the LETSystem (Local Employment Trading System). Founded in Canada in 1982, LETS simply involves a register of goods and services and by whom they are offered, and a simple computer system for keeping an account of transactions in a unit of account that may or may not be related to the national monetary unit. The country with the most LETSystems is Australia, where at least 35 were operating by the end of 1990. The first was set up in Queensland in 1987 and now has 350 members, including many local businesses. Their currency is called the "bunya", after a local nut. Members accept that bunya-income is taxable, but insist on paying in bunyas – a form of payment that has yet to be accepted by the authorities.

Taxation reform

The purposes and effects of taxation are: the raising of revenue, and the discouragement (or encouragement) of certain activities. In the majority of countries most taxation is raised from income taxes. This increases the cost of labour and promotes investment in labour-saving technology, a bias that is increased by such investment's tax deductibility. In societies with high unemployment, this discrimination against labour makes no sense.

In the current situation, taxes need to be shifted away from labour and on to the use of resources and the environment. One such tax, first proposed by the American reformer Henry George more than a hundred years ago, is land value taxation. Like other property taxes it has the advantage of being easily levied locally. The other important new tax in a Green economy is a charge on the use of energy. As detailed work at the University of Edinburgh by Malcolm Slesser has shown, the different sources of energy entering an economy are relatively easy to identify, are convertible to a common unit, and can therefore be taxed effectively. Such a tax would provide a powerful incentive for conservation and efficiency throughout the whole economy. An energy tax is just one of the taxes that can be applied to reduce environmental impacts. The book *The Green Budget* explored several such environmental taxes for the UK economy, including a carbon and nitrogen tax, pollution charges, and taxes on minerals and tropical hardwoods, and places them in a coherent fiscal context.

It is important to stress that all these new taxes could be applied in a fiscally neutral way by removing other taxes to compensate for them. If income taxes were to fall, the reduction in wages that could result, while leaving purchasing power unchanged, could promote a significant increase in employment. It would mark a major shift in industrial society toward a resource efficiency that encouraged the work of people rather than machines.

Environmental taxes

German policy analyst Ernst von Weizsäcker has argued convincingly that environmental taxes represent the single best policy response to the environmental crisis. He advocates having a tax on all products that damage the environment, such as energy, chlorine, heavy metals, and so on, at a rate that increases annually over three or four decades by 5-7% of the products' prices, and cutting other taxes to compensate. The gradual increase gives time for conservation and efficiency technologies to be introduced and for substitutes with less environmental impact to be developed. The reduction of other taxes shifts the balance of advantage in the economy to labour- rather than resource-intensive activities but ensures that the reform has no overall effect on international competitiveness.

Land value taxation

Rising land values are a human and an economic curse, pricing low-income families out of housing and farmland and encouraging the speculative, unproductive hoarding of land in inner cities and elsewhere. Land value taxation would tax these values at a rate determined by the economic use to which the planning system permitted the land to be put. Land for industry, offices, houses, farms, or nature reserves, for example, would each pay a different rate, which would also vary depending on location, prime sites paying more in line with their economic rent. In the book *Costing the Earth*, Ronald Banks estimates that this tax in the UK could yield £58 billion a year, about 44% of 1985 government revenue. The tax has been successfully introduced in cities in the US and Australia, and is advocated by Oxford University economist John Muellbauer as a way of tackling the negative effects on the British economy of booming land and house prices.

Government

Government is the organization of a group of people in a given community; it is the institutions, people, and offices by and through which the rule of state is exercised. Though a relatively recent phenomenon, the modern nation-state, of which there are about 170 of differing size and political complexion, has become the most important unit of government in the world.

Systems of government are best understood historically: former colonies tend to echo many of the repressive aspects of their colonial period; the neo-colonialism of the major industrialized nations, through which they have attempted to expand their economic and ideological influence, has contributed to political instability in the developing world. It has also often involved arms transfers to autocratic and totalitarian regimes, which persist in many parts of the world (see map, right).

The road to a democratic form of government can be long and hard. Such government has three key features: first, it must have the legitimacy needed to govern; second, decision making and implementation must be possible; and third, there must be stability and continuity in political life.

Totalitarian tendencies still lurk in so-called advanced countries. In her books, Hannah Arendt pointed to the extent to which Nazism and Stalinism were nightmare extensions of widely prevalent modern tendencies – the devaluing of the political process, leading to the undue influence of the powerful without proper accountability and control; mass-media propaganda to make it impossible for people to think; an instrumental view of human beings, who tend to be seen as replaceable consumers or ciphers, rather than responsible citizens.

The collapse of East European communism has opened up the possibility both of an increased number of democratic governments and of increased international co-operation. In most countries of Eastern Europe a differentiated politics is struggling for expression; new groupings and new parties are forming and re-forming. The history of Eastern Europe in recent years has underlined the power of popular movements, the potentially huge symbolic importance of leaders, such as Lech Walesa and Vaclav Havel, and the significance of political courage, unity, and organization. It is also noticeable that in every Eastern European country, environmental protest has proved to be an important factor in the democratization process.

The challenge in Europe

In 1990 the protest movements Charter 77 and later Civic Forum in Czechoslovakia, and Solidarity in Poland saw two of their leaders, Vaclav Havel (right) and Lech Walesa (far right), elected Presidents of their countries. Their challenge is to escape from economic central planning and establish genuine markets, while avoiding the excesses of Western capitalism. Most critical will

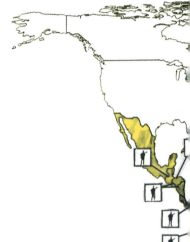

Violent government

For some years Ruth Sivard in *World Military and Social Expenditures* has published data showing the incidence of "Official violence against citizens", defined as torture, brutality, disappearances, and political killings, in Third World countries. The map illustrates her findings, distinguishing between the extent of such violence according to the categories given in the key below. Countries where in 1988 the military had direct power or a controlling influence are also noted.

Official violence against citizens

Frequent

Some

None

  Military-controlled govt

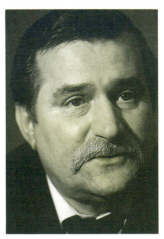

be the way property rights are established and how their economies are "privatized". Will the old ruling class become the new self-serving capitalists? Or will new structures emerge, embodying partnerships between labour and capital; community ownership of land, with secure rights of individual use and tenure; equitable access to finance; and sustainability rights for present and future generations?

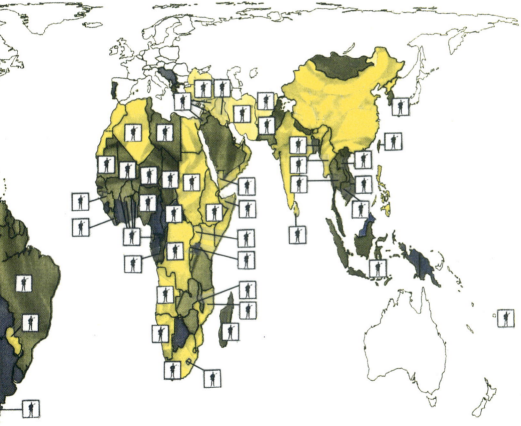

Systems of government

Three broad systems of government can be identified:

○ Totalitarian systems, in which there is an official ideology, a single mass party usually led by one person, a system of terror to enforce obedience, government monopoly of communications, and usually a centrally directed economy.

○ Autocratic systems, with the basis for rule in a traditional political or military elite. There are important limitations on open political competition, very little judicial or media independence, and often state-sponsored violence.

○ Liberal democratic systems, in which competition for power is open and where there are regular elections for more than one party. Civil liberties are recognized within the system and the judiciary and media are independent.

From democracy to sustainability

The role of government is easily stated in theory, but immensely complicated in practice. By establishing property rights, enforcing contracts, and preserving competition where appropriate, government establishes the conditions for markets to operate. But it also has responsibility for redistribution and justice, and for looking after the interests of future generations. Few governments have seriously begun to develop and test policies for long-term environmental sustainability.

Most Western democracies remain unsatisfactory: their political processes are heavily biased toward the affluent; political parties and individuals have a great advantage if they are wealthy enough to buy attention for themselves and their objectives; and the electoral cycle means that short-term considerations weigh heavily in the political scales.

The last decade has seen a surge of environmental awareness, which, through Green parties and otherwise, is having a profound impact on local, national, and international politics. In broad terms the direction in which societies must evolve, reconciling sustainability and equity with economic efficiency, is clear; what is urgently needed is the practical implementation of new policy approaches.

A new model of politics is needed, one that gets away from the present battleground approach. In its place can be put, in the words of David Marquand from his book *The Unprincipled Society*, "a notion of . . . the political domain as a public realm, where the members of the political community listen to, argue with, and persuade each other as equal citizens, so as to find solutions to their common problems." This leads to the idea of government providing a vision and a framework for the long-term sustainable development of a nation.

It must act as a collective brain, developing holistic approaches to politics, economics, and the environment, setting longer-term goals and constantly monitoring and adjusting its plans for reaching those goals. Probably the most impressive current example of such an approach is the National Environmental Policy Plan of the Netherlands (see pp. 84-5).

Science cannot deliver unequivocal answers to environmental problems. The ecological approach to politics necessitates shared approaches between government and society, combining devolution and decentralization with the exercise of power from the bottom up.

The precautionary principle

The 1990 intergovernmental conference on the environment in Bergen, Norway, articulated this political principle in environmental management: "Policies must be based on the precautionary principle. Environmental measures must anticipate, prevent, and attack the causes of environmental degradation. Where there are threats of serious or irreversible damage, lack of full scientific certainty should not be used as a reason for postponing measures to prevent environmental degradation."
Bergen Ministerial Declaration

Local political networks

Independent from, but linked to, the Seikatsu Club Consumers' Co-operative in Japan (see pp. 182-3), are local political networks that have been a significant force in the prefectures in which they are based. In 1987, 33 of their candidates, all of them women, were elected to municipal councils on platforms emphasizing peace, local democracy, ecological conservation, and the advancement of women. In the 1991 local elections, the networks more than doubled their representation to 70. The picture above shows municipal councillors of the Kanagawa Network.

Security

Security means freedom from care – living in peace with others in a healthy environment with varied opportunities to develop personal and interpersonal skills. Security is a state of mind, not an order of battle. The more we pursue security by building arsenals of awesome destructive potential, the less secure we become. National security policies have yielded international insecurity. Each year since 1945, when the first atomic bomb was detonated, the number of nuclear weapons has grown, until now there are about 50,000 warheads with an explosive capacity more than a million times that of the Hiroshima bomb.

These weapons of mass destruction have produced a fundamental security dilemma. In a world governed by a varied mix of systems – from democracies to dictatorships – non-nuclear military force has a part to play in maintaining international order. It is, however, no guarantor of security. The accumulation of military power tends to reduce the security of those perceived as enemies. Their insecurity then reinforces latent hostility, creating further insecurity in its turn and negating the deep-rooted idea that more weapons equate to security. In fact, because of today's global interdependencies nobody is secure unless everybody is. Weapons, in any case, do nothing to generate the security that derives from global wellbeing, social justice, material sufficiency, and ecological stability.

Since the end of World War II, the world has spent about $16 trillion on the military. Industrial countries have doubled their real military expenditure since 1960, while such expenditure in the Third World has increased six-fold. Worldwide, 40 million people are either employed in the arms industries or serve in the armed forces. The US, NATO, the USSR, and Eastern Europe are responsible for three-quarters of all global military expenditure and indirectly for most of the rest of it by promoting the international arms trade.

Global military spending, more than $1 billion a minute, amounts to more than the total incomes of the poorest half of humanity. Industrialized countries spend more on the military than on either health or education. And arms imports in many Third World countries have contributed to and exacerbate their already crippling debt burden.

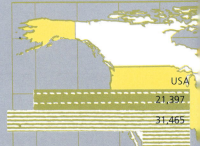

USA
21,397
31,465

The true costs

The Brundtland Report states: "The true cost of the arms race is the loss of what could have been produced instead with scarce capital, labour skills, and raw materials." Half a million scientists are wasting their time and our money on weapons research and military projects. It is no coincidence that two countries with relatively small military budgets, West Germany and Japan, have had the most buoyant economies in recent decades.

Leading exporters of major weapons (1985-89)

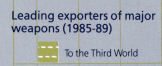

To the Third World

To the industrial world

(figures in millions of constant 1985 US$)

Nuclear weapons people

What are the people like who commission or build nuclear weapons? *The Nuclear Weapons World: Who, How and Where* (Oxford Research Group) provides important insights. "The Strategic Initiative was initiated by President Reagan with the backing of a small group of advisers . . . only one of whom had any real knowledge of defence issues." The others were a brewer, a paper products magnate, an inventor and rancher, and a food magnate. "It was they who con-vinced Reagan to launch the enor-mously expensive and controversial program . . ." The Oxford Research Group highlights how decisions on nuclear weapons are kept secret until work has gone so far that it is virtually impossible to stop it.

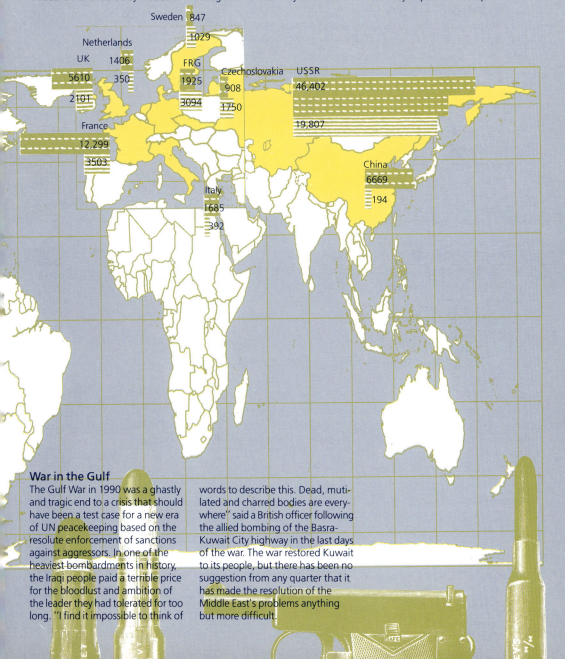

Sweden 847
1029
Netherlands
UK   1406
5610   350   FRG
2101   1925   Czechoslovakia   USSR
              3094   908   46,402
France   1750
12,299   19,807
3503
                    China
Italy   6669
1685   194
392

War in the Gulf

The Gulf War in 1990 was a ghastly and tragic end to a crisis that should have been a test case for a new era of UN peacekeeping based on the resolute enforcement of sanctions against aggressors. In one of the heaviest bombardments in history, the Iraqi people paid a terrible price for the bloodlust and ambition of the leader they had tolerated for too long. "I find it impossible to think of words to describe this. Dead, muti-lated and charred bodies are every-where" said a British officer following the allied bombing of the Basra-Kuwait City highway in the last days of the war. The war restored Kuwait to its people, but there has been no suggestion from any quarter that it has made the resolution of the Middle East's problems anything but more difficult.

The conversion to peace

Peace is indivisible. With nuclear and other weapons of mass destruction spreading around the world, the sombre truth is that a war with these weapons would not just kill millions of the populations of the protagonists; all civilized life on the planet could well be rendered impossible. The need for disarmament is urgent, as emphasized by President Gorbachev in his speech to the UN General Assembly in December 1988. The 1987 INF Treaty, removing some 2000 out of the total 50,000 nuclear warheads, made history as the first agreement to destroy existing weapons. Then November 1990 saw the signing of the Treaty on Conventional Forces in Europe, which made massive reductions in central Europe. The dramatic changes in Eastern Europe and in Soviet foreign policy have brought about a faster, more extensive military relaxation than treaty negotiators ever dreamed possible. To capitalize on this opportunity, future policy must be based on nonprovocative defence involving a fundamental restructuring of a country's armed forces to a defence-only capability.

The prospect of widespread disarmament has rekindled interest in strategies for converting arms industries to socially useful production. This "peace bonus" is evident in countries such as China, where, despite escalating arms exports, the military industry now manufactures nearly 400 different consumer items, from bicycles to television sets. But major obstacles to the implementation of disarmament exist, not least from a powerful coalition of vested interests – those of the industrial workforce, managers, and owners fearing a loss of jobs, incomes, and profits; and of the military fearing an erosion of their *raison d'etre*.

Yet civilian spending generally creates more jobs than does spending on weapons. In India, $13,500 is needed to generate one job in an ordinance factory, while $3800 is needed in industry generally, and only $80-90 in road construction or agriculture.

Finally, peace and security will not prevail without social justice and the universal acceptance of human rights, including those to basic subsistence and environmental health. The resolute pursuit of these objectives by the more democratic countries would indeed constitute a new world order to be prized.

The UN as peacekeeper

The United Nations was founded amid the internationalist enthusiasm following World War II, since when, despite some credits, its effectiveness as a peacekeeping body has been severely hampered by the cold war of mutual suspicion and hostility between the superpowers. With the improved relations between, and the declining influence of the US and USSR, and the emergence of a multipolar world, the UN has a new opportunity to fulfil the peacekeeping role envisaged by its founders. An early imperative is the establishment of an international structure within which UN peacekeeping initiatives and forces can operate, to prevent their domination by any one power, as the US dominated in the Gulf crisis in 1990. And the UN needs the ability to make sanctions more effective, so that they can be relied on to enforce UN resolutions without the need to resort to war.

The need for disarmament

"We have to think ambitiously. If the armament process extends into every corner of society, then disarmament must eventually do the same. Practical aims, such as getting rid of certain weapons or initiating experiments of industrial conversion, need to be located in a wider vision of the future to which we aspire. . . we are going to have to create a society that does not need armaments."
The Baroque Arsenal, Mary Kaldor

Comprehensive international security

"Without disarmament none of the problems of the coming century can be solved . . . We are witnessing the first efforts to build a new model of security through the reduction of armaments, not through their build-up. The use of the threat of force can no longer and must no longer be an instrument of foreign policy. . . One-sided reliance on military power ultimately weakens other components of international security . . . The concept of comprehensive international security is based on the principles of the United Nations Charter and is predicated on the binding nature of international law for all states." From President Gorbachev's speech to the UN, 8 December 1988

Spreading the Helsinki Process

The Conference on Security and Co-operation in Europe (CSCE), also called the "Helsinki Process" after the city where its great Final Act was signed in 1975, was probably the greatest contributor to the end of the cold war. First convened in 1973 and involving all European states except Albania, its Final Act linked military security with human rights, economic and technical co-operation, and cultural and educational exchanges. A defined follow-up process kept the talking and confidence-building going in succeeding years, enabling progress on the various issues to be reviewed, and allowed constructive pressure to be applied to ensure that commitments were met. CSCE clearly has a major role to play in the post-cold-war Europe and could usefully be adapted as a model in other troubled parts of the world, most notably the Middle East.

A new security strategy

In the interdependent, fragile global village of today, national security strategy must be many dimensional, with at least the following components:

o *Disarmament* – the destruction of all offensive weapons and weapons of mass destruction and the reintegration of the companies that make them into the civilian economy.

o *Nonprovocative defence* – the retention only of forces and weapons systems that have an exclusively defensive function.

o *Treaties* – commitment to the Non-Proliferation Treaty and to a Comprehensive Test-Ban Treaty to curb the spread of and ultimately abolish nuclear weapons; and to the curtailment of the international trade in arms.

o *Conflict resolution* – commitment to the Conference on Security and Co-operation in Europe ("Helsinki Process"), and to the UN as the ultimate forum for international conflict resolution.

o *Economic security* – commitment to economic security by enabling *all* the nations' citizens to satisfy their basic human needs through a new international economic order.

o *Environmental security* – commitment to environmental security through strict domestic environmental policies and resolute national support for international environmental treaties.

Global institutions

For many purposes, the world has become a rapidly interacting system. As Barbara Ward put it: "The global society built up by four centuries of colonialism, two centuries of industrialism, and a few decades of advanced communication and space technology is an extraordinary mixture of the traditional and the unprecedented." The traditional aspects of global society derive from trading patterns built up over many hundreds of years. More recent is the legally enshrined sovereignty of the nation-state. But today's global problems – security, human rights, economic development, and environment, plus AIDS and the trade in illegal drugs – are no respecters of political boundaries.

Although a relatively recent historical phenomenon, the nation-state is likely to endure for some time yet. Thus, an international order must be built around the concept of sovereignty, as were the two main 20th-century initiatives to establish an international order that followed the world wars. The League of Nations was created in 1920 to preserve the peace after World War I. But the US never joined, Germany belonged to the League only from 1926 to 1933, and the USSR from 1934 to 1939. Unlike the League, membership of the UN, formed in 1945, is truly universal. But the growth of membership – from its founding 51 nations to about 170 now – has brought new problems.

The UN's performance has been mixed, but it remains true that its reform and development is humanity's best hope of creating a system of global governance that can tackle global problems. However, the vision, idealism, and sense of urgency of its foundation need to be renewed if it is to fulfil the legitimate aspirations of "We the people of the United Nations" who are invoked in its Charter.

Just as the UN endeavours to bring peace and stability to international life, the Bretton Woods institutions – the World Bank (WB) and the International Monetary Fund (IMF) – have provided the international organized basis for the postwar, noncommunist economic system. The WB is responsible for long-term investments, aimed at "development", while the IMF's role is to provide bridging finance to meet short-term balance-of-payments difficulties.

The UN: a problem
There is much evidence that the UN and many of its agencies and officials are failing in their historic mission of promoting international co-operation and security. Most recently, and disastrously, there was the hijacking by the US and its allies of the UN's initially promising approach to Iraq's aggression. Among the agencies, probably the one to have gone farthest astray is the Food and Agriculture Organization (FAO), opulently presided over by its autocratic Director General Edouard Saouma, and described by *The Ecologist* magazine as a "famine machine", which, through its enthusiasm for industrial agriculture (see pp. 100-3), was "promoting world hunger". *The Economist* also recently confirmed the UN's flawed record: "For each success story there are half a dozen of UN waste, incompetence and irresponsibility." Then in 1991 the *Independent on Sunday* newspaper reported that hundreds of staff at the UN's New York headquarters, already among the best-paid bureaucrats in the world, had been involved in tax frauds costing millions of dollars. Unless the UN can be cleared of such incompetence and corruption it is clearly going to be in no position to act as the flagship of a new, humane world order.

Both organizations have been criticized for the way their programmes have adversely affected Third World countries and further enmeshed their economies in a global economy weighted toward Northern interests. Before they can truly become part of the global solution, these institutions need to be thoroughly reformed. The IMF must become more representative of Third World needs; the WB needs to rethink its practice of large-scale, environmentally destructive "development" in the Third World.

There exist many other intergovernmental institutions, including the European Community, the Organization of African Unity, and the Arab League, the Organization of Economic Cooperation and Development, the Group of 77 "nonaligned" Third World countries; the Commonwealth; and the Summit Level Group of 15 countries (G15). There is also the G7 group of countries who have, since 1975, surveyed the global economy and co-ordinated a common response to perceived problems. The failure of G7 effectively to address the problems of the environment and poverty led in 1984 to a parallel process, The Other Economic Summit (TOES), which represents a continuing challenge to the activities of G7.

The UN: a solution

The UN is potentially the lynchpin in the new world order that must evolve. And it already has significant successes to its credit. As *The Economist* also wrote (see left): "Some of the UN agencies do their job reasonably well. One makes sure the Law of the Sea is adhered to. Another sets international post and telecommunications standards. WHO plays a leading part in the global efforts that have eradicated smallpox and in starting to contain malaria. The fund for children (UNICEF) has taken a firm and sometimes effective stand to ensure that it is not the poorest of the poor who pay the bill when governments of Third World countries try to adjust their economies to market realities." The Brundtland Commission Report *Our Common Future* attached particular importance to the work of the UN Environment Programme (UNEP), which, it argued: "should be the principal source of environmental data, assessment, reporting, and related support for environmental management as well as be the principal advocate and agent for change and co-operation on critical environmental and nature resource protection issues." It was UNEP that paved the way for the Montreal Protocol on ozone layer depletion, and set up the Inter-Governmental Panel on Climate Change in 1988 (see pp. 162-3). Just these few examples give a tantalizing taste of what the UN, and only the UN, could achieve with international co-operation.

Toward a global society

While the UN system embodies one key set of global
institutions, and the transnational corporations (see
pp. 72-3) comprise another, these are not the only ones.
Most important in addition are the global nongovernmental organizations (NGOs), about 900 of
which in fact have consultative status with the UN. Over
the last 30 years these organizations have expanded so
that there are global NGOs active on practically every
important world issue. Three examples of NGOs working
in the fields of human rights, consumer affairs, and
international scientific co-operation are described right
and opposite, but there are many others.

 With regard to indigenous peoples, Survival International was founded in 1969 and is now campaigning
in several dozen countries. On the environment, the
World Rainforest Movement has already been looked at
(see pp. 136-7). Important as well is the Environment
Liaison Centre International in Nairobi, a clearing
house for 340 environment NGOs worldwide, two-
thirds of them in the Third World.

 The necessary global institutional framework for the
future is far from complete. Development economist
Paul Streeten has identified ten institutional innovations
that are required in the new context of global
interconnectedness: an international bank to co-ordinate
financial markets and international liquidity; an international debt facility to resolve the Third World debt
crisis; a co-ordinating body for large-scale durable
investments; an international investment trust to
channel the surpluses of rich countries to currency-
needy countries on mutually beneficial terms; an energy
forum involving producers and consumers seeking to
agree a stable pricing structure for, especially, oil; a
global environmental protection agency; a scheme for
commodity price stabilization; a global antimonopoly
and antirestrictive practices body; an international
income or consumption tax for redistribution to poorer
countries; and an independent, international body to
ensure that this aid is spent effectively.

 Several of these proposals would require what is
already desirable: a more developed and binding
system of international law to be administered through
the International Court of Justice in the Hague. At the
national level, the rule of law is a prerequisite of civilized
life. Global interdependence now requires that the same
rule be instituted and enforced internationally.

Global interconnections

Modern communications get people
around the planet in hours and
transmit ideas and information
almost instantaneously. Transnational
corporations are one institutional
result. Institutions of global governance and global NGOs must be,
and increasingly are, another.

The IPCC

In 1988 the international
community established the Inter-
Governmental Panel on Climate
Change, operating under the
auspices of the UNEP and the
World Meteorological Organization.
Its task was to study the science of
climate change, consider its possible
impacts on the world, and suggest
response strategies that could be
used to tackle the problem. The
IPCC is a remarkable exercise in
collaboration between 300 of the
world's leading climate scientists.
No less remarkable is the level of
consensus they managed to achieve
on the notoriously difficult issue of
climate change, declaring themselves
"certain" of global warming unless
significant efforts are made to cut
greenhouse gas emissions (see
p. 15). Stopping global warming will
require another concerted institutional response—a tough, enforceable
Global Climate Convention. This is
one of the main foci of the prepara-
tions of the 1992 UN Conference
on Environment and Development in
Brazil and is sure to remain a central
element of the global environmental
agenda thereafter.

The IOCU

With governments unwilling or unable to enforce accountability for their international activities on transnational corporations, this task has increasingly fallen to consumer advocacy and pressure groups. Most important among these at the global level is the International Organization of Consumer Unions. Founded in 1960 by a number of national consumer associations to carry out product testing and lend cohesion to the fledgling consumer movement, by 1990 IOCU's membership numbered 170 groups in 65 countries. Its role has broadened to turn it into an influential force for change, tackling such problems as ozone layer depletion and toxic waste dumping, the marketing of dangerous drugs and pesticides in the Third World, baby foods, tobacco, food irradiation, and biotechnology. To help address these and other issues, IOCU has been instrumental in setting up about 20 highly effective international networks beyond its formal membership. Its monthly magazine, *Consumer Currents*, carries reliable information of consumer interest on a wide range of subjects, in the context of IOCU's "five consumer responsibilities": critical awareness, action, social concern, environmental awareness, and solidarity. Former IOCU President and Director of IOCU's Asia-Pacific office, Anwar Fazal, explains the shift of IOCU's emphasis as one from "value for money" to "value for people". He goes on: "People are not just concerned about the cost of living. In most places they are concerned with the cost of survival."

Amnesty International (AI)

AI, founded in 1961, is now the world's largest voluntary human rights organization, with a 1989 membership of more than 700,000, and more than 4000 groups in 150 countries. It is a movement that aims to work impartially for the release of all prisoners of conscience provided that they have neither used nor advocated violence. AI opposes torture and the death penalty in all cases without reservation and campaigns for fair and prompt trials for all political prisoners. These are objectives that are clearly in the interests of "We the people" and should be vigorously pursued by the UN's own Commission of Human Rights.

Institutions of development

In his set of essays "On the Archaeology of the
Development Idea", Wolfgang Sachs, of Essen's Institute
of Cultural Studies, has explored the origin and
preconceptions of "development", an impulse that has,
since World War II, ridden on the back of three
ubiquitous and powerful assumptions: that Western
science is the only true way of understanding the world,
which dismisses the accumulated wisdom of most of
humankind; that progress and "development", using
this science, are essentially embodied in the increasing
output of market commodities; and that the relatively
new invention of the nation-state is sovereign within its
often artificial borders, which allows "development" to
be imposed on its subject populations.

The project known as development has essentially
been an alliance between the governments and other
powerful interests in the North and the governing elites
of the South, many of whom were converted to the
Northern worldview during the colonial period. Its
objective was to create a world in the image of the most
"developed" country – the United States. The
mechanisms that were set up between the North and the
South to achieve this end were debt, trade, and aid.

They have been outstandingly successful. In Third
World debt (see pp. 24-5), the North has found an
unlimited means of extracting resources from the South.
Foreign loans have enabled Southern elites to finance a
variety of self-aggrandizing projects. Contrary to banking
and natural justice, repayments are extracted by IMF-
imposed structural adjustment and other means from
the labour and resources of the poorer people, those
who have had no share in the loans themselves.

Much aid and trade has very similar effects; aid being
promoted through bilateral government programmes
and multilateral institutions, such as the World Bank, and
trade being imposed by the ideology of free trade (see
right) through such institutions as GATT (see pp. 100-1)
and the IMF. If development is defined as a means of
further enriching the already relatively rich, irrespective
of the effect on the poor, then aid, trade, and debt have
proved powerful development tools. As Luis Lopezllera,
founder of the Mexican group Promocion del Desarrollo
Popular (Movement for People's Development), has
observed, development for the South has meant
"progress for the few and poverty for the many".

Schatan's MAPRAL

To illustrate the physical reality of
the effect on Southern economies
of rising interest rates and falling
export prices, Chilean economist
Jacobo Schatan invented MAPRAL
(Materias Primas de America Latina),
a weighted composite of the 18
most commonly exported Latin
American primary commodities.
Between 1980 and 1986 the world
price of MAPRAL fell by about
30%. Schatan assumed the
repayment of Latin America's debt
at the 1982 level of $45 billion per
year, and calculated two different
quantities of MAPRAL exports to
repay this debt: a low quantity,
taking 1980 prices and a 6% rate of
interest; or a high quantity taking
1986 prices and a 10% rate of
interest. Schatan shows that the
difference between the two
amounts is a massive 9 billion
tonnes of MAPRAL.

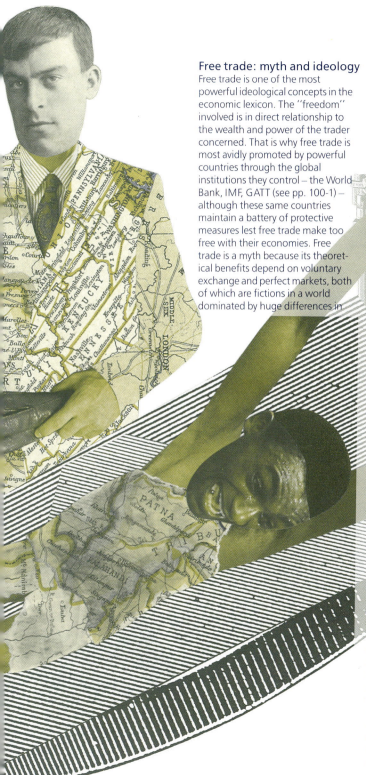

Free trade: myth and ideology

Free trade is one of the most powerful ideological concepts in the economic lexicon. The "freedom" involved is in direct relationship to the wealth and power of the trader concerned. That is why free trade is most avidly promoted by powerful countries through the global institutions they control – the World Bank, IMF, GATT (see pp. 100-1) – although these same countries maintain a battery of protective measures lest free trade make too free with their economies. Free trade is a myth because its theoretical benefits depend on voluntary exchange and perfect markets, both of which are fictions in a world dominated by huge differences in political and economic power, by corporations that dwarf governments, and a high degree of market concentration (see pp. 72-3).

GATT is now seeking to open Third World economies to Northern services, as they are already open to Northern manufactures, in exchange for Third World primary commodities. The North has so far done very well out of this swap, for the primary exports of the South declined in price relative to Northern manufactures by more than 2% per year from 1972 to 1986; for Southern manufactures the relative decline over roughly the same period was about 1%. No wonder the North likes "free trade".

Aid that hurts

Although, in a neo-colonial way, rich countries profit from the poor through debt and trade, they do provide a flow of finance to the Third World, known as "official development aid", which is widely assumed to help the poor. From personal experience and deep study of the aid process Graham Hancock comes to the conclusion that in fact it does not. Rather, the $60 billion a year overwhelmingly benefits three definitely not poor groups: the donor countries themselves, through aid-trade agreements that tie aid to buying often inappropriate goods from donor countries; the relatively rich in the recipient countries, who often manage to turn aid projects to their own advantage; and the well-paid bureaucrats who administer the process, whom Hancock calls the Lords of Poverty. John Madeley's book *When Aid is no Help* also cites many different studies that come to the same conclusion. Hancock's conclusion is that: " . . . aid is a waste of time and money, that its results are fundamentally bad and that far from being increased, it should be stopped forthwith before more damage is done."

Another Development

A different definition of development was proposed by the Dag Hammarskjöld Foundation of Sweden in 1975. Called "Another Development", it has five key characteristics. First, it is oriented toward satisfying people's fundamental human needs. Second, it is a development enacted by the people concerned on the basis of their own knowledge, experience, and culture, rather than being imposed from outside. Third, it is a self-reliant development achieved largely through the mobilization of local resources to meet perceived local needs. Fourth, it is ecologically sound. And, fifth, as is apparent from the discussion of aid, trade, and debt (see pp. 164-5), it cannot be achieved without fundamental reform both of domestic power relations and international development institutions.

The key to achieving these five components is a phenomenon that has already been extensively discussed: the rise of popular movements and people's organizations which increasingly are forming networks across the North–South divide. At their best, such as in the case of the Six S Association and the Working Women's Forum (see right), these organizations exhibit all five of Another Development's aims.

The largest and best organized of these movements operate almost as parallel governments. They are increasingly recognized as the most effective conduits of aid, and even official assistance programmes are now often channelled through such organizations as Six S. Where they produce goods for export, there is an increasing opportunity for them to find sympathetic new markets in the North through Alternative Trading Organizations (see right), another expression of the progressive market at work (see pp. 80-1).

Side by side with these popular movements, an increasingly coherent body of theory and practice is growing to address the inequities of the trading system and Third World indebtedness. Through such concepts as "trade for mutual self-reliance" and the studies of Third World debt by Susan George in the North and Jacobo Schatan in the South, a distinctive Green alternative to the current world economic disorder is being defined.

It is up to the South to decide how it should "develop", but it is not possible both to play the aid-trade-debt game in order to maintain Western lifestyles for an elite few, and to promote Another Development. The two

Alternative trade

Alternative trading organizations (ATOs) have been steadily gaining strength since their beginnings in the 1960s. As a reaction against the exploitative nature of much North–South trade, they seek to give Southern producers and Northern consumers a fair price on goods traded; and, in addition, to give Southern producers insights into Northern markets, and Northern consumers some idea of the realities of Southern production. More than 300 ATOs from more than 40 countries, with a combined turnover of some $200 million, are now associated through the International Federation of Alternative Trade, based in Amsterdam.

Aid that helps

Some Northern countries will continue to give aid on humanitarian grounds to a substantially delinked South, albeit in smaller amounts. To promote Another Development for the poorest, this aid should be directed toward the following:
o Sustainable livelihood security (see pp. 126-7), especially through the regeneration, under the control of poor people, of environmental resources.
o Increasing community capability through programmes of education, primary health care, and appropriate technological development.
o Establishment of revolving loan funds and small-grant programmes, to enable people to acquire productive assets.
Bodies such as the World Bank could not implement such a development strategy. New institutions would be needed.

strategies are exclusive and contradictory. This point does not seem to have been grasped by *The Challenge to the South*, the Report of the South Commission, a group of eminent Southerners under the chairmanship of Julius Nyerere, which was set up in 1987 following a Summit of the Non-Aligned Movement. The Report frequently calls for greater integration of the South into the global economy, albeit on more favourable terms, *and* more equitable, people-centred, culturally appropriate Southern development. All the experience of the development decades suggests that the "more favourable terms" of the integration will not materialize; and that whether or not they did, this integration would lead at best to inequitable, people-marginalized, Western-style development. It is difficult to see how Another Development can be achieved without significant "delinking" of the South from the aid-trade-debt institutions controlled by the North, entailing the severing of many of the ties involved and a determined expansion of South–South solidarity and co-operation.

Working Women's Forum (WWF)

WWF is based in Madras, south India, and is a grassroots union for poor women workers in the informal sector. Founded in 1978, it had more than 150,000 members by 1990. It operates a successful loan scheme for its members, which by 1990 had lent $16 million, and runs a large health and family care scheme. These activities and the collective power and solidarity generated by WWF have trans-formed the lives of thousands of India's most disadvantaged women.

Six S Association

Six S was founded and led in 1976 by Bernard Ouedraogo of Burkina Faso. The purpose of the Association was to spread, strengthen, and link popular mobilizations throughout West Africa. By 1989 it supported 4000 village groups in six countries, all dedicated to self-reliant and eco-logically harmonious development.

Mutual self-reliance

Trade based on comparative advantage has locked most Third World countries into the export of primary commodities, distorting their economic development and inducing profound technological dependency. Such trade in future should be part of a strategy of overall increased self-reliance. Its objective would be increasing both parties' domestic productive capabilities, through the import of appropriate technologies to update indigenous production, and the construction of the infrastructure and acquisition of the skills needed to make them operational.

Resolving the debt crisis

Susan George and Jacobo Schatan have several suggestions for a fair resolution of the debt crisis, which, with debtor solidarity, are realistic. These include writing down the debt, probably by about two-thirds, by subtracting the amount lost to the South due to falls in commodity prices, increases in interest rates and illegal capital flight; formulation of a fixed repayment schedule for the balance based on 1980 commodity prices and a 6% interest rate; or, instead of repayments, either investing the balance in local currency in democratically controlled environment and development projects in the debtor countries, or using it to buy essential imports from creditors. Such a programme would revolutionize debtor country economic prospects and could even generate widespread popular political support in the North.

Introduction: manufactured capital

Manufactured capital comprises *buildings*, and their agglomeration into the villages, towns, and cities that comprise the built environment; *infrastructure*, the physical fabric supporting social and economic life, such as transport networks, schools, hospitals, and media, communications, energy, water and sewerage systems; and *technologies*, the means by which goods and services are produced, from simple tools to the "high" technologies of information and biotechnology.

More than at any other time in human history, the world of the late 20th century is the product of the technologies that have been developed over the past two centuries. With the pace of technological change still quickening, and with the changes becoming more profound and far reaching, it is worth asking what are the forces propelling this technological development.

The answers are not reassuring. Most obviously technology is driven by the quest for profit, through innovation, the development of new products, or through the cost-saving substitution of capital for labour. A second force is the quest for power and control, most clearly expressed in the massive investment in military technology. And a third force is that of basic scientific inquiry, the belief that whatever can be known must be known and, thence, whatever can be done must be done. This last force is closely related to the belief that technology has answers to any and all problems that may arise, a view commonly expressed, for example, with regard to the environment.

The creation of a new driving force for developing technologies and its establishment in industrial form is probably the single largest and most pressing task today. This force will need to spring from an ethical consensus about what is good and right, and will need to place certain technological development off limits. More positively, it will need to give prominence to environmental conservation and efficiency, and be more concerned with the quality of working life than increasing labour productivity. Embodying these complex values in institutional form so that democratic decisions can be made is an immense challenge. But the alternative is the continuing domination of technological development by market forces and powerful interest groups, bringing technology increasingly into conflict with the most basic human and democratic values.

Healthy cities

By the year 2000 it is envisaged that 75% of Europeans, and more than half the world population, will live in cities. The nature of these cities will therefore dominate two of the three aspects of manufactured capital: buildings and infrastructure. At present, as John Ashton, a key figure in the World Health Organization's (WHO) Healthy Cities project, has written: "The divorce of city dwellers from the wider environment and from an ecological understanding has led to a rapacious attitude to the world's natural resources which threatens the sustainability of the planet itself." As a response to this, a new movement for public health, closely linked to the WHO project, is mobilizing around the idea of an ecological city, based on four principles: human interventions should work with natural topography and biological systems; diversity and variety should be objectives in the physical, social, and economic structuring of communities; artificially created systems should be as closed as possible, through recycling and the use of renewable resources; and there should be a balance between population and resources. Twenty-five European cities are formal participants in the Healthy Cities project, but through networking as many as 200 are involved in what has become a movement "based on recognition of the ecological context of health and the need to reconcile human lifestyles with their environmental and planetary impact".

Technological impact

No modern economist has better understood the key importance of technology to the quality of life, as well as to the material standard of living, than Fritz Schumacher. He wrote in *Good Work* that technologies have a profound impact on every aspect of people's lives: "... how they produce; what they produce, where they work; where they live; whom they meet; how they relax; what they eat, breathe and see; and therefore what they think, their freedom or their dependence." Because technology has such an effect on who we *are* it must be appropriate – socially, environmentally, and economically.

Biotechnology

"If ever you needed to understand at least the rudiments of a new technology, that time has come." Thus the authors of *The Laws of Life* begin their explanation of biotechnology, which has been said to promise the end of illness, hunger, pollution, resource shortages, and even of death itself. Biotechnology manipulates existing, and creates new, life forms, and is the most powerful technology the world has ever seen. It has already created a "geep" (a sheep–goat cross) and a human–chimpanzee embryo, a humanoid. As it develops it will affect all aspects of human life through applications in agriculture, medicine, food processing, pharma- ceuticals, energy, mining, resource recovery, and warfare. The develop- ment of biotechnology is being driven by the age-old human lusts for money and power, economic and military. The estimated genetic engineering market is $50 billion a year by the year 2000. Most research is in the private sector, and the technology seems likely to be largely controlled by transnational corpora- tions with extensive patent rights. Never was there a better case for public evaluation and rigorous social control of a new technology. Neither are yet in prospect.

The built environment

Since earliest times, people have chosen habitats to serve their basic needs for shelter and protection from the elements or as places of privacy or security. As civilization evolved, communities of self-interest were formed and buildings constructed ranging from places of mystical significance to ones with agricultural, industrial, or leisure functions.

Communities have increased in size, thus deriving the benefits of special facilities that can be supported by large populations. Improvements in comfort have come with the advent of cheap fuels – coal and then oil, gas, and electricity – and the infrastructure on which communities are based has become more complex. Once relatively self-sufficient communities have out-grown the capacity of food supplies from their hinterlands and of local sites for their waste products. They have expanded to the point at which they have coalesced to form conurbations.

Wealth creation in this area has been seen to lie largely in keeping pace with the demand for this type of settlement pattern. With motorized transport replacing feet or animal-drawn vehicles, there now appears to be no limit to settlement size. Cities of up to 25 million are envisaged, especially in the Third World where migration from the countryside continues. In the West, with its extensive road and rail systems, it is the urban regions rather than the cities that have grown as the pressure to provide for the urban population has spilled over into adjacent rural areas.

Both forms of development – the high-density, relatively compact cities with ever-increasing populations, and the dispersed, low-density urban regions with historic high-density cores – are unsustainable in the longer term. They consume more wealth than they produce. In the absence of proper planning and regulations to reduce externalities, market forces have resulted in unacceptable levels of pollution, noise, wasteful practices, danger, and urban decay, which together combine to lower the quality of life of all those living and working there. At the same time, inflexible or corrupt government agencies have too often failed to provide an enabling context in which the urban poor can themselves improve their living conditions.

The growth of cities
The UN predicts an urban population of about 3 billion by the year 2000, about half the world's population. There will be 60 cities with more than 5 million people, three-quarters of them in the developing world. Both migration and natural increases are important sources of urban population growth, linked by the fact that migrants tend to be young. The urban explosion has put enormous strain on public services. By 1990, the end of the UN Decade on Water and Sanitation, still only 66% of Third World urban residents had access to a satisfactory water source, and satisfactory sanitation services were limited to 35%.

Dehumanizing the city

Because of the increasing value of land close to city centres, inner urban housing in relatively easy reach of jobs is lost to commercial development – the profit from office blocks is greater than that from housing. The comprehensive redevelopment of slum areas is often associated with the destruction of the historical urban fabric. This process leads to a loss of community, of buildings that are worth preserving, and the unique sense of place that gives towns and cities their distinctive character. As the process of modernization continues, site values rise, and it then becomes economical for owners to demolish sound buildings and construct ever higher ones in their place. The open-plan, artificially lit, and mechanically ventilated offices that often result bear little relation to the preferences of users and can cause sick building syndrome. The car-choked, fume-laden streets outside are no more agreeable.

Urban sprawl

Extensive developments on inexpensive land on the edges of cities produce the phenomenon known as urban sprawl, the chief characteristic of which is an orientation toward the use of the car, with all the attendant ''external'' social and environmental costs. Low-density suburban housing and dormitory satellites usually entail longer commuter journeys to work. They cannot be warmed by district heating schemes, nor can they be served by viable public transport services, which encourages multicar ownership and lifestyles dependent on car use. Out-of-town shopping malls requiring cars for access reduce the viability of small, local shops accessible on foot. All these developments increase the distance that needs to be covered, and place anybody without a car at a disadvantage. More people then ''have'' to have a car, further intensifying the spiral of automobile inefficiencies.

Communities for people

Wealth creation in the built environment is not just concerned with the buildings and infrastructure for the wide range of urban functions it contains. It has to do with improving the quality of urban life, producing decent housing with basic amenities, easy and safe access to the facilities of daily life and to open public space, adequate opportunities for social contact and cultural needs, and a sense of community and identity; this in a context of economic lifestyles that minimize adverse environmental impacts.

Sustainable "cities for people" would have certain characteristics: a diversity of land uses and compactness of urban form; streets that are the focus for social life and activity; buildings that use solar energy or otherwise allow for reductions in the use of fossil fuels for heating and lighting; conservation and refurbishment for flexible use of older buildings rather than demolition and redevelopment; high residential densities to allow for economy of construction and in the provision of heating and waste-disposal services; accessible open public spaces; and sufficient private open space for families with children.

In such cities, walking and cycling would be the primary means of travelling to locally based facilities, and amenities would also be located at the nodes of public transport networks so that longer journeys could be conveniently made by bus, tram, or rail. Teleworking, teleshopping, and home-delivery services would further reduce the need for personal transport. To minimize the waste from product packaging, and elsewhere, discounts on waste-disposal service would be given to households and businesses that separated refuse for recycling. The planning process would discourage the development of greenfield sites in favour of the regeneration of derelict urban land. Audits of energy use, traffic generation, and environmental impact would be mandatory for new developments, and the energy efficiency of buildings calculated on change of ownership with the results made available to the public.

The success of this type of development requires great public awareness of the environmental and economic issues involved. It also requires public participation in policy formulation and decision making if the people that live in it are to respect and care for the urban environment that is produced.

A working utopia

In a recent study of pioneering approaches to environmental action, Joan Davidson, in *How Green is Your City*, wrote: "The new vision is that citizens themselves have the skills and imagination to green the city. But they need practical help, not just goodwill." The 60,000 people of Davis, California (above) helped themselves to greening when in the early 1970s they elected three students as local Green councillors. One is now the mayor and Davis has become a "city for people": tens of thousands of trees planted, energy use cut by more than half, bicycles outnumbering cars by 4 to 1, 42km of city cycle lanes constructed, local markets for fresh organic food, $12-a-year allotments, and 70% public participation in recycling schemes. The citizens put these achievements down to their participatory and democratic local politics.

Housing as a verb

At least two-thirds of the world's houses have been built entirely or in major part by those occupying them. The activity of building and maintaining them is important not only to cost-effective shelter but also to community cohesion. As John F C Turner noted in a passage from his book *Freedom to Build*: "Where dwellers control the major decisions and are free to make their own contributions in the design, construction or management of their housing, both this process and the environment produced stimulate individual and social well-being. When people have no control over nor responsibility for key decisions in the housing process . . . dwelling environments may become instead a barrier to personal fulfilment and a burden on the economy." In his later work, Turner stresses that the process of community building needs to be served and supported by technical expertise and by the mechanisms of both the market and the state.

Rural regeneration

The key to halting the headlong growth of cities is to make the countryside, where more than 50% of the world's population still lives, a more viable place to both live and work. This will reverse the rural depopulation that has thus far marked all industrializing societies. This policy, in turn, requires not only an equitable distribution of land based on secure titles, and a cessation of the public policies of the developing world that subsidize the urban consumer at the expense of the rural producer, but also the mobilization of rural communities, as in Finland's Village Action Movement (see pp. 138-9) or West Africa's Six S Association (see pp. 164-7), to revive the local economy, culture, and environment.

Urban regeneration

In Hyderabad, India, the Urban Community Development Department has worked with the community to transform over ten years the neighbourhoods housing the poorest 25% into new settlements of clean, well-lit, modest brick houses with piped water and an efficient sewage system. "Families were given the deeds to their own plot of land, plus a 1000 rupees ($78) subsidy and a 7000-rupee ($546) low-interest loan. With a further 2000 rupees ($156) of their own capital, families could then construct their own home, normally consisting of two rooms and a separate toilet." UNICEF, 1989

The nature of technology

There is a popular misconception that technology is embodied in a tool or machine. While this is a reasonable approximation when a technology is simple, when it is complex, as with modern technology, it is best envisaged as a web of physical and social relationships (see right), stretching into the deepest recesses of the planet and society. Such webs could similarly be constructed for all the new technologies – information technology and artificial intelligence, biotechnology, military and space technology, environmental technologies of conservation, efficiency and waste reduction, solar technologies, and so on. The choice between technologies with greatly different webs is never merely one of cost-benefit analysis; the interest groups concerned inevitably seek to use their power to influence the social choice toward their desired outcome.

Since the Industrial Revolution new technologies seem to have been developed in waves, with the simultaneous mass dissemination of several key inventions. This has led to "long-wave" theories of economic development (see right), in which each new group of innovations provides the impetus for intensive growth, generated by great increases in labour productivity.

Technical change itself is generally one of the least understood social and economic processes. It begins with invention, which is inherently unpredictable. The invention must then be developed commercially into new products and processes. If it is to become a core technology contributing to a new long wave, then it needs to be incorporated throughout the economy and interact synergistically with other technologies. At both the invention and commercialization stages, social values influence the technological choices that emerge and are made. What is invented depends very much on the orientation of basic scientific research, the sort of problems that are both interesting and prestigious to tackle, and the nature of the solutions that are sought. Which inventions are then exploited, and how, is determined by the relative power of the social interests that hope to benefit from them. At present, the most powerful interests emphasize labour productivity, profitability, and military potential. Very different objectives are needed for a technological development appropriate for solving problems of unemployment, Third World poverty, and environmental destruction.

The nuclear technology web

Nuclear power's priorities come from the military, anxious to maintain their weapons capabilities; the nuclear industry, who like the power and profit it entails; and from the nuclear research establishment. The way these interests subvert the social good has been documented in the UK. The public has been misled by claims that nuclear electricity is cheaper than other sources (see pp. 88-91); and that it can make a significant contribution to reducing the greenhouse effect, when in fact its colossal cost crowds out the investment in energy conservation and renewables that could do so. Projected costs of other energy options have also been falsified. A 1982 report on wave power by the Energy Technology Support Unit, based at the heart of nuclear research at Harwell, England estimated wave power costs at 9.8p (pence) per kWh, compared with nuclear's 6.25p, causing wave research to be axed. Eight years later, the true wave figure of 5.2p was conceded. But in 1988-89 nuclear research still received £247 million from public funds, compared with £37 million and £19 million, respectively, for non-nuclear and energy-efficiency research.

Long cycles of technology

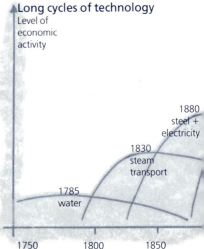

Level of economic activity

1880 steel + electricity

1830 steam transport

1785 water

1750   1800   1850

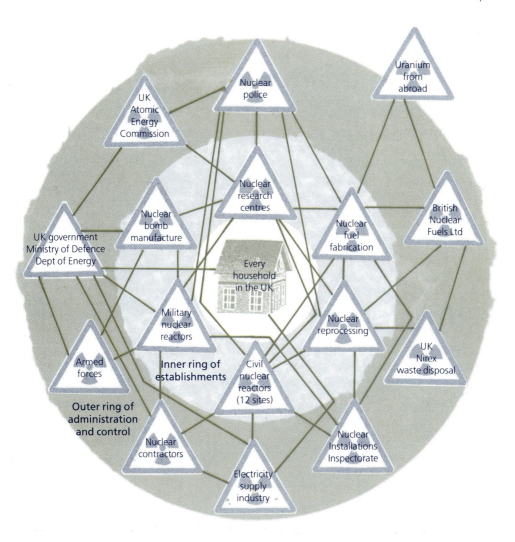

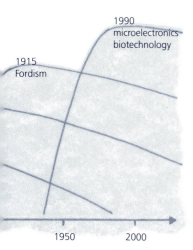

1990
microelectronics
biotechnology

1915
Fordism

1950   2000

Long waves of technology

It is Russian economist Nicolai Kondratiev who is generally credited with the notion that economic growth proceeds in long waves of approximately 50 years. It is now more generally perceived that it is the development of new technologies, or the diffusion of clusters of interrelated innovations, that proceeds in waves, while the translation of this process into economic activity is dependent on the receptivity of the socio-institutional framework and external events such as wars. The economist Carlota Perez called these clusters "technological styles", of which Andrew Tylecote of Sheffield University has identified five since the 18th century: *water* – water power, water transport, and fixed steam engines burning coal in factories; *steam transport* – most importantly the railways, with communications also improved by the electric telegraph; *steel and electricity* – other innovations being textile-related chemicals and the telephone; *Fordism* – mass production, fuelled by oil, and epitomized by the car, plus petrochemicals; and *microelectronics* (computers) *and biotechnology*. For a new style to emerge requires the drastic cheapening of a factor of production.

Appropriate technology

The concept of appropriate technology (AT) begs two questions: appropriate for what and for whom? All functioning technologies must be appropriate for somebody or something, or they would be discontinued. Fritz Schumacher, writing in *Small is Beautiful,* saw large-scale technologies as: ". . . a denial of wisdom. Wisdom demands a new orientation of science and technology toward the organic, the gentle, the non-violent, the elegant and beautiful . . ." For Raphael Kaplinsky in *The Economies of Small,* ATs are those "which operate on a small scale, have a benign effect on the environment and which improve conditions of work". In Third World countries ATs will, in addition, relate to the needs of the poor, be relatively labour intensive, use local resources, enrich work, and improve the quality of social life.

Thus considered, technological appropriateness has three dimensions: social, environmental, and economic. The practical implications of each of these dimensions are likely to be both complex and specific to particular situations. However, conducting technological assessment along narrowly economistic lines is almost certain to lead to inappropriate outcomes in situations, often found in the Third World, of pervasive externalities and highly imperfect markets.

In his analysis of bakeries, brick-making, and sugar-processing in several Third World countries, Kaplinsky shows how ATs have failed to be introduced, despite profitable market opportunities and even economic advantages over prevailing inappropriate techniques, because of market failure, government failure, ignorance, and prejudice in favour of large-scale "modern" technologies. He draws attention to a new trend of "flexible specialization" (see right), which in some areas is undermining economies of scale and gives new opportunities for ATs. In the mix of state and market that is required to take advantage of these, "the AT-enabling state" will have a social base in the small-scale entrepreneurs who tend to benefit from ATs and a capacity for appropriate policy administration both to frame the market and intervene directly in it as necessary. In the absence of such states, much of the initiative for spreading ATs in the Third World has come from NGOs such as Appropriate Technology International in the US and Intermediate Technology Development Group in the UK.

Flexible specialization
Since Henry Ford built his Model T, the dominant technological style has been mass production, defined by US analysts Michael Piore and Charles Sabel as "the use of special-purpose (product-specific) machines and of semiskilled workers to produce standardized goods", in large numbers and at low cost. Piore and Sabel have marshalled an impressive body of evidence that this style is coming under increasing pressure from what they call flexible specialization; ". . . a strategy of permanent innovation . . . based on flexible – multi-use – equipment; skilled workers; and the creation, through politics, of an industrial community that restricts the forms of competition to those favouring innovation." The strategy is a response to the increasing market uncertainty and fragmentation of the 1970s and 80s. Piore and Sabel show that the strategy has been an important part of restructuring in industries as diverse as steel making, chemicals, textiles, and machine tools. Flexible specialization is preferable to mass production in several important respects. First, workers are no longer seen as a cost to be minimized, they are a key resource. Second, as Piore and Sabel say, flexible specialization entails "the fusion of productive activity, in the narrow sense, with the larger life of the community. It is hard to tell where society ends and economic organization begins." It remains to be seen whether this approach will come to replace mass production or whether it will remain subordinate to it.

Beyond labour productivity (LP)

Increasing LP (output per person) is a principal goal of modern techno-logical development. Success – LP in OECD countries up 2.7% per annum on average since the 1960s – has been achieved largely at the expense of the productivity of capital – down nearly 1% per annum over the same period. Capital-intensive techno-logies are badly suited to the surplus-labour/scarce-capital conditions of the Third World, and yet they are often those installed by business, government, and aid agencies. Thus in Kenya, small bakeries are three times as profitable as large-scale baking technology, but they produce only 2.2% of national bread output, as against 70% for the large plants. In sugar-processing, large plants cost more per unit of output, and 22 times more per workplace, than small ones.

Infrastructure

Infrastructure is the name given to the fundamental technological constructs that underpin the productive capacity of, or basic services to, society as a whole. It includes airports, road, rail, telephone, and media networks, water and sewage systems, energy utilities, schools, hospitals, libraries, health services, and so on. Their technology webs determine many of the characteristics of society.

Post 1945, the dominant view was that infrastructure was best organized by the state, and much is still so provided. However, the gale of privatization that has blown through the UK and other countries in the 1980s and 90s, has meant that an increasing amount of infrastructure is now in private hands.

Because of the enormous public investment that infrastructure represents, its greening could proceed only slowly. To be effective, therefore, it would have to be in the context of firm political commitment to a clear strategy commanding a high level of public agreement. Perhaps the leading indicator of this commitment is the extent to which infrastructural provision seeks to foster alternatives to the private use of the car (see pp. 96-9), the archetypal symbol of consumer status and convenience, and of external social and environmental costs. The comparable symbol of the Green economy is the bicycle.

What is entailed in greening the infrastructure relating to energy, transport, health, and education has already been discussed. With regard to the mass media, greening will require their progressive decentralization and democratization, so that they become more directly accessible to the community at a local level, and more representative of social diversity nationally.

A final element of infrastructure, the absence or inappropriateness of which is currently responsible for widespread disease and pollution, is the treatment and disposal of sewage. Even in water-rich temperate climates, flush-toilet sewage systems are proving increasingly wasteful and costly. Their extension to arid zones could only spell disaster for the availability of water there. Chinese experience clearly shows the agricultural value of human wastes (see right). Yet in Western society, this potential resource has become a major pollutant. Remedying this situation is a priority for infrastructural reform.

"The bicycle is the vehicle of a new mentality. It quietly challenges a system of values which condones dependency, wastage, inequality of mobility and daily carnage." James McGurn, quoted in *The State of the World 1990*

Private or public infrastructure?

Political acceptance of privatization in the UK probably derived from the 1970s when, according to Gillian Morris's study *Strikes in Essential Services*: "British industrial relations were transformed by a growth in militancy in the public sector." Disputes affected electricity, local authorities, and health and other essential services for which there was no alternative source of supply. Mrs Thatcher's 1979 government at first had no privatization programme, but soon realized its ideological, political, and financial attractions. By 1991, privatization of all or part of 16 industries had brought in more than £44 billion. One suspects that it is as much this revenue that has made privatization attractive worldwide as the supposed improvements in economic performance.

Night soil

Throughout their history, frugality has been second nature to the Chinese, so that human excrement, or night soil, has traditionally been put to good use as a valuable source of nutrients for soil and plants. Simple methods of treating shistasome and hookworm ova have been employed to prevent the transmission of diseases. The fertilizer is stored in closed containers over a four-week period prior to applying it to the soil.

People's infrastructure

Infrastructure does not have to be provided by the state. Communities are often better placed to provide it, as shown by experience with sanitation facilities in Orangi. This is one of the largest and still-growing squatter settlements in Asia, with a million residents, on the outskirts of Karachi, Pakistan. The Orangi Pilot Project (OPP) began in 1981 involving 20-40 households. By 1990 67,700 households had laid self-managed, self-financed underground sewage lines, involving an investment of $2.3 million. In contrast, a UN project in Orangi spent $650,000 of external aid on developing sewage facilities for just 552 households. Moreover, as OPP mobilizing architect Arif Hasan says: "In the process of acquiring these services, (people) can bring about a change in the unequal political relations that they have with those who rule them."

Control of the media

In the so-called information age, dominated by mass media, who has access to those media and on what terms is a vitally important issue of infrastructure. First, media ownership is highly concentrated. The chart, left, shows the percentage of the market owned by the top five UK companies in each media sector. For UK national newspapers, the market share of the three leading corporations increased from 62 to 75% for dailies, and 60 to 83% for Sundays, between 1947 and 1985. Second, the interests of the corporations are now global and diversified. Rupert Murdoch's News Corporation, for example, with the UK's largest-selling daily and Sunday papers, has 100 other papers stretching from Hong Kong to New York, and worldwide television, satellite, book publishing, and film interests, that give him more potential influence over global information flows than anybody else in history.

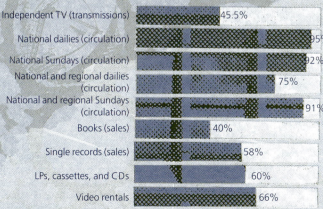

Independent TV (transmissions)	45.5%
National dailies (circulation)	95%
National Sundays (circulation)	92%
National and regional dailies (circulation)	75%
National and regional Sundays (circulation)	91%
Books (sales)	40%
Single records (sales)	58%
LPs, cassettes, and CDs	60%
Video rentals	66%

Redefining industrialism

The foregoing policies amount to taking the industrial economy back to the drawing board in order to redefine its nature, purpose, and acceptable forms of expression. The policies are linked by certain common principles.

First, humanity must escape from an excessive emphasis on individualism and competition. The situation characterized by the Tragedy of the Commons (see right) occurs all too frequently. Even if it were desirable, it is not possible to privatize all the inter-dependencies of today's situations of this sort. There is no alternative to the construction of democratic, institutional frameworks of mutuality and co-operation, rights and responsibilities, together with the mechanisms for their impartial enforcement.

Second, humanity must recognize ecological limits to its activities. The sustainability conditions (see pp. 86-7) that flow from such limits need to be internalized deep within the social fabric, and practical sustainability standards for all environmental impacts need to be derived from them. The consumer society must become the conserver society.

Economic conservatives and the business establishment are already assuming that, thanks to technology, GNP growth can continue practically unimpeded, albeit in somewhat different directions, and that such growth is even necessary for environmental conservation. The problem with these siren voices is that they undermine the impetus for essential change through their endorsement of the most basic objective of "business as usual". We need to be grateful for more sober assessments of the environmental-economic predicament, from such economists as Herman Daly and Roefie Hueting, which point to more difficult, but more realistic, conclusions.

"It is changes in the size of the photosynthetic product that determine ultimately how many of us the earth can support and at what level of consumption. . . . At a time when demand for various biological products is rising rapidly, the earth's biological production is shrinking. The ever-greater annual additions to world population in prospect for the nineties will further reduce the earth's ability to supply our food and raw materials. These two trends cannot continue indefinitely."
State of the World 1990

The Tragedy of the Commons
University of California biologist Garrett Hardin's famous article "The Tragedy of the Commons" describes a situation analogous to many environmental problems. A pasture with common grazing rights is systematically over grazed by herders, each of whom decides on the basis of individual self-interest to increase his herd beyond the carrying capacity of the pasture: if nobody else does it, then the individual who does will obtain a clear advantage with only minor degradation of the field; if others do it, the herder who holds back will have least by the time the field is destroyed. Obviously there is a moral argument for individual restraint, on the basis of which leadership by unilateral example could be effective. Or it might be possible to subdivide the commons into plots protected by private property rights. But with the wider environment, such as the ozone layer and climate, the only secure way out of commons' tragedies is through negotiation, co-operation, and enforceable agreements between the parties concerned.

"Faith in technology as the ultimate solution to all problems can divert attention from the most fundamental problem – the problem of growth in a finite system – and prevent us from taking effective action to solve it." *The Limits to Growth*

The Ehrlich equation (see pp. 86-7) indicates that, even without growth in industrial countries, growth in developing countries, moves to sustainability, and population increase will require that the environmental impact of each unit of consumption decrease by more than 75 per cent, by 2050. The belief that, to accommodate rich country growth, technology can cut this impact still further, is born of blind, desperate faith rather than science.

This does not at all imply economic decline in industrial countries. With modest redistribution, all people in those countries could enjoy a healthy, varied, prosperous life, and a steady-state economy, which would have been the envy of earlier centuries, with a far higher environmental quality than at present. It is the ideology of growth that rules out such an economy: the myth that bigger or more is always better; the business imperative of growth enforced by merger and compe-tition; the relentless fuelling of consumer expectations and dissatisfaction. In rejecting the steady-state solution, this ideology has brought humanity to the brink of global impoverishment.

Toward conserver tourism

Travel and tourism is now the world's biggest industry, with 1987 sales of $2 trillion a year and employing 6.3% of the global workforce. According to the Ecumenical Coalition on Third World Tourism (ECTWT) it is an industry that "exploits local people, damages the environment, promotes consum-erism, widens the gap between rich and poor and reinforces the global status quo." The way mass tourism seeks out the Earth's choicest locations, and then destroys the very social and environmental features that make them attractive, make it an archetype of unsustain-ability. Remedying this situation requires an approach based on several of this book's principal themes. First, local mobilization against social, economic, and environmental exploitation. Second, the application of ecological prin-ciples, such as total carrying capacity to regulate the number of tourists to be accommodated in a particular place and the associated facilities. Third, the enforcement of the regulations by government. At each stage the most influential voice should be that of the people adversely affected by the develop-ment of tourism. There are now many groups, including the ECTWT, working along these lines, but the industry will need to be totally transformed before it can become, in the words of Pope John Paul II, "a real force for world peace".

The 4Rs

Repairing, reconditioning, reusing, and recycling are the key processes of wealth creation in the circular flow that is the hallmark of nature's, and the Green human, economy (see pp. 50-1). Opportunities for repairing and reconditioning are a function of durable design and depend on rolling back the consumer-society phenomena of disposables, fast-changing fashion, and planned obsolescence. A study by the Battelle Research Centre in Geneva, reported in Davis and Bollard's book *As Though People Mattered*, indicated that using design, repair, and reconditioning to increase the average life of a car from 10 to 20 years, total energy consumption in keeping it on the road could be cut by 40%, while employment would increase by 57%. The promotion of reuse is exemplified by deposits that encourage bottles to be reused, which saves more energy than crushing and recycling the glass. In the US, the states of New York,

Massachusetts, and Oregon all have legislation requiring such deposits. Recycling is the sustainable alter-native to landfill and incineration. Compared with using virgin materials, savings of energy in production using scrap are 90% for aluminium, 60% for paper, 50% for steel, and 30% for glass. In the US 17 communities are now approach-ing a 40% recycled waste-stream, the outstanding large-scale example being Seattle in Washington state, which in 1988 set a target of 60% recycling by 1998. According to the Institute for Local Self-Reliance, based in Washington DC, the success characteristics of these schemes are comprehensive costing programmes, mandatory partici-pation, economic incentives, targeting a wide range of materials, recovery from households, busi-nesses, and institutions, kerb-side collections, appropriate containers, and education and publicity. The Institute estimates that 75% of waste is potentially recyclable.

Conclusion

This book's principal conclusion is that humanity will not achieve sustainability, equity, harmony, or happiness while the pursuit of industrial growth, measured by GNP, remains its main economic objective. This does not mean that the new objective should be no growth, which is, in principle, equally compatible with unsustainability and injustice. It does mean the progressive bounding of economic activity by tight sustainability constraints, and the explicit direction of that activity by and toward positive human values: personal development and quality of life, participation in society, democracy, and justice; and the monitoring of economic performance according to these goals. For poor nations, achievement of these goals requires significant production growth; for rich nations, it does not. Should technological change, driven by people-centred values in transition to a largely solar economy manage to achieve it, however, it would be a welcome benefit.

Economics, as Adam Smith knew, is a branch of moral philosophy. If today it seems more like financial idolatry, that is because its central moral value is self-interest. Smith's hope that this self-interest could be the chief engine of social progress has been in vain. Glorifying greed has led to the shopping mall on the one hand and gross exploitation on the other. Green economics would confine to those areas where individual and social self-interest really do coincide.

Smith knew too that people are also powerfully moved by individual conscience and fellow-feeling but thought little of them as an economic force. Green economics in contrast has high hopes of both. They are energizing and inspiring, and consonant with the sort of economy it is seeking to create. But moral sensibility and fellow-feeling do not require self-sacrifice. The biblical injunction is to love thy neighbour as, not instead of, thyself. Green economics' sympathy for others proceeds from a healthy concern for personal growth and fulfilment for oneself. Whether this concern can build a power that will put greed and markets in their place, we cannot yet know. The only way to know is to try it and find out.

Going Green

The Green economy will not be legislated from above. The most government will do is consolidate good practice. There is a huge amount everybody can do here and now in their own lives to become part of the Green economic solution, as producers, consumers, investors, parents, partners, friends, and neighbours. In building a Green economy, motivation, information, and moral commitment are more important than money. It is perhaps fitting that, just as Japan is undisputed master of the industrial economy, so two Japanese organizations – the Seikatsu Club and PP21 – are among the most successful of the people's initiatives that are pioneering the approaches to transform it.

PP21

August 1989 saw a gathering in Japan of 281 activists from 33 countries in a programme entitled The People's Plan for the 21st Century, PP21: An Alliance of Hope. More than 120,000 Japanese participated in 16 international conferences and other events in Japan to discuss agriculture, trade, land reforms, women's rights, workers, consumers, indigenous peoples, and the impact of Japanese aid. The programme culminated in a meeting at Minamata (see pp. 26-7) and the formulation of the Minamata Declaration, condemning the Japanese economy, which "does not empower its citizens but rather seeks to make them powerless and fragmented", and celebrating trans-border actions and solidarity campaigns.

Going solar

A major objective of the industrial economy has been to escape from energy dependence on the sun, through the use of coal, oil, gas, and nuclear energy, the last of which has been pursued with obsessive, anti-economic vigour. Nuclear fusion has received billions of dollars, while more advanced solar technologies remain relatively unsupported. It is on these solar technologies that the Green economy will rely.

○ Biomass—the major energy source for over half the world's people. A massive investment in the Earth's photosynthetic capability needs to produce wood and energy crops while reversing trends of desertification and deforestation.

○ Passive solar—even in cold climates, buildings can be made comfortable by energy from the sun.

○ Solar collectors—these heat water, either domestically or in power stations for electricity, as in California where one such station produces 354 MW at 8c per kWh.

○ Photovoltaics—these generate electricity directly from the sun. In 20 years, the cost of cells has fallen from $30 to 30c per kWh.

○ Wind—in the last ten years cost per kWh has fallen from 30c to 8c.

○ Waves—Norway is developing wave energy on the basis of 8c per kWh.

○ Hydro—small-scale schemes with minimum ecological and social disruption are now becoming viable.

Different countries will employ different mixes of these technologies, which are diverse enough to ensure that all can participate in the solar revolution, without which sustainability will not be achieved.

Seikatsu Club Consumers' Co-op

The Seikatsu Club, with 170,000 member families, is one of the largest consumer co-operatives in Japan. It is also probably the most significant example of Green economic practice in the industrialized world. Started in 1965 by a Tokyo housewife to buy milk more cheaply in bulk, the Club has grown into an economic powerhouse. Its heart is the distribution of 400 products, all produced according to rigorous ecological and social criteria, to the 20,000 local groups of some eight member-families each. The Club has more than £25 million in member investment, which it uses to produce its own goods when others do not meet its standards. Its other activities include the formation of worker collectives to give employment to its members, campaigns against environmental destruction, and the encouragement of like-minded political networks (see pp. 154-5).

Sources and References

pp.8-9
1 Myers, N. 1986 *Tackling the Mass Extinction of Species*, Horace Albright Lectureship in Conservation, University of California, Berkeley
2 Harman, W. 1988 The Need for a Restructuring of Science, *ReVision* Vol.11, No.2, Fall

pp.12-13
3 Smith, A. 1910 (first published 1776) *An Inquiry into the Nature and Causes of the Wealth of Nations*, 2 vols., J.M. Dent, London
4 Smith, A. 1976 (first published 1759) *The Theory of Moral Sentiments* (edited by D. Raphael & A. Macfie), Clarendon Press, Oxford

pp.14-17
5 Boyle, S. & Ardill, J. 1989 *The Greenhouse Effect*, Hodder & Stoughton, London
6 Brown, L. et al. 1988 *State of the World 1988*, W.W. Norton, New York
7 Brown, L. et al. 1989 *State of the World 1989*, W.W. Norton, New York
8 Brown, L. et al. 1990 *State of the World 1990*, W.W. Norton, New York
9 Clark, J. 1986 *For Richer for Poorer*, Oxfam, Oxford
10 Context Institute 1990 *In Context* No.25, late Spring, Bainbridge Island, Washington
11 Ehrlich, P. & A. 1990 *The Population Explosion*, Simon & Schuster, New York
12 Falkenmark, M. 1990 'Global Water Issues Confronting Humanity', *Journal of Peace Research* 27, pp.177-90
13 Goldsmith, E. & Hildyard, N. Eds. 1988 *The Earth Report*, Mitchell Beazley, London
14 Greenpeace International (GI) 1990 *The Failure of the Montreal Protocol*, GI, Amsterdam
15 Instituto del Tercer Mondo (ITM) 1990 *Third World Guide '91/'92*, ITM, Montevideo, Uruguay
16 Jhaveri, N. 1988 'The Three Gorges Debacle', *The Ecologist* Vol.18 Nos. 2/3, pp.56-64
17 Leggett, J. Ed. 1990 *Global Warming: The Greenpeace Report*, Oxford University Press, Oxford
18 Myers, N. 1990 *The Gaia Atlas of Future Worlds*, Doubleday, New York/Gaia Books, London
19 Sadik, N. 1990 *The State of World Population 1990*, UN Population Fund, New York
20 Seager, J. Ed. 1990 *The State of the Earth*, Unwin Hyman, London
21 World Rainforest Movement (WRM) 1990 *World Rainforest Report* Vol. VI No.3, July – September, Rainforest Action Network, San Francisco
22 World Resources Institute (WRI) et al. 1990 *World Resources 1990-91*, WRI, Washington DC

pp.18-19
23 Hewlett, S.A. 1986 *A Lesser Life: The Myth of Women's Liberation in America*, Warner Books, New York
24 Voluntary Fund for UN Decade for Women *State of World Women 1979*, UN, New York
25 Waring, M. 1989 *If Women Counted: A New Feminist Economics*, Macmillan, London

pp.20-1
26 Central Statistical Office 1991 *Social Trends 21*, HMSO, London
27 Kiernan, K. & Wicks, M. 1990 *Family Change and Future Policy*, Family Policy Studies Centre, London
28 National Association of State Boards of Education (NASBE) 1990 *Code Blue: Uniting for Healthier Youth*, NASBE, Alexandria VA, USA
29 Sivard, R. 1985 *Women: A World Survey*, World Priorities, Washington DC
30 Townsend, P. et al. 1987 *Poverty and Labour in London*, Low Pay Unit, London
31 US Bureau of the Census 1990 *Statistical Abstract of the United States 1990* (110th edition), Washington DC
See also reference 15

pp.22-3
32 Berkoff, S. 1990 'A hell of a town' *The Guardian (Weekend)*, London, December 15/16
33 Center for Community Change (CCC), 1990 *America's Third Deficit: Too Little Investment in People and Infrastructure*, CCC, Washington DC
34 Commission for the Creation of a Yanomami Park, various newsletters, São Paulo, Brazil
35 D'Monte, D. 1989 'The pavement dwellers of Bombay' in Bhaskara, H. et al. 1989 *Against all Odds: Breaking the Poverty Trap*, Panos, London
36 Mishel, L. & Frankel, D. 1990 *The State of Working America, 1990/1991*, Economic Policy Institute, Washington DC
37 Oppenheim, C. 1990 *Poverty: the Facts*, Child Poverty Action Group, London
38 Param, U. 1990 'For years we have resisted but there is no reaction', *The Guardian*, 2 November
39 Rich, B. 1987 'Report of a visit of Lokayan and Environmental Defense Fund (EDF) to Singrauli area', February, mimeo, EDF, Washington DC
40 Rich, B. 1990 *The Emperor's New Clothes: The World Bank and Environmental Reform*, World Policy Journal, Spring

pp.24-5
41 Caplovitz, D.L. 1989 'Credit Card Mania in America and Personal Bankruptcy', mimeo, New York City University
42 Ford, J. et al. 1989 'Unemployment and Consumer Debts in Europe: General Report', Institute for Financial Services and Consumer Protection, Hamburg, Germany
43 Huhne, C. 1989 'Some Lessons of the Debt Crisis: Never Again?' in O'Brien, R. & Datta, T. Eds. 1989 *International Economics & Financial Markets: the Amex Bank Review Prize Essays 1988*, Oxford University Press, Oxford
44 Johnson, S. 1989 'Mortgage Debt in the UK', mimeo, Birmingham Settlement, Birmingham
45 Warner, J.L. 1990 'Guilty Guinness Four Face Prison' *The Independent*, 28 August
See also reference 19

pp.26-7
46 Brackley, P. 1988 *Energy and Environmental Terms: A Glossary*. Energy Papers No.24, Joint Energy Programme, Policy Studies Institute/ Royal Institute of International Affairs, Gower, Aldershot, UK
47 Dinham, B. 1990 'Bhopal – the Struggle and the Lessons' *Community Health Action* 16, Summer
48 Global Tomorrow Coalition 1990 *Global Ecology Handbook*, Beaver Press, New York
49 Greenpeace 1988 *Nuclear Power: a campaign briefing*, Greenpeace, London
50 IOCU 1990 *Consumer Currents*, July, IOCU, Penang, Malaysia
51 Medvedev, Z. 1990 'The Environmental Destruction of the Soviet Union', *The Ecologist*, Vol.20 No.1. January/ February, pp.24-9
52 Oulton, C. 1991 'Dying Scientist says Chernobyl Killed 7,000', *Independent on Sunday* 14 April, London
53 Rich, B. 1987, Letter to Barber Conable, World Bank President, on behalf of Environmental Defense Fund (EDF) and others, 6 August, EDF, Washington DC
54 Rich, B. 1989, Statement on behalf of EDF and others concerning the Environmental Performance of the World Bank before two Subcommittees of the US House of Representatives, 26 September, EDF, Washington DC
55 Sivard, R.L. 1989 *World Military and Social Expenditures 1989*, World Priorities, Washington DC
56 Wohlforth, C. 1990 'Slow Progress in the Wake of Exxon Valdez', *Panoscope*, September, Panos, London
See also references 7, 13

pp.28-9
57 Argyle, M. 1987 *The Psychology of Happiness*, Methuen, London
58 Durning, A. 1991 'Asking How Much is Enough' in Brown, L. et al. 1991 *The State of the World 1991*, W.W. Norton, New York
59 Freedman, J. 1978 *Happy People*, Harcourt Brace Jovanovich, New York
60 McDermott, M. 1990 'The Great Mall Glut', *Adweek's Marketing Week*, 5 February
61 Robinson, J. 1989 'When the Going Gets Tough', *American Demographics* Vol.11 No.2, February

62 Robinson, J. 1990 'I Love My TV', *American Demographics* Vol.12 No.9, September

pp.30-1
63 Etzioni, A. 1988 *The Moral Dimension: Toward a New Economics*, Free Press, New York
64 Lansley, S. & Mack, J. 1983 *Breadline Britain*, LWT/MORI, London
65 Myrdal, G. 1978 'Institutional Economics', *Journal of Economic Issues* 12, December, pp.771-83

pp.32-3
66 Daly, H. 1991 'Elements of Environmental Macroeconomics' in Costanza, R. Ed. 1991 *Ecological Economics: the Science and Management of Sustainability*, Columbia University Press, New York
67 IPCC (Intergovernmental Panel on Climate Change) 1990 *Scientific Assessment of Climate Change*, World Meteorological Organisation, Geneva
68 Repetto, R. 1990 *Promoting Environmentally Sound Economic Progress: What the North can do*, World Resources Institute, Washington DC
69 Vitousek, P. et al. 1986 'Human Appropriation of the Products of Photosynthesis', *Bioscience* Vol. 34 No.6, May, pp. 368-73
See also reference 8

pp.34-5
70 Confederation of British Industry (CBI) 1989 *The Capital at Risk*, CBI, London
71 Pius XI, Pope 1931 *Quadragesimo Anno* in Carlen, C. Trans. 1981 *The Papal Encyclicals 1903-1939*, McGrath Publishing Co., Raleigh NC
See also reference 7

pp.36-7
72 Grameen Trust (GT) 1990 *Grameen Dialogue*, December, GT, Dhaka, Bangladesh
73 Ruitenbeek, H. 1990 *Economic Analysis of Tropical Forest Conservation Initiatives: Examples from West Africa*, World Wide Fund for Nature, Godalming, UK

pp.38-9
74 Aristotle 1853 *The Politics and Economics of Aristotle* (Tr. Walford), H. Bohm, London
75 De Soto, H. 1989 *The Other Path*, Tauris, London
76 House, R. 1989 'Hidden Boom in Brazil', *South*, October

pp.40-1
77 UNDP 1990 *Human Development Report 1990*, Oxford University Press, Oxford/New York

pp.44-5
78 Becker, G. 1976 *The Economic Approach to Human Behaviour*, University of Chicago Press, Chicago
79 Morris, W. 1885 'Useful Work versus Useless Toil' in Morton, A. Ed. 1979 *The Political Writings of William Morris*, Lawrence & Wishart, London

pp.46-7
80 Max-Neef, M. et al. 1990 *Human Scale Development: an Option for the Future*, Dag Hammarskjöld Foundation, Uppsala, Sweden
81 Miles, I. & Irvine, J. Eds. 1982 *The Poverty of Progress: Changing Ways of life in Industrial Societies*, Pergamon, Oxford
See also reference 59

pp.48-9
82 Eatwell, J., Milgate, M. & Newman, P. 1987 *The New Palgrave: a Dictionary of Economics*, Macmillan, London
83 Hicks, J. 1946 *Value and Capital: an Inquiry into some fundamental principles of economic theory*, Clarendon Press, Oxford (first edition 1939) p.176
84 Mishan, E. 1967 *The Costs of Economic Growth*, Staples Press, London

pp.50-3
85 Beckermann, W. 1974 *In Defence of Economic Growth*, Jonathan Cape, London
86 Seathl, a Native Indian Chief, in a letter to the US President in 1865, quoted in Cornford, C. and Wood, J.N. Eds. 1977 *If all the Beasts were Gone: an Anthology of Prophesy, Warning and Aspiration concerning the Natural World*, Royal College of Art, London

87 Thatcher, M. 1989, Speech at the Royal Society Annual Dinner September 27 1988, *Science and Public Affairs*, Vol.4, pp.3-9
See also reference 22

pp.54-5
88 Colbert, V. 'Universalisation of Primary Education in Colombia: The New School Programme', mimeo, Bogota
89 Gillmour, A., Statement at 'The Challenge of Change' conference, National Economic Development Office, September 1988, quoted in Webb, S. Ed. 1989 *Blueprint for Success: A Report on Involving Employees in Britain*, Industrial Society, London
90 Handy, C. 1991 'What is a company for?', *RSA Journal* vol.CXXXIX No. 5416, March.
91 Pscharopoulos, G. 1987 *Critical Issues in Education: a World Agenda*, Education and Training Series Report No. EDT96, World Bank, Washington DC, June
92 UNICEF 1990 *The State of the World's Children 1990*, Oxford University Press, Oxford/ New York

pp.56-7
93 Goyder, G. 1987 *The Just Enterprise*, Andre Deutsch, London 94 Turner, B. Ed. 1988 *Building Community*, Building Community Books, London
95 UNNGLS (United Nations Non-Governmental Liaison Service) 1989 *Newsnet* Vol.6 No.1, March, UNNGLS, New York
See also reference 7

pp.58-9
96 Aghevli, B. & Boughton, J. 1990 'National Saving and the World Economy', *Finance & Development* (issue entitled 'The Decline of Saving'), June, International Monetary Fund, Washington DC

pp.60-1
97 Pearce, D. et al. 1989 *Blueprint for a Green Economy*, Earthscan, London

pp.62-3
98 Daly, H. & Cobb, J. 1989 *For the Common Good*, Beacon Press, Boston / Merlin Press, London
99 Lutz, M. 1992 'Measuring Authentic Socioeconomic Development' in Ekins, P. & Max-Neef, M. Eds. 1992 *Real-Life Economics*, Routledge, London
100 Miles, I. 1985 *Social Indicators for Human Development*, Frances Printer, London
101 Morris, M.D. 1979 *Measuring the Condition of the World's Poor: the PQLI*, Pergamon, Oxford/New York
See also reference 77

pp.64-5
102 Agarwal, A. 1985 *5th Annual World Conservation Lecture*, World Wide Fund for Nature, Godalming, Surrey, UK
103 Artis. M.J. Ed. 1989 *The UK Economy: Manual of Applied Economics*, Weidenfeld & Nicholson, London
104 D. En. (Department of Energy) 1990 *Development of the Oil and Gas Resources of the United Kingdom*, D. En., London
105 El Serafy, S. 1989 'The Proper Calculation of Income from Depletable Natural Resources' in Ahmad, Y., El Serafy, S., Lutz, E. Eds. 1989 *Environmental Accounting for Sustainable Development*, World Bank, Washington DC
106 Lone, O. 1988 'Natural Resource Accounting: the Norwegian Experience', mimeo, OECD, Paris
107 Repetto, R. et al. 1989 *Wasting Assets: Natural Resources in the National Income Accounts*, World Resources Institute, Washington DC
108 World Commission on Environment and Development (Brundtland Report) *Our Common Future*, Oxford University Press, Oxford/New York

pp.66-7
109 Leipert, C. 1988 'Social Costs of the Economic Process and National Accounts: towards the identification of defensive expenditures in the Gross National Product', mimeo, Science Center Berlin
See also reference 97

pp.68-9
110 Durning, A. 1989 'Mobilising at the Grassroots' in Brown, L. et al. 1989 *The State of the World 1989*, W.W. Norton, New York
111 Eurostat 1991 *Portrait Sociale de l'Europe*, Office of European Community Publications, Luxembourg
112 Goldschmidt-Clermont, L. 1982 *Unpaid Work in the Household*, ILO, Geneva
113 Goldschmidt-Clermont, L. 1992 'Measuring Households' Non-monetary Production' in Ekins, P. & Max-Neef, M. Eds. 1992 *Real-Life Economics* Routledge, London
114 Schneider, B. 1988 *The Barefoot Revolution*, Intermediate Technology Publications, London
115 Warrior, B. & Leghorn, L. 1974 *Housewiver's Handbook*, Women's Center, Cambridge MA, USA
See also reference 25

pp.70-1
116 Anderson, V. 1991 *Alternative Economic Indicators*, Routledge, London
117 Irvine, J. & Miles, I. 1982 'The Dominant Way of Life in Britain: a Case Study of Maldevelopment' in Miles, I. & Irvine, J. Eds. 1982 *The Poverty of Progress*, Pergamon, Oxford
118 PCC (Population Crisis Committee) 1990 *Life in the World's 100 Largest Metropolitan Areas*, PCC, Washington DC
119 UNICEF annual *State of the World's Children*, Oxford University Press, Oxford/New York
See also reference 100

pp.72-3
120 *Fortune*, July 30th, 1990
121 International Labour Office (ILO) 1989 *Social and labour practices of multinational enterprises in the food and drink industry*, ILO, Geneva
122 UNICEF 1989 *State of the World's Children 1989*, Oxford University Press, Oxford/New York
123 World Bank 1990 *World Development Report 1990*, World Bank, Oxford University Press, Oxford/New York
See also reference 92

pp.74-5
124 Garton-Ash, T. 1983 *The Polish Revolution: Solidarity 1980-82*, Jonathan Cape, London
125 Kavan, J. & Tomin, Z. Eds. 1983 *Voices from Prague: documents on Czechoslovakia and the peace movement*, European Nuclear Disarmament/ Palach Press
126 Ministerio da Reforma e do Desenvolvimento Agrario (MIRAD) 1988 *Estatisticas Cadastras Annuais*, MIRAD, Brasilia
See also reference 92

pp.76-7
127 UNICEF 1991 *The State of the World's Children 1991*, Oxford University Press, Oxford/ New York
See also reference 8

pp.78-9
128 Agran, L. 1990, Interviewed by Will Swaim, *In Context*, No.25 late Spring, Context Institute, Bainbridge Island, Washington, pp.25-7
129 Franke, R. & Chasin, B. 1989 *Kerala: Radical Reform as Development in an Indian State*, Institute for Food and Development Policy, San Francisco (pp.59-60)

pp.80-1
130 Institute for Community Economics (ICE) 1990 'Highlights of 1990 Accomplishments', information sheet, ICE, Springfield MA
131 Watkins, W.P. 1986 *Co-operative Principles: Today and Tomorrow*, Holyoake Books, Manchester, UK

pp.82-3
132 SEWA 1990 *Annual Report 1989*, Mahila SEWA Trust, Ahmedabad, India

pp.84-5
133 Adams, R. 1990 *Self-help, Social Work & Empowerment*, Macmillan, London
134 DOE (Department of the Environment) and other departments 1990 *Our Common Inheritance: Britain's Environmental Strategy*, HMSO, London

135 Financial Times Editorial 1990 'The Palest of Green', *Financial Times*, London 26 September
136 Lutz, M. & Lux, K. 1988 *Humanistic Economics*, Bootstrap Press, New York
137 MOHPPE (Ministry of Housing, Physical Planning and Environment) 1988 *To Choose or to Lose: National Environmental Policy Plan*, MOHPPE, The Hague

pp.86-7
138 Forbes, J. 1971 'The Native American Experience in Californian History', *Californian Historical Quarterly*, September pp. 234-42
139 Hueting, R. 1980 *New Scarcity and Economic Growth*, North Holland, Amsterdam (first published in Dutch 1974)
140 Planet Drum Foundation (PDF) 1989 'North America Plus: a Bioregional Directory', *Raise the Stakes: the Planet Drum Review*, Fall, PDF, San Francisco
141 Sale, K. 1984 "Bioregionalism - a New Way to Treat the Land" *The Ecologist* Vol. 14, No.4
142 Schumacher, E.F. 1974 *Small is Beautiful*, Abacus, 1974 (first edition 1973)
See also reference 11

pp.88-91
143 BBC 1990 'A town like Davis'. *BBC Wildlife*, BBC, London, July
144 British Petroleum Company (BP) 1990 *BP Statistical Review of World Energy*, June, BP Corporate Communication Services, London
145 Centre for Alternative Technology, undated leaflet, *Small-Scale Water Power*, Machynlleth, Wales
146 Flavin, C. 1990 'Slowing Global Warming' in Brown, L. et al. 1990 *State of the World 1990*, W.W. Norton, New York
147 International Energy Agency 1990 'Electricity Production by Fuel', *Coal Information* Table 13, OECD, Paris
148 Keepin, B. 1990 'Nuclear power and global warming' in Leggett, J. Ed. *Global Warming: the Greenpeace Report*, Oxford University Press, Oxford/ New York
149 Lovins, A. 1990 'The Role of Energy Efficiency' in Leggett, J. Ed. *Global Warming: the Greenpeace Report*, Oxford University Press, Oxford/New York

pp.92-5
150 Business International 1990 *Managing the Environment: the Greening of European Business*, Business International, London
151 Business in the Environment (BIE) 1990 *Your Business and the Environment: an Executive Guide*, BIE, London
152 Colchester, M. 1990 'The International Tropical Timber Organisation: Kill or Cure for the Rainforests', *The Ecologist* Vol.20, No.5, September/October
153 International Chamber of Commerce (ICC) 1991 *The Business Charter for Sustainable Development: Principles for Environmental Management*, ICC, Paris
See also references 97, 108

pp.96-9
154 Central Bureau voor de Statistiek (CBS) 1990 *De Mobiliteit van de Nederlandse Bevolking 1989*, CBS, Voorburg/Heerlen
155 Chapman, A., Wade, F. & Foot, H. Eds. 1982 *Pedestrian Accidents*, John Wiley & Sons, Chichester, UK
156 Department of Transport 1988 *National Travel Survey: 1985/86 Report – Part 1, An Analysis of Personal Travel*, HMSO, London
157 Department of Transport 1990 *Transport Statistics Great Britain 1979-89*, HMSO, London
158 Hillman, M. & Whalley, A. 1983 *Energy & Personal Travel: Obstacles to Conservation*, Policy Studies Institute, London
159 Tolley, R. 1990 *Calming Traffic in Residential Areas*, Brefi Press, Tregaron, Wales
160 Whitelegg, J. 1990 *Auswirkungen der EG Politik auf den Gutertransport und die Folgen fur Nordrhein-Westphalen*, ILS, Dortmund, Germany

pp.100-103
161 Brown, L. 1989 'Feeding Six Billion', *World Watch*, September-October, Worldwatch Institute, Washington DC (p.32)

162 Conway, G. & Barbier, E. 1990 *After the Green Revolution: Sustainable Agriculture for Development*, Earthscan, London
163 Coopers & Lybrand Deloitte (CLD) 1990 *Going Organic: The Future for Organic Food and Drink Products in the UK*, CLD, Birmingham
164 Jenkins, T.N. 1990 *Future Harvests*, Council for the Preservation of Rural England, London/World Wide Fund for Nature, Godalming, Surrey
165 Lampkin, N. 1990 *Organic Farming*, Farming Press, Ipswich
166 National Research Council 1989 *Alternative Agriculture*, National Academy Press, Washington DC
167 Postel, S. 1987 *Defusing the Toxics Threat: Controlling Pesticides and Industrial Waste*, Worldwatch Paper 79, Worldwatch Institute, Washington DC
168 Shiva, V. 1991 'The Green Revolution in the Punjab', *The Ecologist*, Vol.21 No.2, March/April
169 Third World Network (TWN) 1990 *Return to the Good Earth: Damaging Effects of Modern Agriculture and the Case for Ecological Farming*, TWN Dossier, Penang, Malaysia
170 United Nations (UN) 1979 *Selected World Demographic and Policy Indicators 1978*, UN, New York
See also references 8, 22

pp.104-5
171 Momsen, J. 1991 *Women and Development in the Third World*, Routledge, London
172 WLUML (Women Living Under Muslim Laws) 1987 'Zina: the Hudood Ordinance and its Implications for Women', *Alert for Action* 21 November, WLUML, Grabels, France
173 WLUML 1990 'Open Season for Women', *Alert for Action* 24 March 1990, based on Editorial in *The Muslim*, 16 March 1990, Lahore, Pakistan, WLUML, Grabels, France
See also references 82, 114, 127

pp.106-7
174 Berry, W. 1975 *A Continuous Harmony*, Harcourt Brace, New York
175 Fox, M. 1983 *Original Blessing*, Bear & Co., Santa Fe NM
176 O'Brien, J., Palmer, M. & Prime, R. 1992 (forthcoming) *A Wealth of Faiths*, World Wide Fund for Nature, Godalming, Surrey, UK

pp.108-9
177 Commoner, B. 1988 'Rapid Population Growth and Environmental Stress', mimeo, paper presented to Expert Group on Consequences of Rapid Population Growth, August 24- 26, UN, New York
178 HRH the Duke of Edinburgh 1990 'Population in Crisis', *The New Road* No.16, World Wide Fund for Nature, Godalming, Surrey
179 Myers, N. 1990 'Population and Environment: Issues, Prospects and Policies', mimeo, paper for UNFPA, New York, November
180 Sadik, N. 1991 *The State of World Population 1991*, UNFPA, New York
181 Shaw, P. 1989 'Rapid Population Growth and Environmental Degradation: Ultimate versus Proximate Factors', *Environmental Conservation* Vol.16, No.3, Autumn
182 UN 1984 *Fertility and Family*, UN, New York
183 UN 1991 *Demographic Yearbook 1989*, UN, New York
See also references 8, 19

pp.110-13
184 Bidinger, P. 1990 'Health in Rural South India: new approaches', *British Medical Journal*, December 22-29, pp.1441-2
185 Erlichmann, J. 1990 'Vested interests "push deadly diet" ', *The Guardian*, 12 December, London
186 Hillman, M. 1991 *Cycling Towards Health and Safety*, Report to the British Medial Association (BMA), BMA, London
187 IOCU (International Organisation of Consumers' Unions) 1990 'The Formula Pushers', *Consumer Currents* No.126, May/June, IOCU, Penang
188 Jeyaratnam, J. 1990 'Acute Pesticide Poisoning: a Major Global Health Problem', *World Health Statistical Quarterly* No.43
189 Rahman, A. 1990 'Rational Use of Drugs', *HAI News* No.54, August, Health Action International, Penang, Malaysia

190 World Health Organisation (WHO) 1986 *World Health Statistics Quarterly* Vol.39 No.4, WHO, Geneva
See also reference 92

pp.114-17
191 Brewster, Sir D. 1855 *Memoirs of the Life, Writings and Discoveries of Sir Isaac Newton*, Constable, Edinburgh
192 Cooley, M. 1987 *Architect or Bee?* Hogarth Press, London (First edition 1980)
193 Datamation 1989 'Where Global IS Power Lies', *Datamation*, June 15
194 Eliot, T.S. 1944 *The Four Quartets*, Faber & Faber, London
195 Frankel, M. 1990 'Parliamentary Accountability and Government Control of Information' in Lewis, N. Ed. 1990 *Happy and Glorious: the Constitution in Transition*, Open University Press, Milton Keynes, UK
196 Line, M. 1990, Presidential Address to UK Library Association, *The Bookseller* 2 November
197 Machlup, F. 1962 *The Production and Distribution of Knowledge in the United States*, Princeton University Press, Princeton NJ
198 Polanyi, M. 1967 *The Tacit Dimension*, Routledge & Kegan Paul, London
199 Posey, D. 1990 'Intellectual Property Rights and Just Compensation for Indigenous Knowledge', *Anthropology Today*, August
200 Rocky Mountain Institute (RMI) 1990 'Efficiency Notebook', *RMI Newsletter* Vol.VI No.111, Fall/Winter
201 Stapledon, G. 1971 *Human Ecology*, Charles Knight, London (first published 1964)

pp.118-21
202 Freire, P. 1972 *Pedagogy of the Oppressed*, Penguin, London (first published 1970)
203 Harper, K. 1990 'Britain Worst for Worker Training', *The Guardian* 6 June, London
204 Kirby, N. 1981 *Personal Values in Primary Education*, Harper & Row, London
205 Prakasha, V. 1983 *Our Future is Our Children: the Case for Early Childhood Care and Education*, UNESCO, Paris
206 UNESCO 1989 *Statistical Yearbook*, UNESCO, Paris
207 Van Rensburg, P. 1981, Speech given in Stockholm on receipt of the 1981 Right Livelihood Award, Stockholm
See also reference 92

pp.122-5
208 Anti-Slavery International (ASI) 1990 *Anti-Slavery Reporter*, ASI, London
209 Anti-Slavery International (ASI) 1988 *A Pattern of Slavery: India's Carpet Boys*, ASI, London
210 Commission of the European Communities 1990 'New Partnerships for Employment Creation at Local Level', report of a LEDA conference in Dublin, 21-22 March, EC, Brussels
211 Handy, C. 1984 *The Future of Work*, Basil Blackwell, Oxford
212 ICFTU (International Confederation of Free Trade Unions) 1991 'ICFTU Annual Survey Cites Union Rights Abuses in 72 Countries', press release 14 March, ICFTU, Brussels
213 Muller-Jentsch, W. et al. 1990 'Labour Market Flexibility and Work Organisation: expert's report on Germany', mimeo, OECD, Paris
214 OECD 1990 *Employment Outlook*, OECD, Paris
215 Robertson, J. 1985 *Future Work*, Gower/ Temple Smith, Aldershot, Hampshire
216 Warr, P. 1983 'Work, Jobs and Unemployment', *Bulletin of the British Psychological Society*, quoted in Handy 1984
217 Windmuller, J. Ed. 1987 *Collective Bargaining in Industrialised Economies: a Reappraisal*, ILO, Geneva

pp.126-9
218 Basic Income Research Group (BIRG) 1989 *Basic Income*, pamphlet, BIRG, London
219 Commission of the European Communities 1989 *Community Charter of the Fundamental Social Rights of Workers*, EC, Luxembourg
220 Conroy, C. & Litvinoff, M. Eds 1988 *The Greening of Aid: Sustainable Livelihoods in Practice*, Earthscan, London
221 Dore, R et al. 1989 *Japan at Work: Markets, Management and Flexibility*, OECD, Paris

222 Dreze, J. & Sen, A. 1990 'Public Action for Social Security' in Ahmad, S., Dreze, J., Hills, J. and Sen, A. Eds. 1990 *Social Security in Developing Countries*, Oxford University Press, Oxford
223 Morita, A. 1986 *Made in Japan*, Dutton, New York
224 Pestoff, V. 1991 'The demise of the Swedish Model and the rise of organised business as a major political actor', mimeo, Stockholm School of Economics
225 Townsend, P. & Davidson, N. Eds. and Whitehead, M. 1990 *Inequalities in Health*, Penguin, London (inc. *The Black Report*, first published 1980, and *The Health Divide*, first published 1987)
226 Wicks, M. 1987 *A Future for All: Do We Need A Welfare State?*, Penguin, London
See also reference 123

pp.130-1
227 Hirsch, F. 1976 *Social Limits to Growth*, Harvard University Press, Cambridge MA

pp.132-5
228 Childcare Network of the EC 1990 *Childcare in the European Community 1985-1990*, Commission of the European Communities, Brussels
229 Ennew, J. & Milne, B. 1989 *The Next Generation*, Zed Books, London
230 Institut de l'Enfance et de la Famille 1990 *Families and Policies: Evolution and Trends in 1988-1989*, Commission of European Communities, Brussels
231 Moss, P. (for Childcare Network of the EC) 1988 *Childcare and Equality of Opportunity*, Commission of the European Communities, London
232 United Nations 1989 *Demographic Yearbook 1987*, UN, New York See references 122, 182, 183

pp.136-9
233 Cockroft, L. 1990 *Africa's Way*, Tauris, London
234 Hardoy, J., Cairncross, S. & Satterthwaite, D. Eds. 1990 *The Poor Die Young*, Earthscan, London
235 Klamer, A. & Cosgell, M. 1990 'The Amish: a Case of Cultural Resistance', mimeo, George Washington University/University of Connecticut, March
236 Pietila, H. 1989 'Village Action Movement as the only Broad Social movement in Finland for humanity and self-determination of people', mimeo, Helsinki
237 Siiskonen, P. 1986 'Participation of families in the decision making process in rural communities', paper given to FAO seminar, Rome
238 Tourancheau, P. 1990 'Superbarrio, le super-heros des sans-abri mexicains', *L'Autre Journal* No.7, December, Paris
239 Wilmott, P. 1989 *Community Initiatives*, Policy Studies Institute, London
See also reference 110

pp.140-3
240 Corry, S. 1989, Address in London on receiving the 1989 Right Livelihood Award on behalf of Survival International, Survival International, London
241 Fischer, E. 1963 *The Necessity of Art*, Penguin, London
242 Insight Guides 1981 *Bali*, Apa Productions, Singapore
243 Lethaby, W.R. 1922 *Form in Civilisation*, Oxford University Press, Oxford
244 Malik, R. Ed. 1990 'An Evening of World Television', *Intermedia* May, International Institute of Communications, London, pp.141-2
245 Morris, W. 1881 'Some Hints on Pattern-Designing' in Briggs, A. Ed. 1962 *William Morris: Selected Writings and Designs*, Penguin, London
246 Playfair, G.L. 1990 *The Evil Eye*, Jonathan Cape, London

pp.144-7
247 Adams, R. et al. 1991 *Changing Corporate Values*, Kogan Page, London
248 Adams, R. et al. 1991 *Shopping for a Better World*, Kogan Page, London
249 Callenbach, E., Capra, F. & Marburg, S. 1990 *The Elmwood Guide to Eco-Auditing and Ecologically Conscious Management*, Global File Report No.5, Elmwood Institute, Berkeley CA
250 Council on Economic Priorities (CEP) 1989 *Shopping for a Better World*, CEP, New York

251 Elkington, J. 1990 *The Environmental Audit*, World Wide Fund for Nature, Godalming, Surrey/ SustainAbility Ltd., London
252 Gray, R. 1990 *The Greening of Accountancy: the Profession after Pearce*, Chartered Association of Certified Accountants, London
253 Lydenburg, S. *et al.* 1986 *Rating America's Corporate Conscience*, Addison-Wesley, Reading MA
254 NEC 1990 *The NEC Credo*, NEC, Tokyo
255 Oakeshott, R. (for Job Ownership Ltd.) 1987 *Employee Stock Ownership Plans in the United States*, Partnership Research Ltd., London
256 Pope John Paul II 1991 *Centesimus Annus*, Papal Encyclical, May
257 Wells, P. & Jetter, M. 1991 *The Global Consumer*, Victor Gollancz, London
258 Wisman, J. Ed. 1990 *Worker Empowerment*, Bootstrap Press, New York
See also reference 131

pp.148-51
259 Bakhoum, I. et al. 1989 *Banking the Unbankable: Bringing Credit to the Poor*, Panos Institute, London
260 Banks, R. Ed. 1989 *Costing the Earth*, Shepherd Walwyn, London
261 CERES 1990 *The 1990 CERES Guide to the Valdez Principles*, CERES, Boston MA
262 EIRIS 1991 'Ethical Investment: an idea whose time has come', pamphlet available from EIRIS, London
263 Grameen Trust (GT) 1990 'Updates: Amanah Ikhtiar Malaysia', *Grameen Dialogue* Vol.1 No.4, September, GT, Dhaka, Bangladesh
264 Hutton, W. 1991 'Counting the Cost of Freedom', *The Guardian* 11 February, London
265 Kemball-Cook, D., Baker, M. & Mattingly, C. Eds. 1991 *The Green Budget*, Green Print, London
266 Makhijani, A. & Browne, R. 1985 'Restructuring the International Monetary System', *World Policy Journal*, Winter 1985-6
267 Muellbauer, J. 1990 *The Great British Housing Disaster and Economic Policy*, Economic Study No.5, Institute for Public Policy Research, London
268 Robertson, J. 1989 *Future Wealth: a New Economics for the 21st Century*, Cassell, London
269 Shields, J. 1988 'Controlling Consumer Credit' *National Institute Economic Review*, August
270 Slesser, M. 1989 *Unitax: A New Environmentally Sensitive Concept in Taxation*, Resource Use Institute, Ross-on-Wye, Herefordshire
271 Tobin, J. 1987 'A Proposal for International Monetary Reform' in *Essays in Economics* Vol.3 (Theory and Policy), MIT Press, Cambridge MA
272 Von Weizsäcker, E. 1991 'Sustainability: a Task for the North', *Journal of International Affairs* Vol.44 No.2, Winter
273 Wang, P. 1991 'Finish First', *Money*, June

pp.152-5
274 Arendt, H. 1958 *The Origins of Totalitarianism*, Macmillan, London
275 Ball, A. 1977 *Modern Politics and Government*, Macmillan, London (first edition 1971)
276 Marquand, D. 1988 *The Unprincipled Society*, Jonathan Cape, London
See also reference 55

pp.156-9
277 Booth, K. et al. 1991 *European Security: The New Agenda*, Saferworld Foundation, Bristol, UK
278 Fitchett, J. 1990 'After Europe's Thaw, a Pact to Ward off the Cold', *International Herald Tribune*, 17/18 November
279 Kaldor, M. 1982 *The Baroque Arsenal*, Andre Deutsch, London
280 Melman, S. 1974 *The Permanent War Economy: American Capitalism in Decline*, Simon & Schuster, New York
281 SIPRI (Stockholm International Peace Research Institute) 1990 *SIPRI Yearbook*, SIPRI, Stockholm
282 Wills, C. & Airs, G. 1991, 'Burnt bodies litter highway after bombing', *The Guardian*, 2 March
See also reference 108

pp.160-3
283 Crosby, L. 1990 'Consumers on the March', *Consumer Lifelines*, IOCU, Penang
284 Economist 1989 'The United Nations Agencies: a Case for Emergency Treatment', *The Economist* December 2, London

285 Hildyard, N. 1991 'An Open Letter to Edouard Saouma', *The Ecologist*, Vol.21 No.2 (FAO issue), March/April
286 Starke, L. 1990 *Signs of Hope*, Oxford University Press, Oxford/New York
287 Urquhart, B. & Childers, E. 1991 'A World in Need of Leadership: Tomorrow's United Nations', *Development Dialogue* 1990: 1-2, Dag Hammarskjöld Foundation, Uppsala, Sweden
288 Streeten, P. 1992 'The Evolution of Development Thought: Facing up to Global Interdependence' in Ekins, P. & Max-Neef, M. Eds. 1992 *Real-Life Economics*, Routledge, London Ward, B. 1988 *Progress for a Small Planet*, Earthscan, London
289 Ward, B. 1979 *Progress for a Small Planet*, Penguin, London
290 Waterhouse, S. 1991 'UN Staff Net Millions in Tax Fraud', *Independent on Sunday*, May 19, London
See also references 17, 108

pp.164-7
Amin, S. 1990, *Delinking*, Zed Press, London
291 Dag Hammarskjöld Foundation (DHF) 1975 *What Now? Another Development*, DHF, Uppsala, Sweden
292 Ekins, P. 1989 'Trade for Mutual Self-Reliance', *The Ecologist* Vol.19 No.5, September/October
293 George, S. 1988 *A Fate Worse than Debt*, Penguin, London
294 Hancock, G. 1989 *Lords of Poverty*, Macmillan, London
295 Madely, J. 1991 *When Aid is no Help*, Intermediate Technology Publications, London
296 Sachs, W. 1989 'On the Archaeology of the Development Idea: six essays', mimeo, Pennsylvania State University
297 Sarkar, P. 1988 'The South-South economic cooperation in the world of North-South unequal exchange' mimeo, CICD, Ljubljana, Yugoslavia
298 Sarkar, P. & Singer, H. 1991 'Manufactured Exports and their Terms of Trade since 1965', *World Development* Vol.19, No.4
299 Schatan, J. 1987 *World Debt: Who is to Pay?* Zed Books, London

pp.168-9
300 Ashton, J. 1990 'Urban Lifestyle and Public Health in the City', *The Statistician* 39, pp.147-56
301 Ashton, J. 1991 'Sanitarian becomes Ecologist: the new Environmental Health' *British Medical Journal*, 26 January, London
302 Ashton, J. 1991 'The Healthy Cities Project: a Challenge for Health Education' *Health Education Quarterly* Vol.18 (1): 39-48
303 Fowler, C., Lachkovics, E., Mooney, P. & Shard, H. 1988 'The Laws of Life, Another Development and the New Biotechnologies', *Development Dialogue* 1988: 1-2, Uppsala, Sweden
304 Schumacher, F. 1980 *Good Work*, Sphere Books, London

pp.170-3
305 Davidson, J. 1988 *How Green is Your City?* Bedford Square Press, London
306 Harpham, P., Lusty, T. & Vaughan, P. 1988 *In the Shadow of the City: Community Health and the Urban Poor*, Oxford University Press, Oxford/New York
307 St. George, R.L. 1989 'No Mean City', *Resurgence* No.134, May/June
308 Turner, J.F.C. & Fichter, R. Eds. 1972 *Freedom to Build: Dweller Control of the Housing Process*, Collier Macmillan, New York
See also references 22, 122

pp.174-5
309 Brown, P. 1990 'Wave power undercuts nuclear cost', *The Guardian*, 1 June, London
310 Department of Energy/H.M. Treasury 1991 *The Government's Expenditure Plans within the Energy Sector*, Cm.1505, HMSO, London
311 Freeman, C., Clark, J. & Soete, L. 1982 *Unemployment and Technical Innovation: a Study of Long Waves in the World Economy*, Frances Pinter, London
312 Jeffery, J. 1990 'Dirty Tricks: How the Nuclear Lobby Stopped the Development of Wave Power in Britain', *The Ecologist* Vol.20 No.3, May/June
313 Perez, C. 1985 'Structural Change and Assimilation of New Technologies in the Economic and Social System' in Freeman, C. Ed. 1985 *Design,*

Innovations and Long Cycles in Economics Development, Frances Pinter, London
314 Tylecote, A. 1991 *The Long Wave in the World Economy*, Routledge, London
315 Valentine, J. 1985 *Atomic Crossroads: Before and After Sizewell*, Merlin, London

pp.176-7
316 Daly, H. 1991 'Ecological Economics and Sustainable Development' mimeo, World Bank, Washington DC
317 Englander, S & Mittelstadt, A. 1988 'Total Factor Productivity: Macroeconomic and Structural Aspects of the Showdown', *OECD Economic Studies* No.10. Spring, OECD, Paris
318 Kaplinsky. R. 1990 *The Economies of Small: Appropriate Technology in a Changing World*, IT Publications, London
319 Piore, M. & Sabel, C. 1984 *The Second Industrial Divide: Possibilities for Prosperity*, Basic Books, New York
See also references 142, 304

pp.178-9
320 Curran, J. & Seaton, J. 1988 *Power Without Responsibility* (third edition), Routledge, London
321 Hasan, A. 1986 'The Low Cost Sanitation Project of the Orangi Pilot Project and the Process of Change in Orangi, unpublished seminar paper, and private correspondence with P.Rahman 6.11.90)
322 Hyman, H. 1989 'Privatisation: the Facts' in Veljanovski, C. Ed. 1989 *Privatisation & Competition: a Market Prospectus*, Institute of Economic Affairs, London
323 McGarry, M. 1976 'The Taboo Resource: the Use of Human Excreta in Chinese Agriculture', *The Ecologist* Vol.6 No.4
324 Price Waterhouse 1989, 1990 *Privatisation: the Facts*, Price Waterhouse, London

pp.180-1
325 Bernstam, M. 1991 *The Wealth of Nations and the Environment*, Institute of Economic Affairs, London
326 Davis, J. & Bollard, A. 1986 *As Though People Mattered*, Intermediate Technology Publications, London
327 Ekins, P. 1991 'The Sustainable Consumer Society: a Contradiction in Terms?' *International Environmental Affairs*, University Press of New England, Hanover NH, Autumn
328 Elliott, M. 1991 'The Pleasure Principle' in *The Economist* 'Survey: Travel & Tourism', 23 March
329 Hardin, G. 1968 'The Tragedy of the Commons', *Science* Vol.162, 13 December
330 Heaton, J., Repetto, R. & Sobin, R. 1991 *Transforming Technology: An Agenda for Environmentally Sustainable Growth in the 21st Century*, World Resources Institute, Washington DC
331 ICC (International Chamber of Commerce) 1991 *The Business Charter for Sustainable Development*, ICC, Paris
332 Kourik, R. 1990 'What's So Great About Seattle?', *Garbage*, November/December, Old House Journal Corporation, Brooklyn NY
333 Meadows, D.H. et al. 1972 *The Limits to Growth*, Universe Books, New York
334 O'Grady, A. Ed. 1990 *The Challenge of Tourism*, Ecumenical Coalition on Third World Tourism, Bangkok, 1990
335 Platt, B. et al. 1991 *Beyond 40 Percent: Record-Setting Recycling and Composting Programs*, Institute for Local Self-Reliance, Washington DC
See also references 8, 108

pp.182-3
336 Ampo 1990 'Righting a World Turned Upside Down' *Ampo: Japan Asia Quarterly Review* Vol.21, Nos. 2-3, Pacific-Asia Resource Center, Tokyo
337 Flavin, C. & Lenssen, N. 1991 'Designing a Sustainable Energy System' in Brown, L. et al. 1991 *The State of the World 1991*, W.W. Norton, New York
338 Gershon, D. & Gilman, R. 1990 *Household Eco-Team Workbook*, Global Action Plan, Olivebridge NY
339 New Consumer 1991 'The Great Japanese Supermarket Revolt', *New Consumer* Spring, New Consumer, Newcastle, UK

Index

Bold type indicates main entry